Chinese:
Communicating in the Culture

A publication of The Ohio State University
National East Asian Languages Resource Center

funded by
The U.S Department of Education

Distributed by The Ohio State University
Foreign Language Publications

Managing Editor: Dr. Minru Li
Distributions Manager: Greg Wilson

Cover design: Dan O'Dair
Cover photos: Eric Shepherd
Page design: Yong Lang and Dan O'Dair

Chinese:
Communicating in the Culture

Performance Text One

Beginning Course in Spoken Mandarin

Galal Walker

Yong Lang

Published by
Foreign Language Publications
National East Asian Languages Resource Center
The Ohio State University

This volume prepared and published by
    National East Asian Languages Resource Center
    The Ohio State University
    Hagerty Hall
    1775 S. College Road
    Columbus, OH 43210-1309
    614-292-4361 • fax: 614-688-3355
    flpubs.osu.edu

Library of Congress Cataloging-in-Publication Data

Walker, Galal, 1945–
    Chinese: communicating in the culture : beginning course in spoken Mandarin :
performance text one / Galal Walker, Yong Lang.
      p. cm
    ISBN 978-0-87415-352-1 (alk. paper)
    1. Chinese language--Textbooks for foreign speakers--English. I. Title: Beginning
course in spoken Mandarin. II. Lang, Yong, 1954- III. Title.

    PL1129.E5
    951.05'9'092--dc22
    [B]

    2004053759

Manufactured in the United States of America
Printed and bound by Thomson-Shore, Inc., Dexter, MI

ISBN 978-0-87415-352-1

Table of Contents

ACKNOWLEDGMENTS

In the making of this course there are many sources of direct and indirect help and support. The authors would first like to acknowledge the influence of the late Ronald Walton. Many of the concepts that underlie the structure and content of these lessons emerged in discussions and studies conducted with Ron over many years. Secondly, we thank the numerous students of Chinese over twenty years of individualized instruction and classes who permitted us to observe, interview, and inquire after their learning practices. The design of this course is focused on the autonomous learner such as we find in our individualized instruction program. Without their willingness to share their learning experiences with us, we could not have produced these lessons.

The production of this audio program and book has involved the dedication and knowledge of many persons. Wu Lijuan has been a persistent checker for authenticity and a keen detector of mishaps and errors. Li Minru has been a strict and devoted editor. Chen Henning has helped us keep the different components of this project coordinated. Liu Jun has edited and compiled the audio program. Dan O'Dair has seen to the formatting and graphics. Without the skills of these key persons, this program would never have reached this point. For their dedication, we are profoundly grateful. Other important contributors to this project include Steven Knicely, Tom O'Connor, Wang Jianqi, Eric Shepherd, Jian Xiaobin, and Wang Yuanyuan.

Funding for this course came from the Defense Language Institute, a U.S. Department of Education International Research and Study grant, and the Freeman Foundation.

This course will eventually cover many volumes and audio disks. In thanking our families for showing understanding when we have spent too much time and attention to this project, we hope we can extend their good graces into the future until it reaches completion.

INTRODUCTION

Chinese: Communicating in the Culture is designed for the rank beginner who wants to speak Mandarin Chinese. This set of materials starts the learner off with sufficient support to prepare for a class or to develop fundamental speaking skills in self-study. These materials include a "Performance Text" and an audio program. The text serves as a guide through the audio program where the teaching and learning occurs. The content covers three general areas: instructional expressions, people, and places.

In Unit Zero you learn instructional expressions in order to interact with your instructor in Chinese. The expressions presented here have been selected as the most frequently observed communications between teacher and student in a Chinese class that is focused on the student's performance. Although there are alternatives to many of these expressions, a careful instructor can keep to these expressions until the student has internalized them in his or her class performance. After that, perhaps the instructor will want to use other expressions.

The unit focusing on people practices you on recognizing, addressing, and discussing a variety of persons. The point is to direct your attention on how Chinese address one another and to give you enough language resources to discuss the good and not-so-good aspects of people around you.

People in places is the focus of Unit Two. Here you can practice talking about where people are and what they are doing there.

These materials are designed for the learner who understands that learning a language entails not only what to say, but also how to say it and when to say it. We try to give the learner sufficient support to be well prepared to work with a competent instructor. But for this to happen, the learner must understand that a lot of listening, repeating, and speaking has to happen before his or her performance reaches the acceptable level.

Chinese: Communicating in the Culture is designed for the learner, whether that learner is part of a class or studying on his or her own. The Performance Text only works in conjunction with the audio program. Anyone using it without the audio program will be lost.

The audio program will either accompany this volume or be available on a class website. When working with this program, the learner will be exposed to recordings in all sorts of conditions. Some excerpts have been recorded on the site of the action and some have been recorded in a sound studio. Some of the speakers are trained professional broadcasters, some are not. Therefore, there is not a consistent quality of voices or of recording conditions. We have chosen this approach because we know it is the best way to prepare the learner to comprehend Mandarin outside the class. We do understand, however, that our choice will require the learner to listen somewhat longer and repeat somewhat more often.

The dialogs in ***Chinese: Communicating in the Culture*** have for the most part been taken from actual conversational exchanges that we have observed or recorded. As a result, the conversations you encounter here are somewhat different from those in other Mandarin textbooks. Actual spontaneous conversation, as opposed to a composed dialog, is somewhat problematic — people do not always behave the way we would like our models to behave. But we have decided that these dialogs will give the learner a better capacity to deal with the Mandarin Chinese he or she will encounter in China or in a Chinese community outside China.

The vocabulary presented in these materials is listed three ways in the appendices: by unit and stage — there you can find all the words and phrases presented in each lesson; by *pīnyīn* — there you can look up the Chinese according conventional spellings; by English — if you remember an English interpretation of a word you have learned, you can try to find the Mandarin equivalent.

Learning Chinese

There are good reasons for you to learn Chinese. Mandarin Chinese is the first language to more speakers than any other language. It is the official language of China and the inheritor of a rich cultural tradition that can be traced back thousands of years. Throughout history, Chinese culture has directly influenced other major cultures of East Asia and contributed broadly to cultures around the world. In present times, the impact of the Chinese people is being felt throughout the world—their growing economic power affects the price of goods and commodities across the planet and Chinese movies, music, and martial arts are gaining aficionados everywhere, just to mention a couple of obvious influences. As the Chinese people encounter the 21st Century, they are bringing social and scientific innovations to the international scene and are steadily establishing a record of Chinese contributions to the modern world. If you are looking at this textbook, you obviously have a sense of all this and are considering beginning the study of Mandarin. A brief introduction to this process might prove useful.

Mandarin is one of seven mutually unintelligible "dialects" of Chinese. It is spoken by approximately 70% of all Chinese speakers and is the language of education and public activities. China is a linguistically complex country: You are likely to find yourself in a bilingual environment wherever you go in the country and even Mandarin has several varieties that appear to be clearly different from one another. We are presenting *pǔtōnghuà* in these materials. We might call it "broadcast standard." It is a version of Mandarin that you will hear on television and radio programs across China. The voices you will hear belong to professional actors and broadcasters in addition to ordinary people from all parts of the country. The reason for this diversity is to give you the opportunity to develop a general familiarity with the way the language is spoken throughout China.

Chinese has distinctive characteristics that will influence the way you approach learning the language. It is a tonal language. This means you have to develop a perception of tones and invest them with phonological value. A tone in Chinese is as necessary as a consonant in English. If you do not get it right, you will not be easily understood.

The basic unit of sound in Chinese is the syllable. And there are relatively few of them and the tones are important in distinguishing one from the other. You will soon learn to distinguish *tāng* (soup) from *táng* (sugar), *tǎng* (to lie down), and *tàng* (scalding). Compare the small number of Chinese syllables (1282) with the English syllables that are over ten thousand. This means that each syllable in Chinese conveys much information, and that pronunciation is an important concern. The time you invest into practicing and improving your pronunciation as you learn to speak the language will yield an impressive rate of return for you as you progress in your Chinese skills.

If you come to Chinese from a background in European languages, the grammatical features of Chinese are not what you might expect. There are no gender agreements, no tense is added to verbs, nouns and pronouns do not decline, and verbs do not conjugate.

The choice of words and word order are basic to expressing your meaning. Therefore, learning vocabulary and practicing patterns of expressions and sentences are other crucial activities on your way to fluency.

Chinese culture itself is perhaps the most distinctive feature influencing communication in this language. Chinese speakers do not behave in their language the way speakers of English are apt to behave in theirs. Learning to communicate in Chinese is not only a matter of learning what to say, but also when and how to say it. In this course of study, when we present the language of a lesson, we try to put you into the situation where that particular piece of language would be used. We expect you to learn to perform the language in the context of the situation just as if you were an overpaid actor on a sitcom. Perform it as if you mean what you say enough times and, as if by magic, you will come to actually mean what you say. The secret to successfully learning to speak Chinese is this: Speak a lot of Chinese in situations you understand.

Chinese: Communicating in the Culture is designed to give you the best possible opportunity to speak Chinese in a way that seems natural to Chinese people. We do this by giving you an opportunity to learn to perform a role in a conversation and to practice the spoken expressions and cultural moves that were introduced in the conversation. The result should be that you are able to use these expressions and moves in new situations. Listening is the key skill. If your listening comprehension is good, you are in a position to develop accurate speech and efficient reading. Your success in this program depends on your willingness to work hard on the audio component. That should absolutely be the focus of your study.

In order to take full advantage of this program, you should pay attention to following five basic principles:

1. The Chinese you need to learn in this course is on the audio program. A successful learner of Chinese will develop the ability to learn it aurally. Life, culture, and language occur on the fly and without the convenience of subtitles that you can refer to when your comprehension falters. The graphic and printed versions of the language are there to help you access and keep your place while you are working with the sounds of the language.

2. The more you perform the language, the better and faster you will learn it. There is nothing mystical about learning Chinese: the more you do, the more you are able to do. When you get the chance, perform the conversations as if you were auditioning for a part in a play, movie, or a lucrative commercial with the possibility of long-term residuals. Get used to speaking the language in a full, natural sounding voice. If you sound strange speaking Chinese at first, that is to be expected. Hey! You're speaking Chinese! With constant performance of the language, you will soon develop a comfortable familiarity with the Chinese coming from your own voice. At that point, let others be amazed at the smooth Chinese emanating from you. No matter how little Chinese you can say, strive to say it in a way that would make someone overhearing you think you know the whole language.

3. Use your imagination. The more vividly you can picture yourself observing or participating in a conversation with a Chinese person, the more quickly you will recall the Chinese you have learned. If you can visualize the event in color, you will be a better student of Chinese than if you can only manage to imagine in black and white. When you learn a new structure or set of vocabulary, take the time to use them in real, virtual, or simply pretend situations.

4. Recall the story of a conversational exchange. Something happens in a particular situation every time two or more persons converse. Keep that event in mind as you practice and review expressions, questions, and responses. Remember newly studied language as a part of communicating with a Chinese person — real or imagined. When you have the opportunity to interact with Chinese people, notice how things are done--what they are like when speaking Chinese or English and how their behavior is similar to or different from your expectations.

5. Look for opportunities to experiment and observe the result. If you are around Mandarin speakers, practice doing with them what you have learned in this program and learn to accurately observe the response. Languages are complex, so do not be disturbed if the responses are not according to the scripts you have learned, and be delighted when they are. Enjoy both the successes and the failures. Your ability to appreciate the process of gaining skills in a new language is a strong indicator of your eventual success. In learning to actually communicate with Chinese, you can learn as much from failure as from success. As you experiment more and learn more Chinese, you will steadily increase the number of successful exchanges. Samuel Beckett encouraged his actors with good advice: "Try. Fail. Try again. Fail better."

Chinese: Communicating in the Culture has different components that are designed to give you opportunities to observe how communication occurs in a specific context, to understand it, and to practice communication moves that are recognized by most Chinese speakers. Some of the activities are easy and some are really hard. However, we have tried to make sure that you know what is going on as you learn to communicate in Chinese culture. This audio program and accompanying textbook are divided into "units" and "stages". A unit focuses on a particular area such as "people" (Unit One). A stage is basically one lesson. There are ten stages in each unit. Most of the stages consist of a dialog and a set of drills, but there are also stages focused on pronunciation and romanization, and on reading and writing. The final stage in a unit is a self test. It is there for you to check out your comprehension and general command of the materials presented in the unit.

In the stages consisting of a dialog and drills, the audio program will have a "coaching" version with extensive English explanations and a "rehearsal" version that presents the Chinese without the explanations. Once you understand the lesson from the coaching, go to the rehearsal audio and concentrate on the Chinese. Do a lot of listening and repeating. Get used to hearing Chinese and hearing yourself speak Chinese. Below are introductions to the various components in these materials.

Instructional Expressions

These are presented in Unit Zero. The time you are together with your instructor is extremely valuable. It should be spent with you speaking as much Chinese as possible and your instructor reacting, responding, and correcting your performance. Whether you study in a classroom or individually, you need to leave your session with the impression that you experienced an intensive Chinese workout and you have an accurate idea of how well you did that. These instructional expressions will help you experience these kinds of sessions. Learn them by listening to the audio program and repeating after the models. From time to time you will have a drill to check out your understanding.

Dialog Coaching

Dialogs are provided for you to see and hear how people communicate in particular situations and to give you the opportunity to assume the roles of those people. In the presentation of a dialog, you will hear a number of different voices belonging to standard Mandarin speakers from different regions of China.

Coaching is on the audio program. Here you are talked through a conversation with descriptions of conversational situations, new expressions, new grammatical concepts, and tips on pronunciation. Listen to the explanation and repeat the new expressions. You should work with the coaching until you are familiar with the dialog. That means until you can place everything you hear in a social context and basically understand what is being said. The dialogs are close to natural conversational performances. Some are more difficult to hear because they were recorded on site with background noise. In such cases, our advice is to listen more carefully and a few more times.

Coaching concludes with a presentation of vocabulary of the expressions introduced in each stage. The vocabulary items are grouped into categories by either part of speech or meaning. You can listen as each item is pronounced, given an English explanation or gloss. When we think it is useful, we will add a few examples of the expression in sentences or exchanges.

Role Play Rehearsals

At the end of the coaching, you will have an opportunity to act out the dialog with the players on the tape. This lets you put yourself into a conversation by assuming the roles of each participant. The idea is to be able to fit your part into the flow of the conversation. You will probably need a number of repetitions to perform a conversation smoothly. Accuracy in pronunciation and delivery takes time. The way to shorten that time is to develop a self-critical ear by noticing where your performance deviates significantly from the native speakers and where it is spot on.

Practice Drills

Drills are designed to generalize your ability to use the new items presented in each dialog conversation. The goal is to prepare you to use these items in a variety of situations. In addition to practicing the items introduced in the conversations, the drills will introduce variations on these items. For example, if you learn to use adjectives to describe what people look like in a conversation, the drills will lead you to practice how to ask about a person's appearance. Some drills are easy and some are very difficult. Be sure you understand what you are to do in the drill and what it means before you spend a lot of time on it. Listen carefully to the examples and the introduction to the drill and review the points focused on there.

You may want to first go through all the drills to get an idea of what is covered in the Stage you are studying. Then go back and perform in each drill repeatedly until you have the response pattern down. After that, repeat the entire set of drills until you reach a sense of familiarity with all the items practiced in the drills. The ability to perform competently in the drills will assure you of success in learning to speak the language.

Pronunciation and Romanization (P&R)

As you begin to learn to communicate in Chinese, you will be encouraged to pay attention to pronunciation. After you have practiced a number of expressions and situations, you will encounter the first P&R. These six stages distributed over three units will present the sounds of Mandarin in a systematic way. Go through them carefully and return to them from time to time to "recalibrate" your perception and pronunciation of particular syllables and combinations.

Chinese is represented in the Roman alphabet in a system called *pīnyīn*. This is the way you will first be introduced to the language in this program of study. *Pīnyīn* uses most of the letters of the English alphabet, lacking only *V v*, and adding an umlaut *Ǔ ǔ*. The tones in Mandarin are indicated by the following marks above the main vowel of each syllable: *ā á ǎ à*. The absence of such a mark indicates a neutral tone.

As you embark on your study of Chinese, learning *pīnyīn* is important—reference works such as dictionaries use it, publications in English represent Chinese by using it, and it is a popular input method for typing Chinese on computers. However, in the early stages, it is best to focus your attention on the audio program and to think of that venue as the source of your Mandarin. The more you train yourself to hear and discriminate Chinese sounds, the faster your listening and reading comprehension develops and the more accurate your speaking becomes.

Reading and Writing

After you have been introduced to the sound system and have had enough time to become familiar with the way Mandarin sounds, we will introduce you to the writing system of Chinese. On your way to becoming a fluent reader of Chinese, you will learn 3000-4000 graphs or *hànzì* (Chinese characters). Each graph represents one morpheme, or a unit of meaning, and one syllable. Words in Chinese are usually written with more than one *hànzì*. There are two versions of *hànzì* (Chinese characters) with which beginning learners of Chinese have to contend—traditional and simplified. Simplified (or *jiǎntǐzì*) is the version used in the People's Republic of China and Singapore. The traditional characters (or *fántǐzì*) are used in Taiwan, Hong Kong, and in Chinese communities throughout the world. Most foreign students of Chinese need to know both versions, especially if they are interested in reading documents from an earlier time than mid-Twentieth Century; however, it is common for a student of the language to be more familiar with one form or the other. In this program of study we offer the option to choose either *jiǎntǐzì* or *fántǐzì*. Decades of observation of students of Chinese and some research indicates that beginning with the traditional and then picking up the simplified results in more learners developing that ability to use both forms. But the choice of which version one starts with most often depends on one's instructor or on what part of the Chinese speaking world one intends to travel to.

In this program the first things you learn to read are name cards. Name cards are very common in Chinese speaking society. They function as a reminder of a person's name and their social status. Most importantly they indicate the title one should use when addressing someone in Chinese. From this simple beginning, we will launch you on a reading career that will open onto a vast landscape of possibilities.

Concluding the Introduction

Learning Chinese is a brave and serious undertaking. Chinese culture represents a huge part of human experience on this planet and often is the major cultural alternative to the Western perspective. Being consistent, patient, and persevering is important here. If you learn to communicate in Chinese culture, it will change the way you see the world and change the way you see yourself. Such transformations are not quick and easy. So plan for the long march.

UNIT 0
Instructional Expressions

These expressions will help you in the instructional sessions with your teacher. Unless you are discussing knowledge about Chinese, your instructional session should be conducted in Chinese. This is difficult at first, but it is the beginning step for preparing you to cope with the predicaments that you as a foreign speaker of Chinese can expect to encounter.

These phrases will permit you to interact with your teacher in Chinese. Learn them as you would learn key phrases before taking a trip to a country you have never before experienced. These expressions are to be recognized so that you can respond to the teacher's expectations. You will want to rehearse some of the expressions until you can say them when the proper time comes. You will know which expressions these are when you encounter them. Now, begin by listening to a segment of the audio program: Unit 0 Stage 1.

Chinese: Communicating in the Culture is fundamentally an audio program. These materials <u>must</u> be used with the audio program. Find the appropriate track before turning the page. Learn the Chinese in the audio program by using these print materials when useful.

Greetings between Instructor and Student(s)

A student greets the teacher and the teacher responds.

Student:	**Lǎoshī hǎo.**
	How are you, teacher?
Instructor:	**Nǐ hǎo.**
	How are you, (student)?

Students greet the teacher and the teacher responds.

Students:	**Lǎoshī hǎo.**
	How are you, teacher?
Instructor:	**Nǐmen hǎo.**
or	**Tóngxuémen hǎo.**
	How are you, (students)?

Instructor Feedback and Guidance

The teacher is approving a student's response.

Instructor: **Duì le.**
                Correct.

The teacher is not approving a student's response.

Instructor: **Bú-duì.**
                Not correct.

DRILL

Look at the equations and practice judging the correctness of an anwer:

Example:

$$\pi = 1.234$$

Student: **Bú-duì.**
Not correct.

1

$$4^2 = 16$$

2

$$\sqrt{16} = 4$$

3

$$7 \div 2 = 4$$

4

$$\sqrt{4} = 16$$

5

$$\sqrt{16} = 2 \times 2$$

The teacher is asking a student to sit down.

Qǐng
Please

Qǐng zuò.
Please be seated.

The teacher is starting a class.

Xiànzài
Now

Kè
Class

Shàngkè le.
Let's begin class.

Xiànzài shàngkè le.
Now let's begin class.

Instructor Directions

The teacher asks the student(s) to repeat after her.

Shuō
Speak

Gēnzhe wǒ shuō
Speak after me

Qǐng gēnzhe wǒ shuō.
Please speak after me.

Qǐng nǐ gēnzhe wǒ shuō.
Please (you) speak after me.

The teacher asks everyone to repeat after her.

Dàjiā
Everyone

Dàjiā gēnzhe wǒ shuō.
Everyone speak after me.

Qǐng dàjiā gēnzhe wǒ shuō.
Everyone speak after me please.

The teacher asks the student(s) to listen to what she says.

Tīng
Listen

Tīng wǒ shuō
Listen to me

Qǐng nǐ tīng wǒ shuō.
Please (you) listen to me.

Qǐng dàjiā tīng wǒ shuō.
Please (everyone) listen to me.

Practice following the teacher's request. Repeat after the example, where you are asked either to repeat or listen to what the teacher says:

Example: Instructor: **Qǐng nǐ gēnzhe wǒ shuō: Qǐng zuò.**
              Student: **Qǐng zuò.**
              Instructor: **Qǐng nǐ tīng wǒ shuō: Qǐng zuò.**
              Student: _____

1. **Dàjiā hǎo.**

2. **Xiànzài**

3.

4.

5. **Bú-duì.**

Instructor Directions and Questions

The teacher asks the student(s) to say it again.

Yíbiàn
Once

Shuō yíbiàn
Say (something) once

Zài shuō yíbiàn.
Say (it) one more time (again).

Qǐng nǐ zài shuō yíbiàn.
Would you please say (it) again?

How do you say (something) in Chinese?

Zěnme shuō?
How do you say (something)?

Zhōngwén
Chinese

(......) Zhōngwén zěnme shuō?
How do you say (...) in Chinese?

"New York" Zhōngwén zěnme shuō?
How do you say "New York" in Chinese?

DRILL

Practice giving the Chinese equivalent:

Example: Instructor: **"Instructor" Zhōngwén zěnme shuō?**
                Student: **Lǎoshī.**

1.   2.   3.   4.   5.

Instructor Questions and Directions

How do you say (something) in English?

Zhōngwén
Chinese

Yīngwén
English

(......) Yīngwén zěnme shuō?
How do you say (...) in English?

(......) Zhōngwén zěnme shuō?
How do you say (...) in Chinese?

DRILL

Practice giving Chinese and English equivalents:

Example: Instructor: **"Qǐng zuò" Yīngwén zěnme shuō?**
            Student: **Please be seated.**

    1.   2.   3.   4.   5.

Please ask your question(s).

Wèntí
A question/Questions

Wèn wèntí
Ask a question/Ask questions

Qǐng nǐ wèn wèntí.
Please ask (your) question(s).

DRILL

Practice asking for the Chinese and English equivalents:

Example: **Lǎoshī**
Instructor: **Qǐng nǐ wèn wèntí.**
Student: **"Lǎoshī" Yīngwén zěnme shuō?**
Instructor: **Instructor.**

1.   **Zhōngwén**

2.   **Question**

3.   **English**

4.   **Wèntí**

5.   **Instructor**

Please answer the question.

Huídá
Answer

Nǐ huídá
(You) answer.

Qǐng nǐ huídá.
(You) answer please.

DRILLS

Drill One: Practice answering questions when requested:

Example: Instructor: **Qǐng nǐ huídá. "Tóngxué" Yīngwén zěnme shuō?**
Student: **Student.**
1.   2.   3.

Drill Two: *Practice asking and answering questions about the Chinese and English words you see:*

Example 1: Cue: Qǐng nǐ huídá.
             Instructor: "Tóngxué" Yīngwén zěnme shuō?
             Student: **Student.**

Example 2: You read: **Wèntí**
             Cue: Qǐng nǐ wèn wèntí.
             Student: **"Wèntí" Yīngwén zěnme shuō?**
             Instructor: **Question.**

1. **Zhōngwén**
     Cue: Qǐng nǐ huídá.
     Instructor: "Zhōngwén" Yīngwén zěnme shuō?
     Student:

2. **Now**
     Cue: Qǐng nǐ wèn wèntí.
     Student:
     Instructor: **Xiànzài.**

3. **Lǎoshī**
     Cue: Qǐng nǐ wèn wèntí.
     Student:
     Instructor: **Instructor.**

4. **Ask a question**
     Cue: Qǐng nǐ huídá.
     Instructor: "Ask a question" Zhōngwén zěnme shuō?
     Student:

5. **Garlic**
     Cue: Qǐng nǐ wèn wèntí.
     Student:
     Instructor: **Dàsuàn.**

Pronunciation and Romanization: Tones

In this stage we are going to introduce a major feature of Mandarin Chinese—the tones. As a beginning learner of the language, one of the first things to do is to distinguish the four tones and neutral tones of the language when you hear them. We will first direct your attention to the four tones and later let you hear variations of the neutral tones.

High-level

Tāng

Rising

Táng

Low-rising

Tǎng

Falling

Tàng

Táng

Tāng   Táng

Pay attention to the heavily aspriated T. Listen to "soup" and "candy" spoken one after another and hear how they are different.

Here is another chance to distinguish these two words. When you hear the word, mark the correct tone:

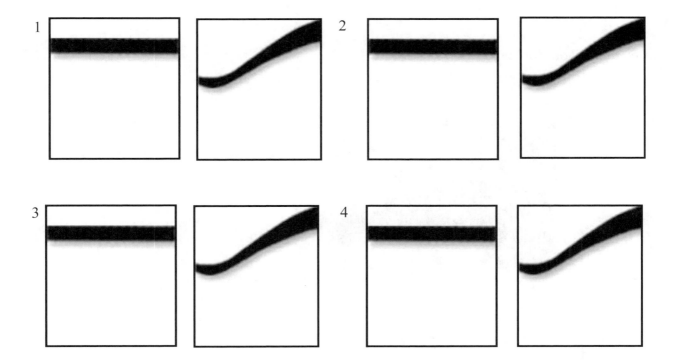

Your correct choice should be as follows:

Listen to the word for "lie down":

   Tăng

Now listen to see if you can hear and mark the tone when the instructor says "soup", "candy", and "reclining".

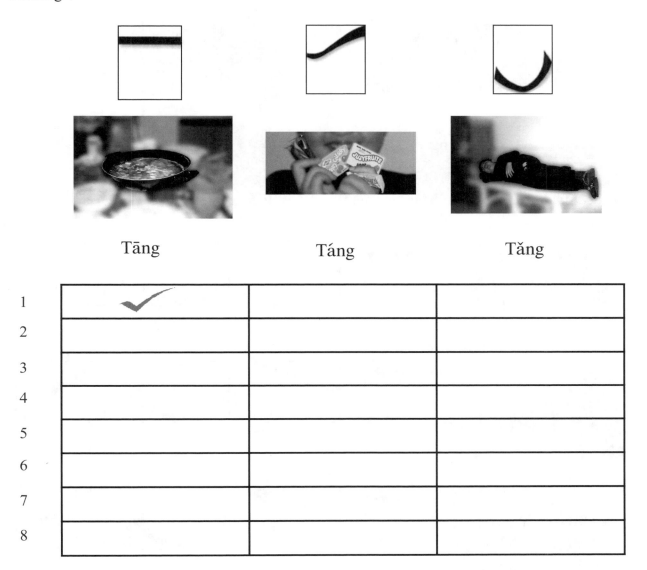

Tāng   Táng   Tǎng

1	✓	
2		
3		
4		
5		
6		
7		
8		

Finally, listen to the word for "scalding hot".

Tàng

Now, listen to the difference between "candy" and "scalding":

Táng   Tàng

Now, identify the tone you hear by checking the appropriate tone mark:

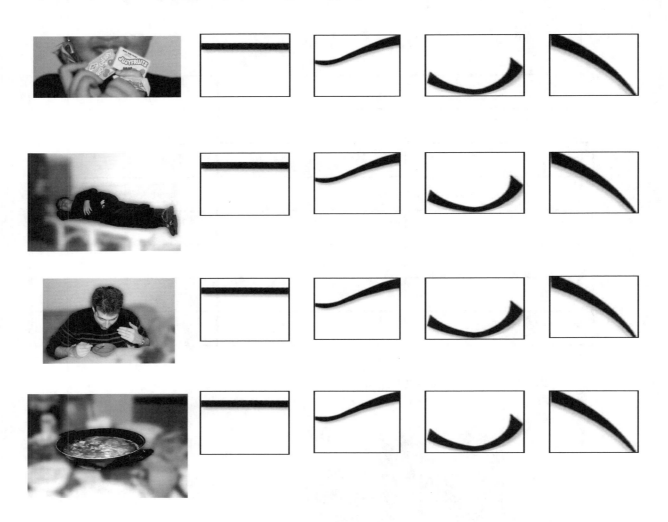

Did you get all four tones correct? This is the end of Unit 0 Stage 6. We'll continue with pronunciation and romanization in Unit 0 Stage 9.

Instructor and Learner Feedback Expressions

Do you understand?

Dǒng le ma?
Understand?

Nǐ dǒng le ma?
Do you understand?

Dǒng le.
(I) understand.

Bù-dǒng.
(No, I) don't understand.

Drill One: Practice answering questions about your understanding of the following five words and expressions:

Example:

"Lǎoshī"

Instructor: **Nǐ dǒng le ma?**
Student: **Dǒng le.**

Example:

"Diànnǎo"

Instructor: **Nǐ dǒng le ma?**
Student: **Bù-dǒng.**

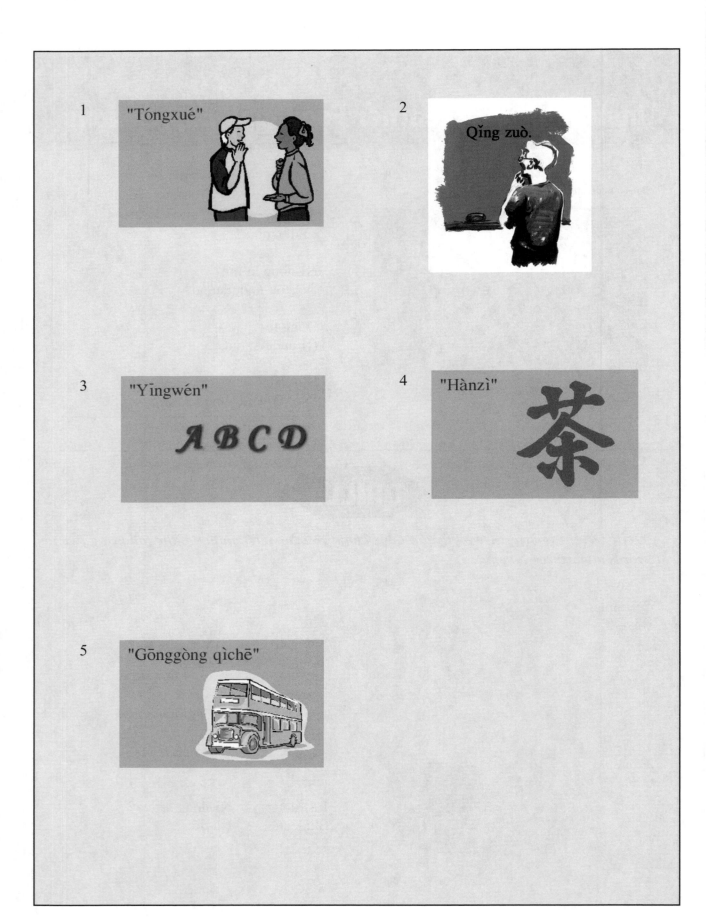

Drill Two: *Practice asking and answering questions about understanding:*

Example:

"Instructor"

Lǎoshī.

Instructor: **Qǐng wèn wèntí.**
Student: **Nǐ dǒng le ma?**
Instructor B: **Dǒng le.**

Example:

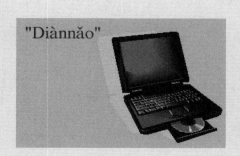

"Diànnǎo"

Instructor A: **Qǐng nǐ huídá.**
Instructor B: **Nǐ dǒng le ma?**
Student: **Bù-dǒng.**

1

"Tóngxué"

2

Qǐng zuò.

3   "Yīngwén"

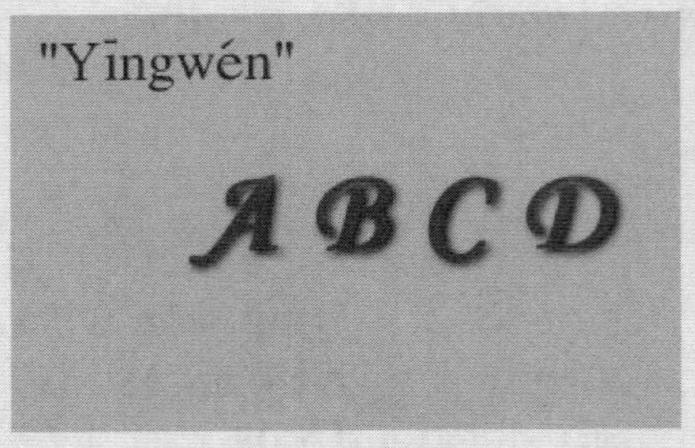

ABCD

4   "Hànzì"

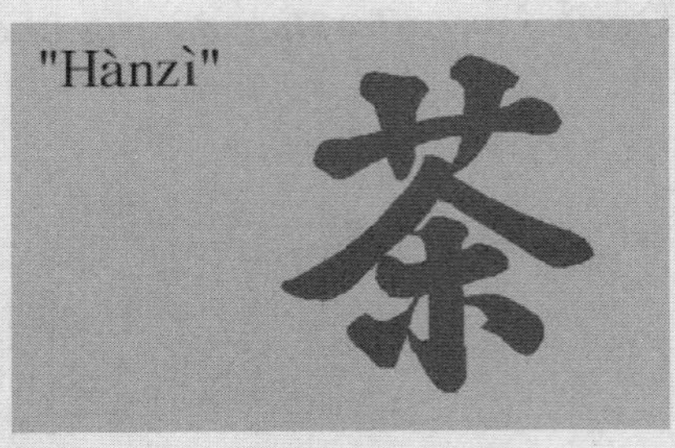

茶

5   "Gōnggòng qìchē"

I don't know.

Bù-zhīdao.
(I) don't know.

DRILL

Practice answering questions according to the directions:

Example:	Instructor:	**"Instructor" Zhōngwén zěnme shuō?**
	Student:	**Lǎoshī.**

Example:	Instructor:	**"Soccer" Zhōngwén zěnme shuō?**
	Student:	**Bù-zhīdao.**

1.   2.   3.   4.

5.   6.   7.   8.

Instructor Verification and Conclusion of Class

Are there any questions?

Yǒu
Have

Méi-you
Not have

Yǒu méi-you?
Are there any?/Is there one?

Yǒu méi-you wèntí?
Are there any questions?

I have (a) question(s).

Yǒu wèntí.
Have (a) question(s).

Méi-you wèntí.
(I) don't have (a) question(s).

Yǒu wèntí.

DRILL

Practice giving the Chinese equivalent:

Example: You see: **Xiànzài = ?**
                   Instructor: **Yǒu méi-you wèntí?**
                   Student: **Yǒu wèntí.**

1.   **Lǎoshī = Instructor**

2.   **Shàngkè = Start class**

3.   **Tóngxuémen = ?**

4.   **Zhōngwén = Chinese**

5.   **Dàjiā = ?**

End of the class

Xiàkè le.
Class is over.

Xiànzài xiàkè le.
Class is over now.

Xiàkè le.

Expressing gratitude to the teacher

Xiè
(To accept with gratitude)

Xièxie.
(To accept with gratitude)

Xièxie lǎoshī.
(To accept with gratitude from your teacher)

Response to expressions of gratitude

Kèqi
Polite; politeness

Bú-kèqi.
No need to be polite/You are welcome.

Good-bye.

Zài
Again

Jiàn
To see

Zàijiàn.
See you again/Good-bye.

Pronunciation and Romanization: Tones

In this stage we are going to see how well you distinguish the four tones. When you hear a syllable, indicate its tone by checking on the appropriate tone representation.

DRILLS

Drill One: tāng vs táng

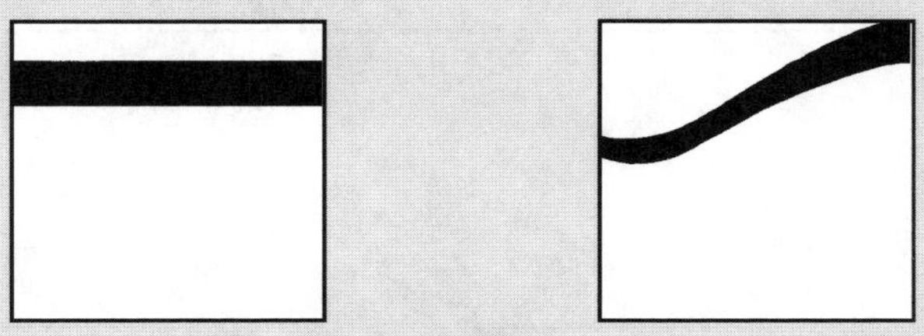

✓	

1
2
3
4
5

Drill Two: tū vs tǔ

1		✓
2		
3		
4		
5		
6		

Drill Three: táo vs tǎo

1		✓
2		
3		
4		
5		
6		

Drill Four: tōu vs tòu

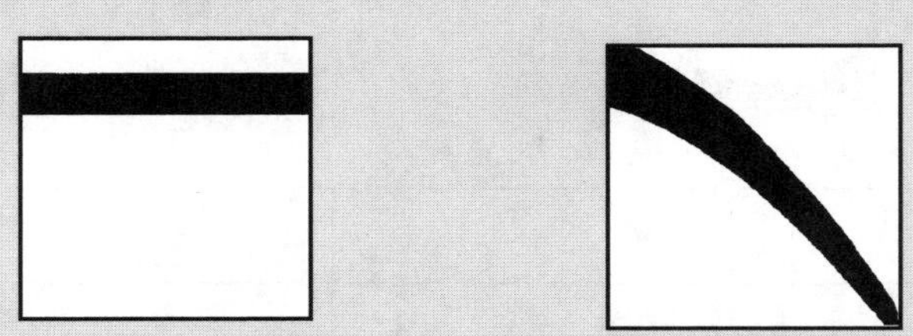

1		✓
2		
3		
4		
5		
6		

Drill Five: tái vs tài

1		✓
2		
3		
4		
5		
6		

Drill Six: tăn vs tàn

1	✓	
2		
3		
4		
5		
6		

Drill Seven: distinguish the four tones.

1	✓			
2				
3				
4				
5				
6				
7				

How did you do with this? You should work with this stage until you are skilled in detecting which of the four tones you are hearing. This is the end of Unit 0 Stage 9.

Self-test One: *Select the appropriate description of the expression you hear.*

Example: You hear: **Zàijiàn**

a) request to repeat a sentence
b) expression of farewell
c) question about understanding
d) statement about correctness

Correct answer: b) expression of farewell

1
a) statement of well being
b) greeting to students
c) request for perfection
d) greeting to an instructor

2
a) requests you to be seated
b) request for an answer
c) statement that a problem exists
d) expression of farewell

3
a) begins class
b) requests you to ask a question
c) statement that you do not have the desired information
d) ends a class

4
a) requests you to repeat what you just said
b) greeting from instructor to class
c) requests you to be seated
d) requests you to listen to what the speaker has to say

5
a) begins class
b) requests you to ask a question
c) statement that you do not have the desired information
d) ends class

6
a) asks how to say something in Chinese
b) asks if there are any questions or problems
c) states the lack of understanding
d) requests you to be seated

7 a) requests you to repeat what you
      just said
   b) greeting from instructor to class
   c) requests you to be seated
   d) requests you to listen to what the
      speaker has to say

8 a) begins class
   b) requests you to answer a question
   c) states that you do not have the
      desired information
   d) ends class

9 a) begins class
   b) requests you to answer a question
   c) states that you do not have the
      desired information
   d) ends class

10 a) begins class
   b) requests you to answer a question
   c) states you do not have the desired
      information
   d) ends class

11 a) states well being
   b) greeting students
   c) requests perfection
   d) greeting to an instructor

12 a) states that something is incorrect
   b) requests you to repeat what the
      speaker says
   c) asks if there are any problems or
      questions
   d) requests you to listen to what the
      speaker is saying

13 a) requests you to repeat a sentence
   b) expresses farewell
   c) asks about understanding
   d) states that something is correct

14 a) asks how to say something in
      Chinese
   b) asks if there are any questions or
      problems
   c) states a lack of understanding
   d) requests you to be seated

15 a) states a lack of understanding
   b) states the absence of the desired
      information
   c) states that something is wrong
   d) states that something is correct

16 a) states that something does not exist
   b) states that something is wrong
   c) states non-comprehension
   d) expresses farewell

17 a) states a lack of understanding
   b) states that something is incorrect
   c) states the lack of the desired
      information
   d) states that something does not exist

18 a) states that something is correct.
   b) states that comprehension has
      occurred
   c) asks about comprehension
   d) expresses greeting from instructor
      to students

19   a) ends class
b) asks about comprehension
c) asks if there are any problems
d) asks how to say something in Chinese

20   a) states that there is a question
b) states comprehension
c) states a lack of understanding
d) asks if there are any problems

Self-test Two: *Select the appropriate expression for each description you hear.*

Example: You hear: **Greet your instructor.**

        a) Zàijiàn.
        b) Lǎoshī hǎo.
        c) Nǐmen hǎo.

Correct answer: b) Lǎoshī hǎo.

1   a) Yǒu wèntí.
b) Tóngxuémen hǎo.
c) Xiànzài xiàkè le.

2   a) Bù-dǒng.
b) Bú-duì.
c) Duì-le.

3   a) Bù-dǒng.
b) Bú-duì.
c) Duì le.

4   a) Bù-zhīdao.
b) Qǐngzuò, xiànzài shàngkè le.
c) Xiànzài xiàkè le.

5   a) Qǐng nǐ gēnzhe wǒ shuō.
b) Qǐng nǐ zài shuō yíbiàn.
c) Zhōngwén zěnme shuō?

6   a) Qǐng nǐ zài shuō yíbiàn.
b) Dàjiā tīng wǒ shuō.
c) Qǐng nǐ gēnzhe wǒ shuō.

7   a) Qǐng nǐ zài shuō yíbiàn.
b) Qǐng nǐ tīng wǒ shuō.
c) Qǐng nǐ gēnzhe wǒ shuō.

8   a) Zhōngwén zěnme shuō?
b) Qǐng nǐ huídá.
c) Qǐng nǐ wèn wèntí.

9   a) Zhōngwén zěnme shuō?
      b) Yǒu méi-you wèntí?
      c) Dǒng le ma?

10   a) Zhōngwén zěnme shuō?
      b) Yǒu méi-you wèntí?
      c) Yīngwén zěnme shuō?

11   a) Zhōngwén zěnme shuō?
      b) Qǐng nǐ huídá.
      c) Qǐng nǐ wèn wèntí.

12   a) Zhōngwén zěnme shuō?
      b) Yǒu méi-you wèntí?
      c) Dǒng le ma?

13   a) Bú-duì.
      b) Bù-dǒng.
      c) Dǒng le.

14   a) Bú-duì.
      b) Bù-dǒng.
      c) Bù-zhīdao.

15   a) Bú-duì.
      b) Bù-dǒng.
      c) Bù-zhīdao.

16   a) Yǒu méi-you wèntí?
      b) Xiànzài xiàkè le.
      c) Nǐ tīng wǒ shuō.

17   a) Zàijiàn.
      b) Bú-duì.
      c) Méi-you wèntí.

18   a) Duì le.
      b) Yǒu wèntí.
      c) Dǒng le.

19   a) Qǐng nǐ gēnzhe wǒ shuō.
      b) Xiànzài xiàkè le.
      c) Bù-dǒng.

20   a) Tóngxuémen hǎo.
      b) Zàijiàn.
      c) Qǐng nǐ zài shuō yíbiàn.

Yǒu wèntí.

UNIT 1
Meeting and Identifying People

Unit One is designed to give you some basic skills at meeting and identifying people.

The general procedure is to guide you through a conversation, rehearse you to participate in that conversation, and then expand your ability to conduct similar, but different, conversations. Your success in learning to perform the Chinese on this audio program will depend on the extent of your involvement with the program. The more you listen and participate using your normal speaking voice, the more you will retain in your memory and the better you will perform.

In Unit One, you will learn to do the following in Mandarin Chinese:

Stage One, *Meeting People*: greet people using appropriate terms of address.

Stage Two, *First Meeting*: exchange names.

Stage Three, *Exchanging Information about Names*: identify people by name and position.

Stage Four, *Discussing Someone's Condition*: ask and answer questions about present and previous conditions of people you know.

Stage Five, *Pronunciation and Romanization: Initials, Medials, and Finals*: pronunciation practice.

Stage Six, *Discussing People*: discuss the appearance of people and compare them with others.

Stage Seven, *Identifying People*: describe people by appearance and personality, find out if people have free time.

Stage Eight, *Pronunciation and Romanization: Initials, Medials, and Finals*: pronunciation practice.

Stage Nine, *Meeting and Introducing People*: introduce yourself, welcome people, and apologize for not meeting expectations.

Stage Ten, *Self Test*: test your command of the Chinese you have studied.

Dialogue Setting

Sino-American Trade Co., Washington, DC

The following exchange of greetings occurs in the Washington office of the Sino-American Trade Company between two co-workers. The two have a close working relationship. We know this because they use familiar terms of address that are based on the relative ages of the two people involved. The greeting itself is the most neutral, or context-free, greeting in Chinese. This suggests that the person initiating the greeting does not intend to stop and talk a while.

Lǎo Bái: Xiǎo Wáng, nǐ hǎo.

Xiǎo Wáng: Lǎo Bái, nǐ hǎo.

Dialogue Information:

* General greeting: **Nǐ hǎo.**

* Greeting a younger friend: **Xiǎo Wáng, nǐ hǎo.**

* Greeting an older friend: **Lǎo Bái, nǐ hǎo.**

Vocabulary (Shēngcí)

1. Chinese Family Names (xìng)
   Wáng
   Lǐ
   Liú
   Zhāng
   Bái
   Huáng

2. Terms of Address (chēnghu)
   lǎo
   xiǎo
   xiānsheng
   nǚshì
   xiáojie
   tàitai

3. Phrase (cízǔ)
   wèn......hǎo

Tāmen dōu jiào wǒ Xiǎo Lǐ......

Xiǎo Lǐ

DRILLS

Drill One: *Greet people outside of China. When you are asked to greet someone, do so:*

Example: Instructor: **Wèn Lǐ xiānsheng hǎo.**
            Student: **Lǐ xiānsheng, nǐ hǎo.**

1.   2.   3.   4.

5.   6.   7.   8.

Drill Two: *Addressing people. Choose the appropriate greeting from the choices given below:*

   a. **Wáng nǚshì, nǐ hǎo.**   b. **Zhāng xiáojie, nǐ hǎo.**

   c. **Liú xiānsheng, nǐ hǎo.**   d. **Lǎo Bái, nǐ hǎo.**

   e. **Xiǎo Lǐ, nǐ hǎo.**   f. **Bái tàitai, nǐ hǎo.**

1. **Bái** is a married woman in Taiwan.   _____

2. **Wáng** is a businesswoman coming to your
   office.   _____

3. **Liú** is a businessman coming to your office. _____

4. **Lǐ** is your younger friend.   _____

5. **Zhāng** is a young woman in Singapore.   _____

6. **Bái** is your older friend.   _____

Drill Three: Greeting the person described. Listen to the description and respond appropriately:

1.   2.   3.

4.   5.   6

Drill Four: Analyzing greetings.

Example: Instructor: **Lǐ tàitai, nǐ hǎo.**
                   Student: **Liú xiānsheng, nǐ hǎo.**

a) Mr. Li is greeting his younger friend, Liu.
b) Mr. Liu is greeting a married woman.
c) Mr. Liu is greeting a younger woman.

1   a) Mr. Wang is greeting his boss.
     b) Bai is greeting his boss.
     c) Wang is greeting his older friend.

2   a) Ms. Liu is greeting her boss.
     b) Miss Liu, a younger unmarried woman, is greeted.
     c) Ms. Liu, a businesswoman, is greeted as she arrives for a meeting.

3   a) Two friends are greeting each other.
     b) Wang is greeting his boss.
     c) Bai is greeting her boss.

Dialogue Comprehension

Lǎo Bái: Xiǎo Wáng, nǐ hǎo.
Xiǎo Wáng: Lǎo Bái, nǐ hǎo.

Nǐ hǎo

First Meeting

Dialogue Setting

**Train
Trip to
Fuzhou**

The train is at Beijing Station, awaiting departure. One of the passengers looks across to the younger man sitting opposite him and decides to get acquainted.

Dù Qiū: Qǐngwèn, nín guìxìng?

Zhāng Tóngshēng: Xìng Zhāng, Zhāng
Tóngshēng.

Dù Qiū: Ò, Xiǎo Zhāng tóngzhì.

Dialogue Information:

* Polite phrase to express your wish to ask a question: **qǐngwèn**

* Polite form of the second person singular pronoun: **nín**

* Polite way to ask for someone's family name: **guìxìng**

* Verb for family name: **xìng**

* A Chinese name: **Zhāng Tóngshēng**

* Interjection: **ò**

* "Junior" Zhang: **Xiǎo Zhāng**

* Comrade: **tóngzhì**

Vocabulary (Shēngcí)

1. Phrases (cízǔ)
   qǐngwèn
   guìxìng

2. Verb (dòngcí)
   xìng

3. Chinese Family Names (xìng)
   Ōuyáng
   Fāng
   Dù
   Chén
   Zhào
   Shī
   Lín
   Wú

4. Chinese Given Names (míng)
   Huàmíng
   Shīzhòng
   Mín

   Mǐn
   Wànxiāng
   Tóngshēng
   Qiū
   Shàntián
   Lìyù

5. Pronouns (dàicí)
   nín
   tā　**tā**

6. Negative Marker (fǒudìngcí)
   bú/bù

7. Terms of Address (chēnghu)
   tóngzhì
   tóngxué
   fùjīnglǐ

8. Interjection (gǎntàncí)
   ò

DRILLS

Drill One: *Verifying family names.*

Qīnghuá University

Zhāng Róng

Professor

Example:

Instructor: **Xìng Zhāng ma?**
Student: **Duì le, xìng Zhāng.**

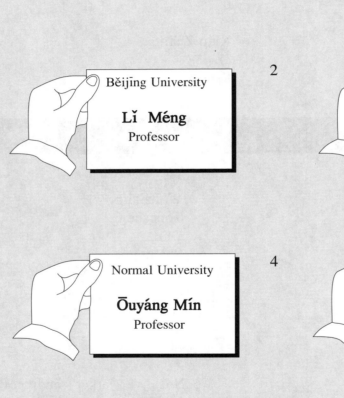

1

Běijīng University

Lǐ Méng

Professor

2

Bǎishēng Center

Chén Xīn

Manager

3

Normal University

Ōuyáng Mín

Professor

4

Chinese Literature Press

Bái Shòuhé

Editor

5

Tāofèn Bookstore

Lín Qīng

Assistant Manager

Drill Two: *Correcting an assumption.*

Example:

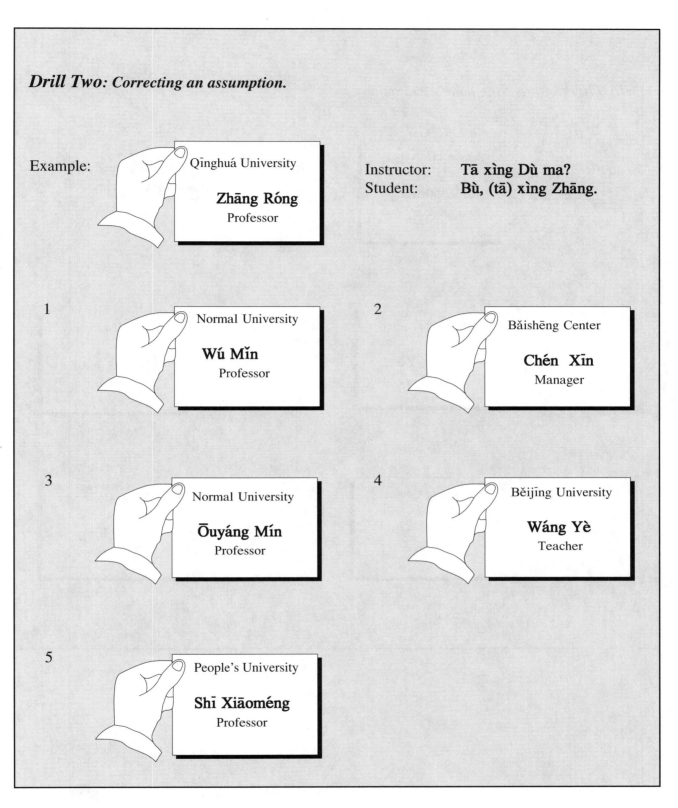

Qīnghuá University

Zhāng Róng

Professor

Instructor: **Tā xìng Dù ma?**
Student: **Bù, (tā) xìng Zhāng.**

1

Normal University

Wú Mǐn

Professor

2

Bǎishēng Center

Chén Xīn

Manager

3

Normal University

Ōuyáng Mín

Professor

4

Běijīng University

Wáng Yè

Teacher

5

People's University

Shī Xiǎoméng

Professor

Zhāng Tóngshēng

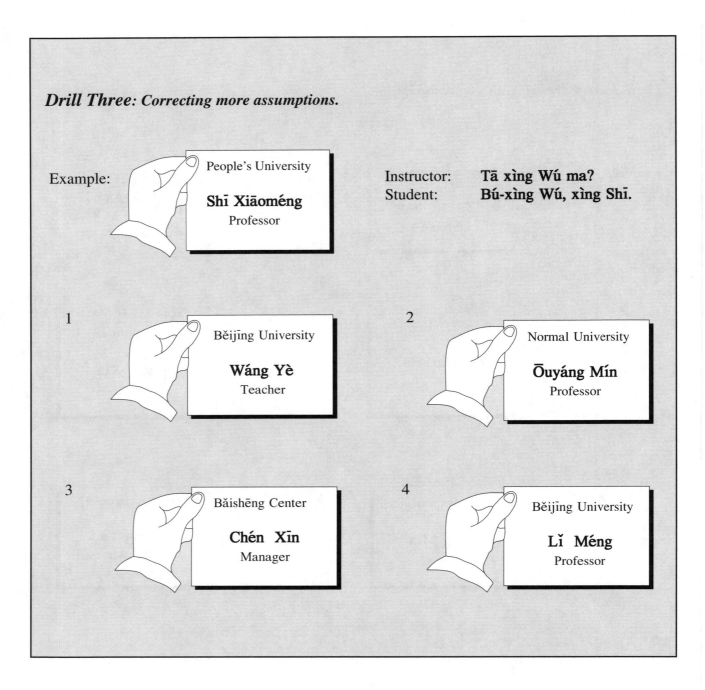

Drill Three: *Correcting more assumptions.*

Example:

People's University

Shī Xiāoméng

Professor

Instructor: **Tā xìng Wú ma?**
Student: **Bú-xìng Wú, xìng Shī.**

1

Běijīng University

Wáng Yè

Teacher

2

Normal University

Ōuyáng Mín

Professor

3

Bǎishēng Center

Chén Xīn

Manager

4

Běijīng University

Lǐ Méng

Professor

Dù Qiū

Drill Four: *Receptionist in an office.*

Example: 9:00: Ms. **Liú**

      Ms. **Liú**:   **Nǐ hǎo......Wǒ......**
      Receptionist: **Qǐngwèn, nín guìxìng?**
      Ms. **Liú**:   **Xìng Liú, Liú Wànxiāng.**
      Receptionist: **Ò, Liú nǚshì, qǐngzuò.**

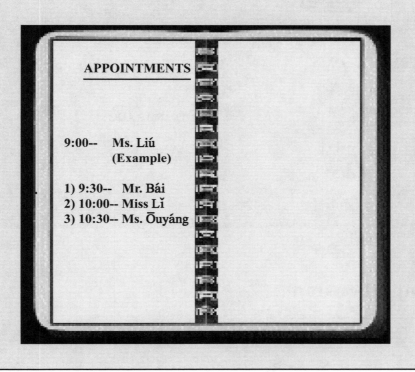

APPOINTMENTS

9:00--   Ms. Liú
       (Example)

1) 9:30-- Mr. Bái
2) 10:00-- Miss Lǐ
3) 10:30-- Ms. Ōuyáng

Míngpiàn

Qīnghuá University
Professor
Zhāng Róng

Drill Five: *Receptionist in a school. Do the same job in the school where you are a student. When students come in looking for Wu laoshi, get their family name, greet them and then ask them to be seated.*

1

Chén tóngxué

2

Zhào tóngxué

Dialogue Comprehension

Dù Qiū:	Qǐngwèn, nín guìxìng?
Zhāng Tóngshēng:	Xìng Zhāng, Zhāng Tóngshēng.
Dù Qiū:	Ò, Xiǎo Zhāng tóngzhì.

Lèi le

Exchanging Information about Names

Dialogue Setting

Sino-American Trade Co., Washington, DC

Back in the Washington office of the Sino-American Trade Company: a new colleague is asking Wang Liyu about another colleague. He is first identified by his position and then by family name and given name.

Lǐ Píng: Tā shi shéi?
Wáng Lìyù: Shì fùjīnglǐ.

Lǐ Píng: Xìng shénme? Jiào shénme?
Wáng Lìyù: Xìng Huà, míngzi jiào Xiǎohuì.

Dialogue Information:

* General question word for asking about identity: **shéi/shuí**

* Copula ("to be" verb):   **shì/shi**

* Assistant manager: **fùjīnglǐ**

* General question word for asking about things: **shénme**

* Verbs of naming: **jiào**

* Names in general: **míngzi**

* A Chinese given name: **Xiǎohuì**

Vocabulary (Shēngcí)

1. Question Words (yíwèncí)
   shéi/shuí
   shénme

2. Copula (xìcí)
   shì

3. Verb (dòngcí)
   jiào

4. Nouns (míngcí)
   jīnglǐ
   fùjīnglǐ
   mìshū/mìshu
   lǎoshī
   xuéshēng/xuésheng
   rén
   míngzi

5. Terms of Address (chēnghu)
   jīnglǐ
   fùjīnglǐ
   mìshū/mìshu
   tóngxué
   lǎoshī

6. Chinese Family Name (xìng)
   Huà

7. Chinese Given Names (míng)
   Xiǎohuì
   Píng

8. Phrase (cízǔ)
   Shénme rén?

DRILLS

Drill One: *Greet the person who has been pointed out to you.*

Example:

Instructor:	Tā shi jīnglǐ, xìng Wáng.
Student:	Wáng jīnglǐ, nǐ hǎo.

1

2

3

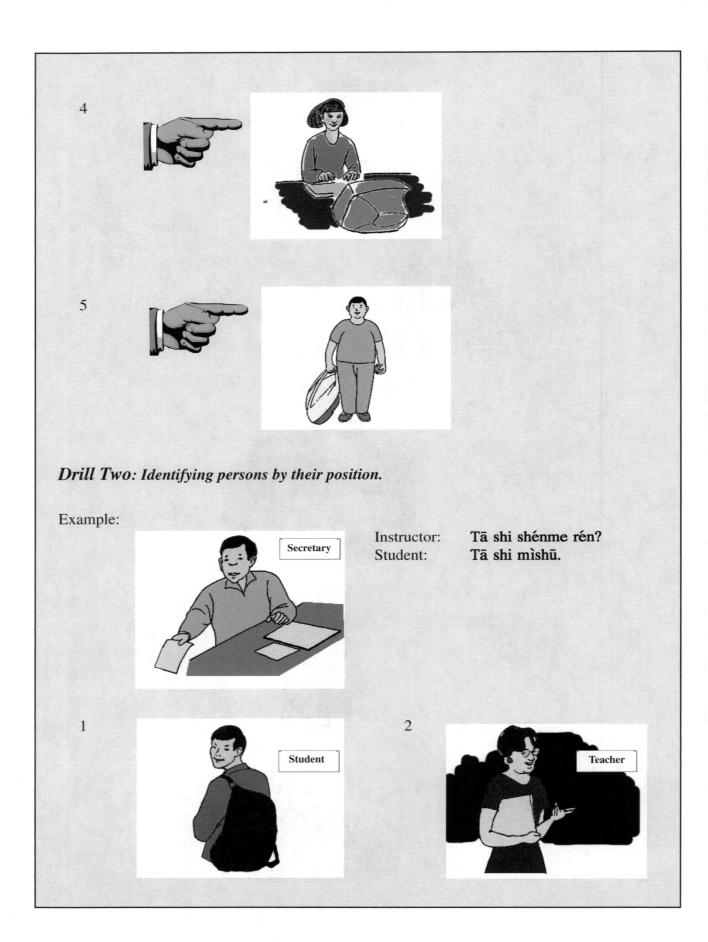

4

5

Drill Two: *Identifying persons by their position.*

Example:

Secretary

Instructor:	**Tā shi shénme rén?**
Student:	**Tā shi mìshū.**

1   Student

2   Teacher

3

Manager

4

Secretary

5

Assistant Manager

Drill Three: *Asking people's names.*

Example: Cue: **Tā shi lǎoshī.**
                  Student: **Lǎoshī jiào shénme míngzi?**

1.   2.   3.   4.

5.   6.   7.

Xuéshēng

Drill Four: *Identifying people.*

Example:

Zhāng Píng

Instructor: **Jīnglǐ shi shuí?**
Student: **Shì Zhāng Píng.**

1

Manager

2

Comrade Dù

3

Secretary

4

Mr. Liú

5

Teacher

Drill Five: *Answering questions about names and position.*

Example:

Instructor: **Lǎoshī xìng shénme?**
Student: **Xìng Liú.**

1

2

3

4

5

Drill Six: Denying identities.

Example:

Instructor: **Tā shi mìshū.**
Student: **Bù, tā bú-shì mìshū.**

1

2

Secretary

3

Zhāng Tóngshēng

4

Bái Shàntián

5

Secretary

Drill Seven: *Correcting an identification.*

Example:

Secretary

Instructor: **Tā shi lǎoshī.**
Student: **Bù, tā shi mìshū.**

1

Dù Qiū

2

Zhāng Tóngshēng

3

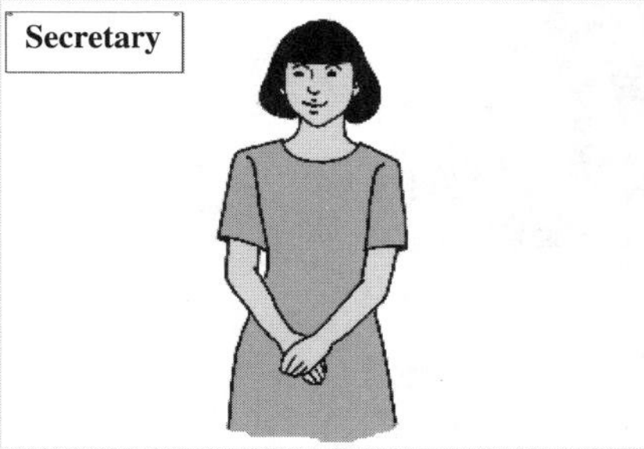

Secretary

4

Dù Qiū

5

Manager

Dialogue Comprehension

Lǐ Píng:	Tā shi shéi?
Wáng Lìyù:	Shì fùjīnglǐ.
Lǐ Píng:	Xìng shénme? Jiào shénme?
Wáng Lìyù:	Xìng Huà, míngzi jiào Xiǎohuì.

Huà Xiǎohuì

Lǎoshī

Discussing Someone's Condition

Dialogue Setting

Sino-American Trade Co., Beijing

This conversation takes place on the telephone. The call is between the Washington and Beijing offices of the company. The Beijing office is experiencing an outbreak of the flu virus. Wang Liyu finds this out as soon as she asks how her Beijing colleague is doing.

Wáng Lìyù: Nǐ zuìjìn zěnmeyàng ne?
Shèng Yīng: Yǒu yìdiǎn(r) bù-shūfu.

Wáng Lìyù: Tóngshìmen ne?
Shèng Yīng: Tāmen yě dōu gǎnmào le.

Dialogue Information:

* General question word for asking about manner: **zěnme**

* General question word for asking about
  condition: **zěnmeyàng**

* Sentence particle which expresses friendliness: **ne**

* Timeword for recent past: **zuìjìn**

* General expression for feeling well/not feeling
  well: **shūfu/bù-shūfu**

* General expression of an undesirable condition: **yǒu yìdiǎn(r)**

* Noun identifying colleagues: **tóngshì**

* Third person plural pronoun: **tāmen**

* Pluralization suffix: **men**

* Phrase for catching the flu: **gǎnmào le**

* Change of state particle: **le**

* Adverb indicating that everything in the subject
  participates: **dōu**

* Adverb indicating that a new subject shares
  previously mentioned condition: **yě**

Dōu hǎo ma?

Vocabulary (Shēngcí)

1. Phrases (cízǔ)
   zěnmeyàng
   yǒu yìdiǎn(r)
   gǎnmào le

2. Nouns (míngcí)
   tóngshì
   tóngshìmen

3. Adjectives (xíngróngcí)
   hǎo
   lèi
   shūfu
   bù-shūfu
   cōngming
   lǎn
   línghuó
   kāitong
   luōsuo
   máng
   wángù
   nǔlì

4. Adverbs (fùcí)
   dōu
   yě
   hěn

5. Time Words (shíjiān fùcí)
   yǐqián
   xiànzài
   zuìjìn

6. Question Particles (yíwèn zhùcí)
   ma
   ne

7. Pronoun (dàicí)
   tāmen

8. Change of Situation Particle (dòngtài zhùcí)
   le

Review the following adjectives and the images we use to represent them for Drills 1 to 3.

máng   **busy**

lǎn   lazy

lèi   tired

cōngming   smart

shūfu   comfortable

hǎo   well

nǔlì   hardworking

wángù   stubborn

bù-shūfu   ill

luōsuo   talkative

línghuó   flexible

Drill One: *Expressing an undesirable condition.*

Example:

Instructor: **Zhāng lǎoshī tā rén zěnmeyàng ne?**

Student: **Tā yǒu yìdiǎn(r) wángù.**

1

2

3

4

5

6

7

8

Drill Two: *Expressing conditions.*

Example:

Instructor: **Lín jīnglǐ zuìjìn zěnmeyàng ne?**
Student: **Tā hěn hǎo.**

1

2

3

4

5

6

Drill Three: *Talking about people.*

Example 1:

Instructor: **Tóngxuémen tāmen rén dōu zěnmeyàng ne?**

Student: **Tāmen dōu yǒu yìdiǎn(r) lǎn.**

Example 2:

Instructor: **Tóngshìmen tāmen rén dōu zěnmeyàng ne?**

Student: **Tāmen dōu hěn nǔlì.**

1

2

3

4

5

Drill Four: *Correcting erroneous hypotheses.*

Example: Instructor: **Wáng Lìyù bù-shūfu ma?**
                 Student: **Bù, tā hěn hǎo.**

1.   2.   3.   4.

Bù-shūfu

Drill Five: Rectifying a misperception.

Example: Instructor: **Nǐ hěn lèi ma?**
                                Student: **Bù, wǒ bú-lèi.**

1.   2.   3.   4.   5.

Drill Six: Desirable responses and question extensions.

Example 1:   Instructor: **Nǐ hěn lèi ma?**
                                Student: **Wǒ bú-lèi. Nǐ ne?**

Example 2:   Instructor: **Nǐ shūfu ma?**
                                Student: **Wǒ hěn shūfu. Nǐ ne?**

1.   2.   3.   4.   5.

Drill Seven: Continuing the conversation.

Example: Instructor: **Wǒ hěn lèi. Nǐmen ne?**
                                Student: **Wǒmen yě dōu hěn lèi.**

1.   2.   3.   4.   5.

6.   7.   8.   9.   10.

Drill Eight: Deducing a previous condition.

Example: Instructor: **Xiànzài jīnglǐmen dōu zhīdao le.**
                  Student: **Yǐqián jīnglǐmen dōu bù-zhīdao.**

1.   2.   3.   4.   5.

6.   7.   8.   9.   10.

Dialogue Comprehension

Wáng Lìyù: Nǐ zuìjìn zěnmeyàng ne?
Shèng Yīng: Yǒu yìdiǎn(r) bù-shūfu.
Wáng Lìyù: Tóngshìmen ne?
Shèng Yīng: Tāmen yě dōu gǎnmào le.

Diànhuà

Pronunciation and Romanization: Initials, Medials, and Finals

Each syllable in Chinese is a basic unit of meaning, what students of language call a "morpheme." This is in contrast to English where a morpheme can be composed of a number of syllables. For example, English *appreciate* is one word consisting of one morpheme composed of four syllables:

ap.pre.ci.ate

And *appreciated* is a word consisting of two morphemes composed of five syllables:

*appreciat*e and *–ed*

The number of syllables in English exceeds ten thousand, but there are considerably less than two thousand syllables in Mandarin Chinese. Compared to European languages, there are relatively few syllables in Chinese and a syllable carries a lot of information. Therefore, it is important to pay careful attention to the pronunciation of syllables when beginning the study of spoken Chinese.

When studying pronunciation of Mandarin Chinese, it is useful to pay attention to four aspects of the syllable:

1) the initial—the first consonant in the syllable
2) the final— the vowel or vowel-consonant concluding the syllable
3) the medial—the vowel that sometimes occurs between the initial and the final
4) the tone— the high-low pitch which characterizes the entire syllable

For our purposes, we can say that every syllable will have a final and a tone even if the tone is a neutral tone. The initial and medial only occur in some Chinese syllables.

In this stage, we will learn and practice some of these elements by listening to contrasting pairs and repeating what you hear. The spellings reflect the conventions of *Hànyǔ Pīnyīn,* the official Romanization of Mandarin in the People's Republic of China. In the beginning pay most attention to the sounds of Mandarin you hear, later you will be able to use *Hànyǔ Pīnyīn* much more accurately.

Let's distinguish different sets of finals.

a	ai

mǎ	mǎi

mǎ  horse

mǎi  buy

| an | ang |

| ān | āng |

ānjìng  quiet, peaceful

āngzāng  dirty

an	ang
mán	**máng**

mántou

steamed bun

máng

busy

en	eng
mèn	**mèng**

mèn  to stew

mèng  dream

in	ing

mín	míng

rénmín  people

míngzi  name

in	ing
yīn	yīng

shēng**yīn**   sound

yīngxióng   hero

Can you hear the difference between *–i-n* and *–i-n-g*? Do you have the sense that the *–n-g* in Chinese is somewhat softer than in English? If you do, you are in good shape. If you have trouble with these finals, spend a little more time on this section.

Listen to the following high-level tone words with the letter "*i*" in their spelling:

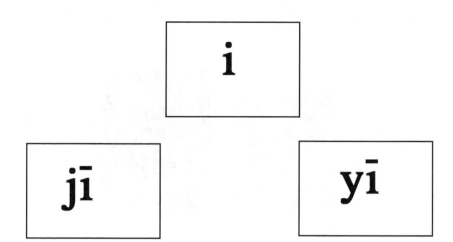

jī   chicken

yī   one

When following the initial consonants s-, c-, and z-, which are formed by passing air past a rigid tongue-tip touching the ridge behind your upper teeth, the letter "*i*" represents a high vowel that sounds like the *–a* in *t-s-a* in the quickly spoken phrase "It's a girl!"

Your teeth are together and you mouth is wide. Let's listen to a series of high-level tone words that have this sound:

sī  silk

zī  capital

cī  tell someone off

The letter "*i*" changes value after the retroflex initials spelled with *ch-*, *zh-*, *sh-*, and *r-*.

ch-

zh-

sh-

r-

chìzi  shark fin

zhìzi  young child

shìzi  math equation

rìzi  calendar day

The letter -*e* also has different qualities in *Hanyu Pinyin,* depending on what it is combined with. It is best to pay attention to the entire final, consisting of a single vowel, a combination of vowels, or vowels plus –*n* or –*ng*.

As a final all by itself, "e" sounds quite similar to the sound made by a person who has been struck in the stomach.

e

è   kě   hē

è

hungry

kě

thirsty

hē  drink

This may be a good time to contrast the finals *–i, -e,* and *–a* in similar environments. Let's listen to falling-tone words all with the initial *s-*.

sì  four

sè  lust

sà  thirty

Now we are going to give you the opportunity to distinguish between the following final sounds you have encountered in this stage:

a, ai	ma, mai
an, ang	man, mang
en, eng	men, meng
in, ing (yin, ying)	min, ming
-i (yi)	ji
-i	si, ci, zi
-i	chi, zhi, shi, ri
e	ke, he

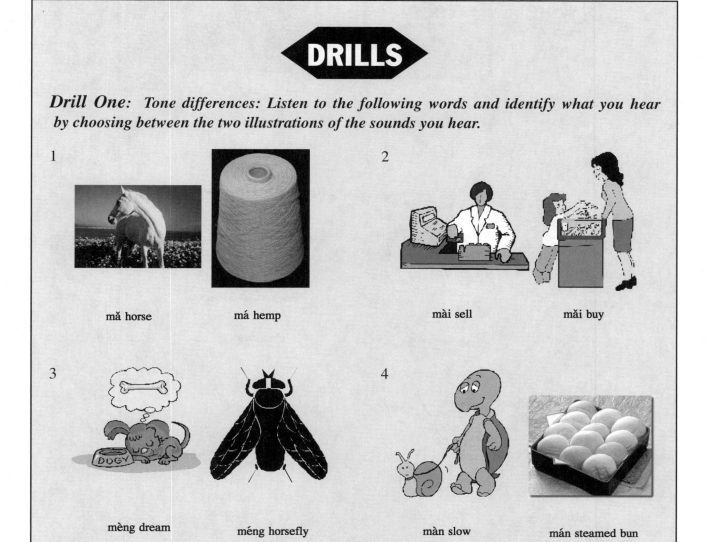

DRILLS

Drill One: Tone differences: Listen to the following words and identify what you hear by choosing between the two illustrations of the sounds you hear.

1

mǎ horse   má hemp

2

mài sell   mǎi buy

3

mèng dream   méng horsefly

4

màn slow   mán steamed bun

5   mìng fate   míng name

6   è hungry   é goose

7   kě thirsty   kē measure for tree

8   sè lust   sī silk

9   shìzi equation   shīzi lion

10   chìzi shark fin   chízi pond

11   zhìzi toddler   zhízi nephew

Drill Two: *Final differences: Listen to the following words and identify what you hear by choosing between the two illustrations provided.*

1

sì four   sè lust

2

sà thirty   sè lust

3

mǎ horse   mǎi buy

4

mǎi buy   mǎ horse

5

mín people   míng name

6

míng name   mín people

7

jī chicken   jīn gold

8

āng dirty   ān peaceful

9

hē drink   kě thirsty

10

sè lust   sī silk

11

āng dirty   ān peaceful

12

kě thirsty   hē drink

13

zī capital   zā bundle

14

cī scold   sè lust

15

kě thirsty   è hungry

16

mèng dream   mèn stew

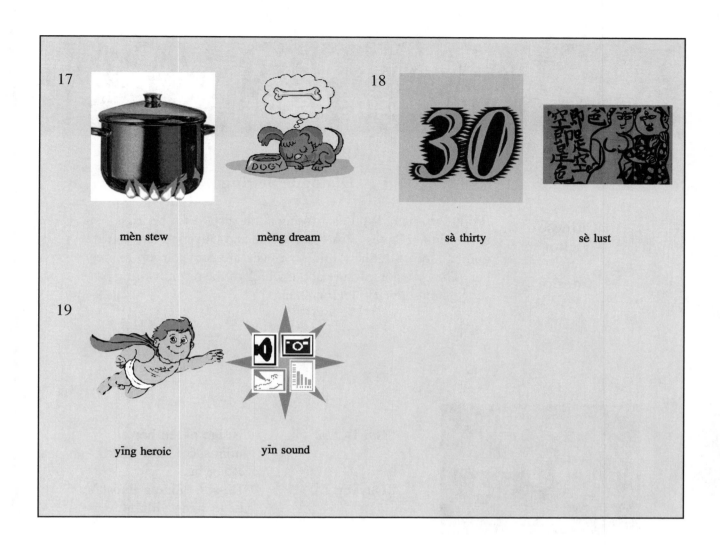

17

mèn stew　　　　mèng dream

18

sà thirty　　　　sè lust

19

yīng heroic　　　　yīn sound

This concludes Unit 1 Stage 5, the third session focusing on pronunciation.

Máng

Dialogue Setting

Chinese Visitor to America

Professor Zhang Rong is arriving at the airport for her first visit to the United States. Professor White and Ouyang Lee, who are going to look after her during her visit, are at the airport to meet her. They are not too sure about which of the disembarking passengers might be Professor Zhang.

| Bái Délún: | Nèige nǚrén hěn miànshóu. Shì Zhāng Róng ba. |
| Ōuyáng Lǐ: | Bú-shì. Zhāng jiàoshòu bǐ tā pàng yìdiǎn(r). |

Bái Délún: Ò, duì le. Nèige nǚde bǐjiào shòu.

Dialogue Information:

* Noun for "female":   nǔrén

* Noun for "human":   rén

* General demonstrative referring to something that is away from the speaker: nèi/nà

* General measure: gè, wèi

* The variant words for "familiar":   miànshóu/miànshú

* Sentential particle indicating an assumption: ba

* General pattern to refer to a "state":   Shì Zhāng Róng ba.

* General phrase for a negative judgement: Bú-shì.

* Adjective meaning "fat", "heavy figured":   pàng

* Adverb meaning "a bit":   yìdiǎn(r)

* verb of comparison: bǐ

* Exclamation of surprise: ò

* General phrase to express agreement: Duì le.

* Adjective describing a slim physique: shòu

* Noun for female: nǔde

* Adverb of comparison: bǐjiào

Shuō

Vocabulary (Shēngcí)

1. Question of Physical Features (yíwèncí)
   zhǎngde zěnmeyàng

2. Verb of Physical Features (Dòngcí)
   zhǎngde

3. Adjectives of Physical Features
   (xíngróngcí)
   pàng
   shòu
   ǎi
   gāo
   miànshóu/miànshú
   lǎo
   dà
   xiǎo
   niánqīng
   zhuàng
   piàoliang
   nánkàn

4. Term of Address (chēnghu)
   jiàoshòu

5. Nouns (míngcí)
   rén
   nánrén/nánde
   nǚrén/nǚde

6. Demonstratives (zhǐshì dàicí)
   nèi/nà
   zhèi/zhè

7. Measures (liàngcí)
   gè
   wèi

8. Conjuction for Nouns (liáncí)
   hé

9. Adverb of Comparison (bǐjiào fùcí)
   bǐjiào

10. Verb of Comparison (bǐjiào dòngcí)
    bǐ
    bǐjiào

11. Particle of Assumption (yǔqì zhùcí)
    ba

Hē

Drill One: Describing people.

Example:

5 ft

Instructor: **Nèige nǚrén zhǎngde zěnmeyàng?**

Student: **Nèige nǚrén hěn ǎi.**

1

98 lb

2

3

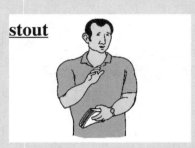

stout

4

Never!

5

stout

6

7
age: 21

8

9
overweight

10

Drill Two: *Critically describing people.*

Example: Instructor: **Lǎo Lǐ hěn zhuàng ma?**
            Student: **Bú-zhuàng. Lǎo Lǐ yǒu yìdiǎn(r) shòu.**

            1.   2.   3.

            4.   5.   6.

Shū

Drill Three: Implied comparison.

Example 1:

Xiǎo Lǚ (23)　Xiǎo Lǐ (25)

Instructor:　**Xiǎo Lǐ bǐ Xiǎo Lǚ dà yìdiǎn(r).**
Student:　**Duì, Xiǎo Lǐ dà.**

Example 2:

Instructor:　**Lín xiānsheng bǐ Lín tàitai gāo.**
Student:　**Bù, Lín tàitai gāo.**

1

Xiǎo Zhū (28)　　Xiǎo Táng (30)

2

Tóngshēng (33)　　Dù Qiū (36)

3
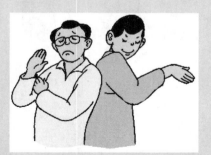

Chén lǎoshī　Wáng lǎoshī

4

Xiǎo Hé　Xiǎo Xǔ

5

Xiǎo Lín   Xiǎo Huáng

6

Zhōu jīnglǐ   Sū nǚshì

7

Dài lǎoshī   Liú xiānsheng

8

Dù Qiū   Zhāng Tóngshēng

9

10

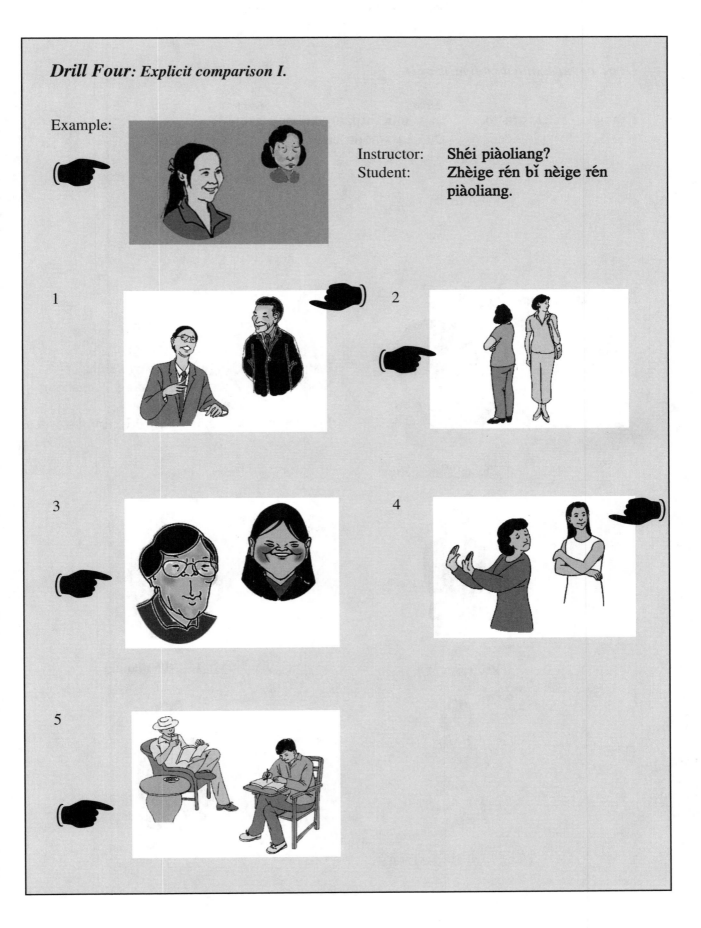

Drill Four: Explicit comparison I.

Example:

Instructor: **Shéi piàoliang?**
Student: **Zhèige rén bǐ nèige rén piàoliang.**

1

2

3

4

5

Drill Five: Explicit comparison II.

Example: Instructor: **Lǐ xiáojie bǐjiào piàoliang ba.**
           Student: **Duì, Lǐ xiáojie bǐ nèige rén piàoliang yìdiǎn(r).**

1.   2.   3.   4.

5.   6.   7.

Drill Six: Introducing folks.

Example:

Zhāng Tóngshēng

Instructor: **Qǐngwèn, zhèiwèi shi......?**
Student: **Zhèiwèi shi Zhāng Tóngshēng tóngzhì.**
Instructor: **Ò, Zhāng tóngzhì, nín hǎo.**

1

Professor Wú

2

Mr. Liú, the manager

3

Wáng Lìyù, the secretary

4

Mr. Tián

5

Ms. Zhào

Dialogue Comprehension

Bái Shàntián: Nèige nǚrén hěn miànshóu. Shì Zhāng Róng ba.
Ōuyáng Lǐ: Bú-shì. Zhāng jiàoshòu bǐ tā pàng yìdiǎn(r).
Bái Shàntián: Ò, duì le. Nèige nǚde bǐjiào shòu.

Jiǎo

Identifying People

Dialogue Setting

Sino-American Trade Co., Washington, DC

A stranger has come to the office looking for the assistant manager. The secretary, Ms. Wang, does not know who the gentleman is. Perhaps for this reason, she isn't very much help at all.

Kèren:	Qǐngwèn, Huà Xiǎohuì fùjīnglǐ shi něiwèi?
Wáng Lìyù:	Huà fùjīnglǐ ma? Tā ya......jiùshi nèige yòu shòu yòu ǎi de nánrén.
Kèren:	Tā xiànzài yǒu kòng ma?
Wáng Lìyù:	Wǒ bù-qīngchu.

Dialogue Information:

* Polite way to ask "which person?":	**năwèi/něiwèi**
* General question word for asking "which":	**nă/něi**
* Polite or formal measure word for person:	**wèi**
* Question sentence particle:	**ma**
* Particle of modification:	**de**
"the woman who looks familiar":	**hěn miànshóu de nǔrén**
"an attractive teacher":	**piàoliang de lăoshī**
"the relatively tall student":	**bǐjiào gāo de tóngxué**
"a manager who isn't opinionated":	**bù-wángù de jīnglǐ**
"lazy colleagues":	**hěn lăn de tóngshìmen**
"talkative people":	**hěn luōsuō de rén**
* Adjective meaning "thin":	**shòu**
* Adjective meaning "short":	**ăi**
* Adverb of coexisting attributes:	**yòu......yòu......**
* The emphatic version of the state verb **shì**:	**jiùshi**
"It's that skinny, short guy"	**jiùshi nèige yòu shòu yòu ăi de nánrén**
* Verb meaning "to have":	**yǒu**
* Adjective meaning "empty":	**kòng**
* Phrase indicating "free time":	**yǒu kòng**
* Adjective meaning "clear, distinct":	**qīngchu**
* Adjective meaning "not sure":	**bù-qīngchu**

Vocabulary (Shēngcí)

1. Question Words (yíwèncí)
   nǎ/nǎge/nǎwèi
   něi/něige/něiwèi

2. Pronouns (dàicí)
   wǒ
   wǒmen
   zánmen
   nǐ
   nín
   nǐmen
   tā
   tāmen

3. Nouns (míngcí)
   kèren (measures: **wèi, ge**)
   kèrenmen

4. State Verb (zhuàngtài dòngcí)
   jiùshi

5. Verbs of Cognition (rènzhī dòngcí)
   zhīdao
   bù-zhīdao

6. Adjective (xíngróngcí)
   qīngchu

7. Adjectives of Social Judgment (píngjià xíngróngcí)
   nénggàn
   wúnéng
   cōngming
   bèn
   dàfang
   xiǎoqi
   jǐnzhāng
   píngjìng
   nánkàn

8. Adverb of Coexisting Attribute (biǎoshì tóngshí cúnzài de fùcí)
   yòu......yòu......

9. Phrases (cízǔ)
   yǒu kòng
   méi-kòng/méi-you kòng
   bù-qīngchu

10. Particle of Modification (xiūshì zhùcí)
    de

Examples of *DE* modified noun:

* **wǒmen de jīnglǐ**	our manager
* **nénggàn de jīnglǐ**	a capable manager
* **wǒmen de nénggàn de jīnglǐ**	our capable manager
* **Tā shi wǒmen de nénggàn de jīnglǐ**	She is our capable manager
* **lǎoshī shuō de zhōngwén**	the Chinese the teacher speaks
* **hěn bèn de rén**	stupid person
* **hěn lǎo de rén**	old person

DRILLS

Drill One: *Confirming a judgment.*

Example: Instructor: **Nǐ hé wǒ dōu shi xuésheng.**
             Student: **Duì le, zánmen dōu shi xuésheng.**

    1.   2.   3.   4.   5.   6.

    7.   8.   9.   10.   11.

Drill Two: *Defending people.*

Example: Instructor: **Xuéshengmen dōu yǒu yìdiǎn(r) bèn.**
             Student: **Bù, tāmen dōu hěn cōngming.**

    1.   2.   3.

    4.   5.   6.

Drill Three: *Asking for confirmation of your conclusions.*

Example: Student: **Liú Wén xiānsheng zěnmeyàng?**
             Instructor: **Tā hěn wúnéng.**
             Student: **Ò, nèige hěn wúnéng de rén shi Liú Wén xiānsheng ma?**

1. **Zhū jīnglǐ**　　　　2. **Lǐ Wǎnxiāng nǚshì**　　　　3. **Lín Báihuá**

4. **Wáng Lìyù mìshū**　　　5. **Xiǎo Sū tóngxué**　　　6. **Shī lǎoshī**

7. **Fàn Jié**　　　　8. **Ōuyáng Lǐ**　　　　9. **Huà fùjīnglǐ**

10. **Kē Yuèhuá**

Drill Four: *Identifying persons.*

Example:

 <u>**6 ft 7 & 275 lbs**</u>

Instructor: **Wáng lǎoshī shì nǎwèi?**
Student: **Nèige yòu gāo yòu pàng de rén jiùshi Wáng lǎoshī.**

1  <u>**5 ft & 105 lbs**</u>

2  <u>**age 72 & 205 lbs**</u>

3  <u>**98 lbs & called Quasimodo**</u>

4  <u>**age 19 & Miss Suzhou**</u>

5  <u>**6 ft 2 & weight champ**</u>

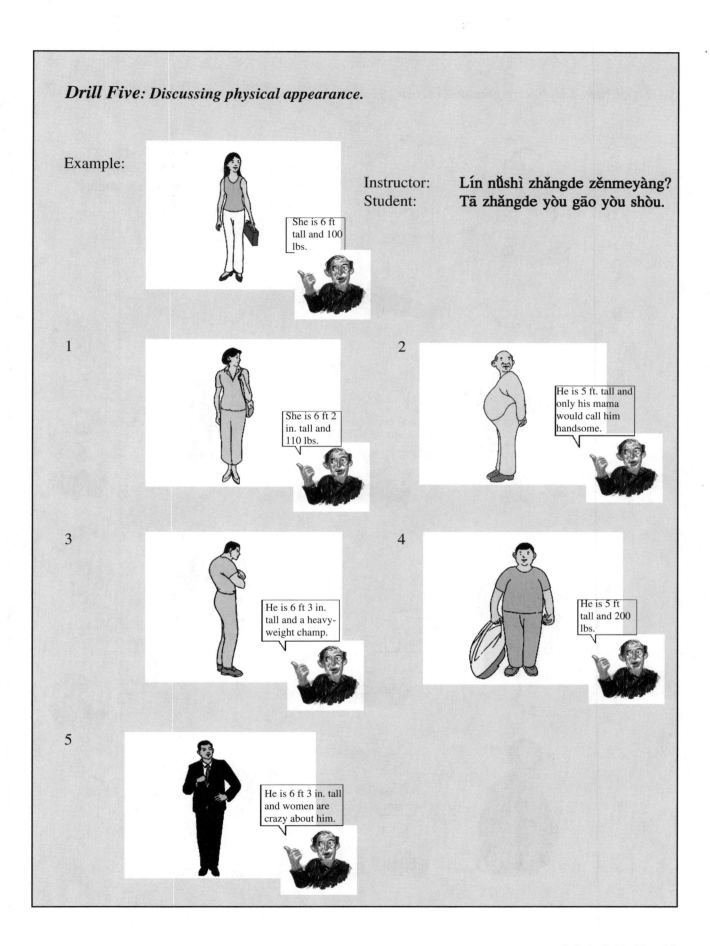

Drill Five: *Discussing physical appearance.*

Example:

Instructor: **Lín nǔshì zhǎngde zěnmeyàng?**
Student: **Tā zhǎngde yòu gāo yòu shòu.**

She is 6 ft tall and 100 lbs.

1

She is 6 ft 2 in. tall and 110 lbs.

2

He is 5 ft. tall and only his mama would call him handsome.

3

He is 6 ft 3 in. tall and a heavy-weight champ.

4

He is 5 ft tall and 200 lbs.

5

He is 6 ft 3 in. tall and women are crazy about him.

Drill Six: *Discussing personal characteristics.*

Example:

Instructor: **Bì jīnglǐ rén zěnmeyàng ne?**
Student: **Tā yòu bèn yòu wúnéng.**

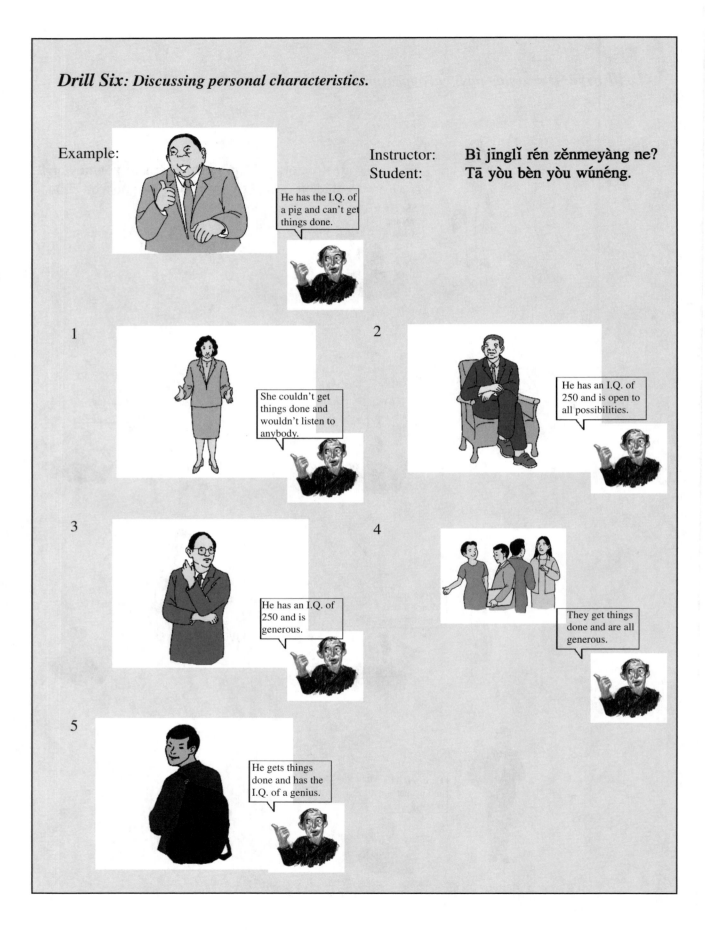

He has the I.Q. of a pig and can't get things done.

1

She couldn't get things done and wouldn't listen to anybody.

2

He has an I.Q. of 250 and is open to all possibilities.

3

He has an I.Q. of 250 and is generous.

4

They get things done and are all generous.

5

He gets things done and has the I.Q. of a genius.

Drill Seven: *Correcting a mistaken impression.*

Example 1:   Instructor: **Wú lǎoshī hěn nénggàn ba.**
                 Student: **Bù-nénggàn. Wú lǎoshī hěn wúnéng.**

Example 2:   Instructor: **Xuéshengmen dōu yǒu wèntí ba.**
                 Student: **Méi-you. Xuéshengmen dōu méi-you wèntí.**

1.   2.   3.   4.   5.

6.   7.   8.   9.   10.

Dialogue Comprehension

Kèren: Qǐngwèn, Huà Xiǎohuì fùjīnglǐ shi něiwèi?
Wáng Lìyù: Huà fùjīnglǐ ma? Tā ya......jiùshi
                 nèige yòu shòu yòu ǎi de nánrén.
Kèren: Tā xiànzài yǒu kòng ma?
Wáng Lìyù: Wǒ bù-qīngchu.

Well and not well

Pronunciation and Romanization: Initials, Medials, and Finals

Although Chinese speakers do not use pronouns as frequently as English speakers do, one of the key words you learn in Mandarin is the one that refers to the speaker, namely the low-rising first person singular:

wǒ  me

The neat thing about this language is that you can use *wǒ* no matter where it occurs in relation to a verb.

wǒ  me

When this sound follows a consonant that is formed with the lips, namely *m-, b-, p,* and *f-*, it is spelled with a single *–o,* but still pronounced as the *–u-o* combination: Here are some common words and morphemes with rising tones that you can practice:

mó

bó	pó	fó

mógū

mushroom

bózi

neck

pózi

old woman

Fó  Buddha

Elsewhere, following all other consonants, this final is spelled *–u-o*. Here are some low-rising tone examples:

duǒ  measure
for flower

huǒ  fire

The number "five" is pronounced with a low-rising tone and spelled *w-u*. Listen carefully: the "w" is either very light or not there, sounding more like a "rounding" of the *-u*. :

wǔ  five

Compare and pronounce the first person singular pronoun and the number "five."

wǒ  me

wǔ five

Here is an opportunity to listen again and repeat falling-tone $-zi$ words with $-u$ finals after the instructor:

bùzi   step

pùzi   shop

dùzi   belly

tùzi  rabbit

sùzi  millet

kùzi  pants

Xiǎohuǒzi (= young guy)

Contrast low-rising tone syllables with *−u* finals to those with *umlaut-ü*.

nǔlì   hard working

nǚshì   lady

The second morpheme, *nü,* is found in words for female humans: "woman, girl, daughter." English does not have the *-ü* sound. Many English speakers have trouble distinguishing it from the more famil-iar *−u* sound, but there is no reason for you to have that difficulty. If you are having trouble making this sound, try starting out by pronouncing *-i*, as in the second-person pronoun *nǐ*, and then without moving your tongue whatsoever, pucker your lips until they are noticeably protruding and stiff in a semi-chaste kiss formation. Try this by repeating after your instructor:

nǐ   you

nǚshì   lady

If there is no preceding consonant, then –*ü* should be spelled *y-u*. The rising-tone word spelled *y-u* means fish. Practice the word for "fish' by repeating after your instructor:

yú  fish

Contrast *nü* the word for "woman" with the morpheme meaning to "put forth (effort)" spelled n-u. Practicing this pair will give you a feeling for this important distinction:

nǚshì  lady

nǚlì hard working

The sound represented by the *umlaut-ü* is spelled with the two umlaut dots over the –*u* when there are only vowels in the final and when following the initials *l-* and *n-*. When there is no initial consonant, these sounds are spelled with an initial *y-*. Here are some falling-tone words to practice that illustrate these rules:

lǜ  law

yuè		month
lüèduó		plunder, rob
luàn		chaos
huái**yùn**		pregnant
kùn		sleepy

yuàn      courtyard

The -a in *yuan* is NOT pronounced the way you might reasonably guess. Instead, it should be pronounced just like the *e* in English "*e*nd," making sure as well that the -*n* is pronounced more emphatically than in English. Listen again and repeat as the instructor gives you the word for a yard, or a small garden.

yuànzi      courtyard

Listen to the word for dragon:

lóng      dragon

The pronunciation of –*o-n-g* is similar to the -o- in "woman" followed by the -*ng* in "long".   Listen to the rising-tone word for dragon again and repeat after the instructor:

lóng  dragon

A falling-tone word with this final following a medial y- is the verb meaning "to use."

yòng  to use

An example of the element *yong* occurring after the *x-* initial is the word for "bear." "Bear" is a rising-tone word.

xióng  bear

The *x-* initial is pronounced with the tip of your tongue resting behind your lower teeth. Try it again in the word for panda a rising tone – level tone combination that is literally "bear"–"cat."

xióngmāopanda

This brings us to the 4 diphthongs, or vowel combinations.

Māo, the word for "cat," is a high level tone as you can see in this word for "kitten," which is formed with the morpheme meaning "young."

xiǎo māokitten

But let's put the cute critter aside and examine these diphthongs in rising-tone words.

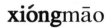

| máo | méi | móu | mái |

máo  wool, fur

méimao  eyebrow

móuhuà  plan

mái  bury

Listen to these four finals once again. Learn to distinguish them when you hear them.

máo    wool

méi 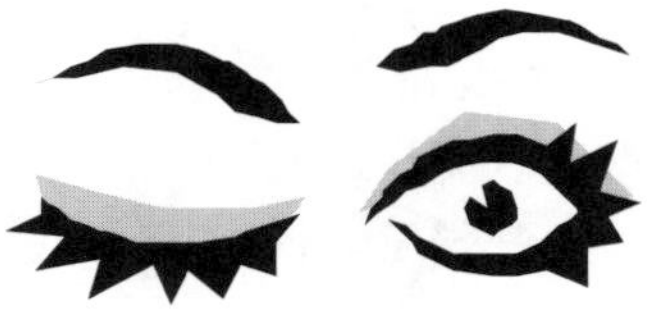   eyebrow

móu    plan

mái    bury

Let's now practice distinguishing medials. These are the vowel sounds that can either pattern between the initial and the final, or occur at the beginning of the syllable. In Chinese, only three vowel sounds can function as medials. They are *-i, -u,* and *-ü.*

yāzi 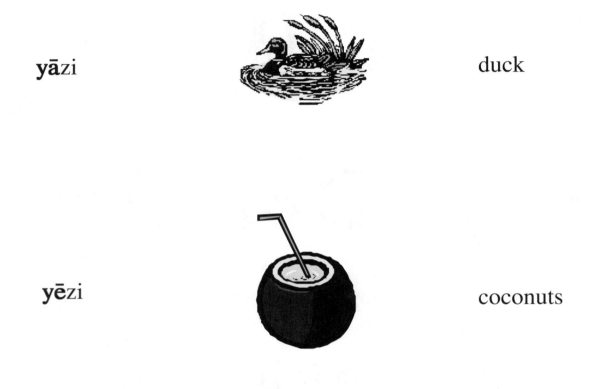 duck

yēzi coconuts

If there is a preceding consonant, then *y-a* will be spelled as *–i-a*. The word for "shrimp" is a high-level tone word with an *x-* initial that starts with the tip of your tongue behind your lower teeth:

xiā  shrimp

If there is a preceding consonant, then *y-e* should be rewritten as *–i-e*. The word for shoes is a rising–tone word with an *x-* initial. Listen and repeat as the instructor says the word for "shoes" beginning with the tip of your tongue behind your lower teeth.

xiézi   shoes

The word for "eggplant" is another rising-tone word with this medial-final combination. The tone mark never goes over the medial, so the rising-tone mark is over the *–e*.

qiézi   eggplant

Listen as your instructor says the words for shrimp and shoes. Click on the syllable you hear.

xiā   shrimp

xié   shoes

Here, we are going to let you hear your instructor order some eggplant in red sauce:

hóngshāo qiézi   fried eggplant

Here are two more pairs of *-i-* medial words: *yào* and *yòu*. The first pair has no initial, and the second pair has the *j-* initial.

yào   sparrow hawk

yòuzi   grapefruit

With a low-rising tone and a *j-* initial, these elements give us the words for "dumpling" and "alcoholic beverages."

jiǎozi   dumpling

The low-rising *jiǔ* means "wine" and occurs in many terms for various alcoholic drinks.

jiǔ  wine

Listen to these two high-level tone words:

wā baby's crying

huā 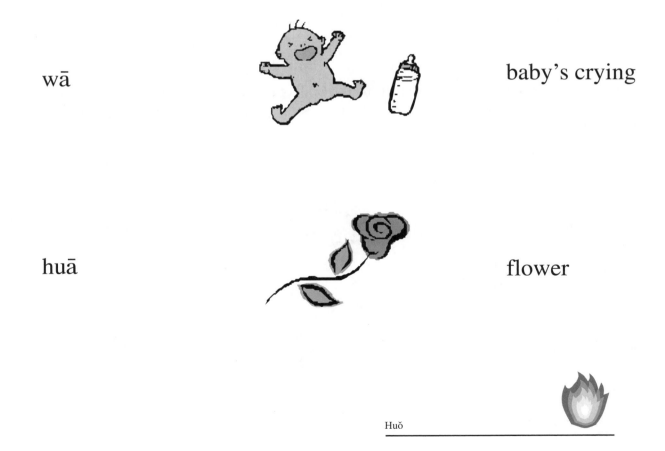 flower

Huǒ

Let's take a closer look at other syllable-morphemes and words with the –u medial.

The locative for "outside" is *wài*. Listen to this word being contrasted to a word with a *h-* initial. The falling-tone word means "bad" or "ruined."

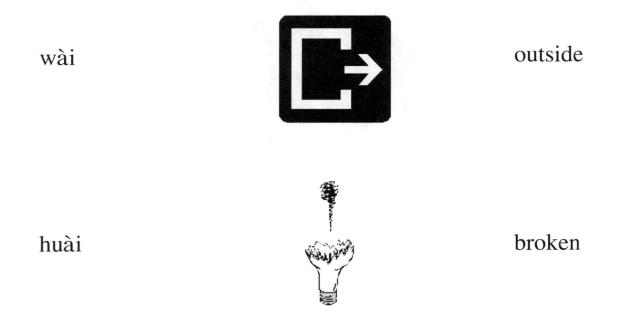

wài   outside

huài   broken

The word for a substance formed into a ball such as a pill or a spherical food, such as a meatball, is the rising-tone word *wán*. Listen as the instructor contrasts this word with a word meaning "ring" that has an *h-* initial.

ròu**wán**   meatball

zhǐ**huán**   finger ring

While we are familiar with this medial–final combination, here is the opportunity to contrast the words for a "sour taste" and "garlic." "Sour" is a high level tone and "garlic" is a falling tone.

suān   sour

suàn   garlic

When *y-a-n* occurs with a rising tone, we get the word for salt. Although you will probably not find a shaker of salt on a Chinese table, you might find this word useful.

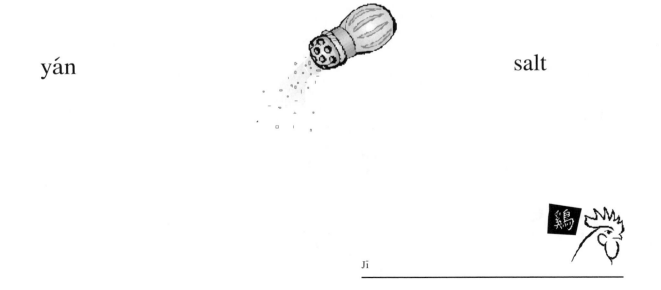

yán   salt

Jī

With an *m-* initial and a falling tone, you get a word that is extremely important when you are involved in the study of Chinese, namely the word for "noodles." When following an initial, the spelling of this final is –*i-a-n.*

miàn

noodle

One of the most common names on this planet is *wáng,* which originally referred to the king or the hereditary ruler of a state. The *w-a-n-g* appears as –*u-a-n-g* when it follows an initial. This gives us the opportunity to contrast the words for "king" and the color "yellow." Both are rising tone words that rhyme with "pong" of "ping pong."   The initial *h-* occurs with the sound for "yellow."

wáng

king

huáng

yellow

To bring up an unpleasant topic, the word for "mosquito" is a rising tone word:

wénzi  mosquito

With an *l-* initial this forms a word that means "wheel." Repeat the word for "wheel" after your instructor. Be sure to keep the rising tone:

lúnzi  wheel

The syllable spelled *w-e-i* is pronounced like the English "way" as in "one-way," with the tip of your tongue forward and high up in your mouth. A low-rising tone word of this syllable is the morpheme for the "tail of an animal."

wěiba  tail

When there is a preceding consonant initial, this final is spelled *-u-i*. Since we are on animal parts, repeat the word for "leg" after your instructor. This word has an additional silent "*t*" initial with a significant aspiration, or spurt of air accompanying it.

tuǐ  leg

DRILLS

Drill One: *Identification of the tones. When you hear a word, indicate the tone of its first syllable by marking on the appropriate tone representation.*

1

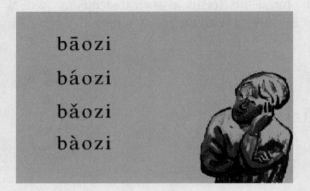

bāozi

báozi

bǎozi

bàozi

2

qiēzi

qiézi

qiězi

qièzi

3

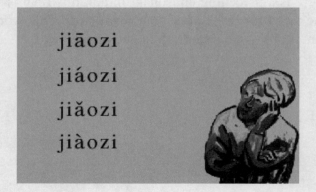

jiāozi

jiáozi

jiǎozi

jiàozi

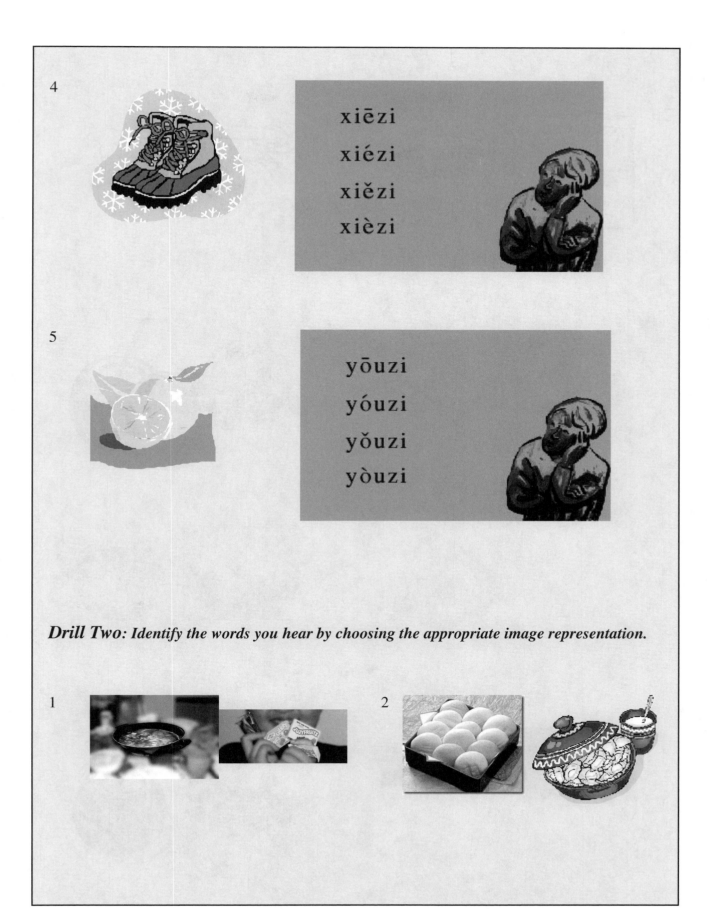

4

xiēzi
xiézi
xiězi
xièzi

5

yōuzi
yóuzi
yǒuzi
yòuzi

Drill Two: *Identify the words you hear by choosing the appropriate image representation.*

1

2

Drill Three: *When you hear a word or morpheme, identify it by circling the appropriate image.*

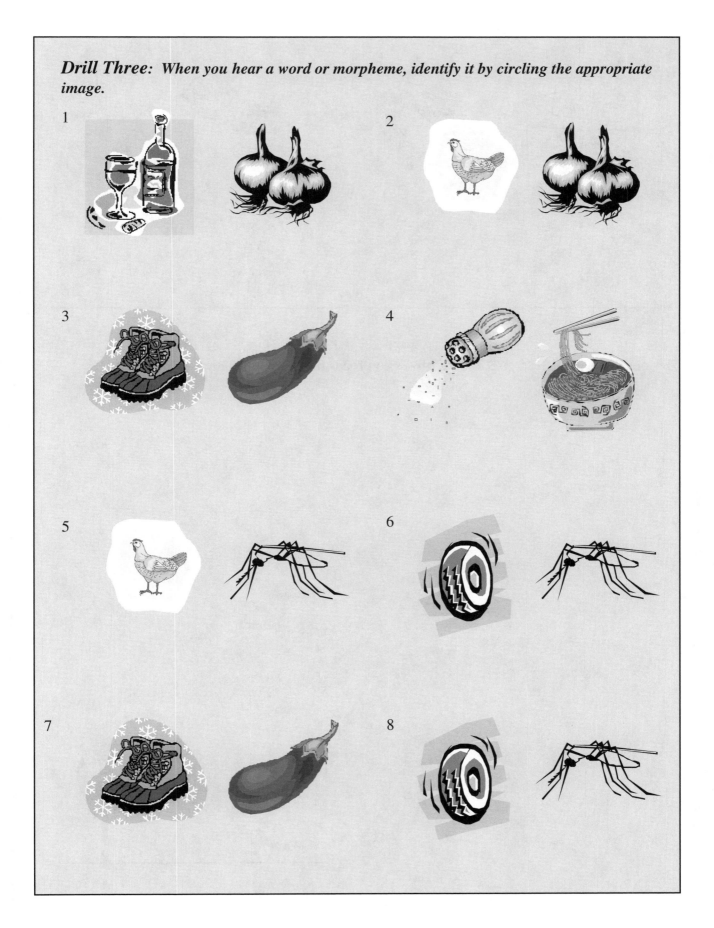

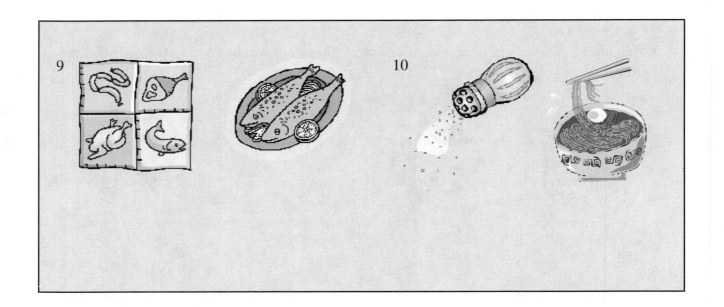

This concludes Unit 1 Stage 8, the fourth session focusing on pronunciation.

Yìduǒ huā(r)

Meeting and Introducing People

Dialogue Setting

Chinese Visitor to America

Professor White and Ouyang Li are trying to find the arriving Professor Zhang. She spots them before they see her and approaches them with a self introduction. Professor White is somewhat embarrassed for not having been more attentive.

Zhāng Róng: Qǐngwèn, nín shi Bái jiàoshòu ma?
Bái Délún: Wǒ jiùshi.

Zhāng Róng: Zìwǒ jièshào yíxià. Wǒ shi Qīnghuá Dàxué de Zhāng Róng.

Bái Délún: Ò, Zhāng jiàoshòu. Huānyíng, huānyíng...... Zhēn duìbuqǐ ya.

Dialogue Information:

* Professor: **jiàoshòu**

* Question particle: **ma**

* Emphatic form of the state verb **shì**:   **jiùshi**

* Reflective pronoun: **zìwǒ**

* Verb meaning "introduce":   **jièshào**

* Time duration: **yíxià**

* Name of a well-known university in Beijing: **Qīnghuá Dàxué**

* Particle of modification: **de**

* Verb for welcoming an outgroup member: **huānyíng**

* Phrase for showing embarrassment and shame: **duìbuqǐ**

* Sentential emphatic particle: **ya, wa, na, nga**

Chī

Vocabulary (Shēngcí)

1. State Verb (zhuàngtài dòngcí)
   jiùshì

2. Question of Verbs (yíwèncí)
   zěnme

3. Verbs (dòngcí)
   chēnghu
   jiào
   jièshào

4. Nouns (míngcí)
   dàxué
   xuéyuàn
   xuéxiào
   gōngsī

5. Terms of Address (chēnghu)
   jiàoshòu
   tóngxué
   zhǔrèn
   yuànzhǎng
   xiàozhǎng

6. Names of Institutions (zhuānyǒu míngcí)
   Qīnghuá Dàxué
   Rénmín Dàxué
   Běijīng Dàxué
   Shīfàn Dàxué
   Běijīng Shīfàn Dàxué
   Táiwān Shīfàn Dàxué
   Hénán Shīfàn Dàxué
   Huáměi Màoyì Gōngsī

7. Adverb (fùcí)
   zhēn

8. Reflexive Pronoun (fǎnshēn dàicí)
   zìwǒ

9. Particle (zhùcí)
   a

10. Time Duration (shíjiān fùcí)
    yíxià   yíxià zi

11. Phrases (cízǔ)
    zìwǒ jièshào yíxià
    wǒ gěi nǐmen jièshào yíxià
    huānyíng
    duìbuqǐ

Hē

DRILLS

Drill One: *Asking about a person's identity.*

Example:

Prof. Bái

Instructor: **Nǐ hǎo.**
Student: **Qǐngwèn, nín shi Bái jiàoshòu ma?**
Instructor: **Wǒ jiùshi.**

1

President Jì

2

Mr. Huà, Assistant Manager

3

Mr. Zhū, the Director

4

Wáng, Fellow Student

5

Mr. Fèi, the Dean

6

Prof. Wú

7

Ms. Fāng, the Manager

Drill Two: *Identifying persons with their work place.*

Example 1:

Qīnghuá University
Professor
Zhāng Róng

| Instructor: | Nèiwèi nǚshì shi shéi? |
| Student: | Tā shi Qīnghuá Dàxué de Zhāng jiàoshòu. |

Example 2:

The Company
Secretary
Lǚ Yīng

| Instructor: | Tā shi shénme rén? |
| Student: | Tā shi wǒmen gōngsī de Lǚ mìshū. |

1

People's University
President
Lǐ Jūn

2

Sino-Am Co.
Manager
Fāng Guànyīng

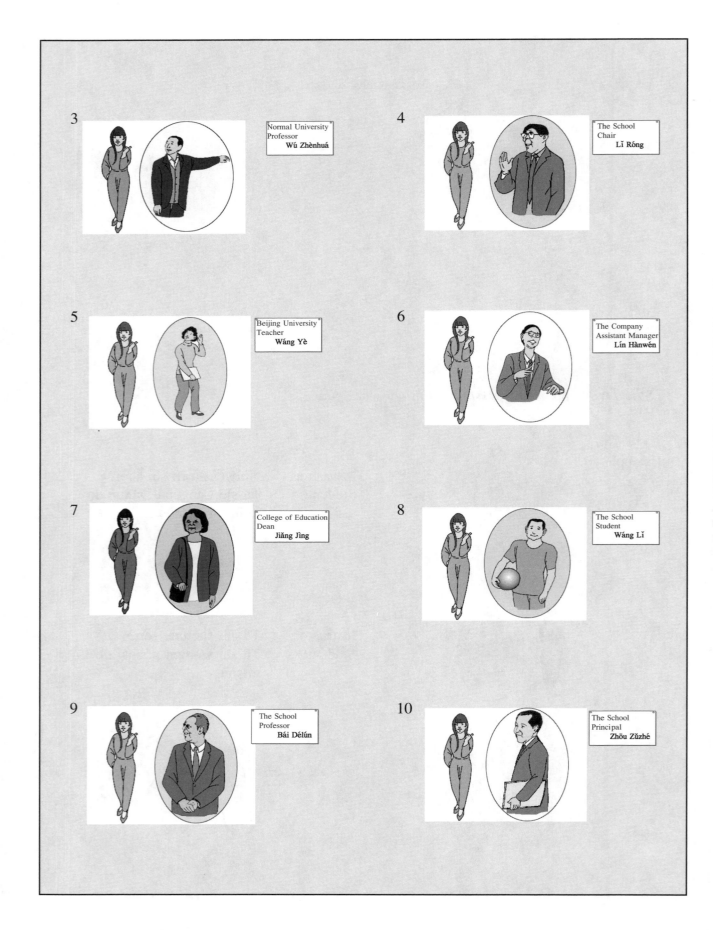

3   Normal University Professor **Wú Zhènhuá**

4   The School Chair **Lǐ Róng**

5   Beijing University Teacher **Wáng Yè**

6   The Company Assistant Manager **Lín Hànwén**

7   College of Education Dean **Jiǎng Jìng**

8   The School Student **Wáng Lǐ**

9   The School Professor **Bái Délún**

10   The School Principal **Zhōu Zǔzhé**

Drill Three: *Identifying yourself.*

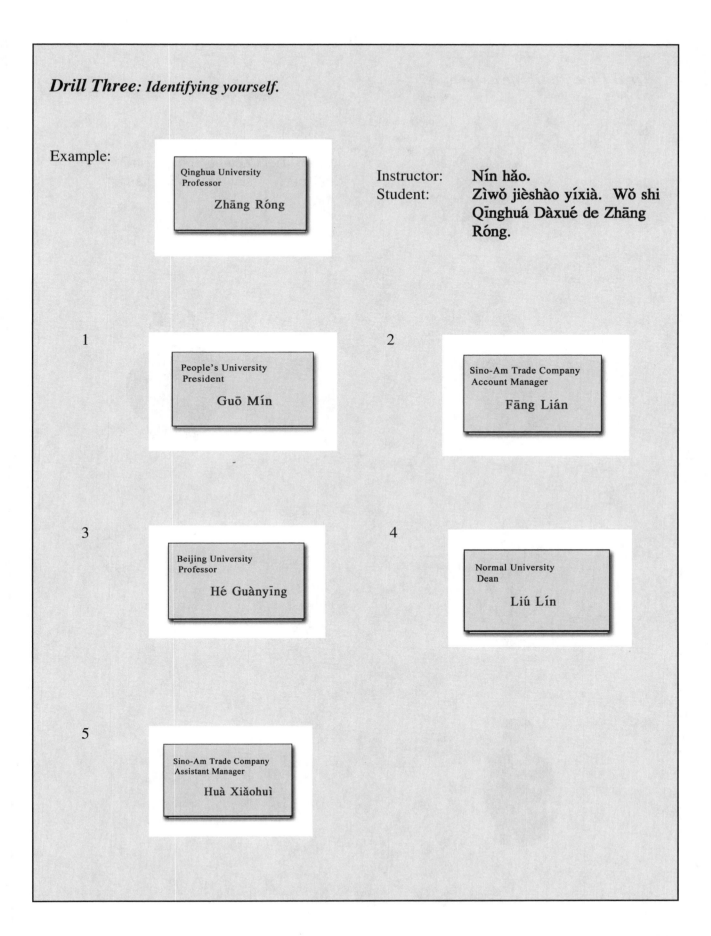

Example:

Qinghua University
Professor

Zhāng Róng

Instructor: **Nín hǎo.**
Student: **Zìwǒ jièshào yíxià. Wǒ shi Qīnghuá Dàxué de Zhāng Róng.**

1

People's University
President

Guō Mín

2

Sino-Am Trade Company
Account Manager

Fāng Lián

3

Beijing University
Professor

Hé Guànyīng

4

Normal University
Dean

Liú Lín

5

Sino-Am Trade Company
Assistant Manager

Huà Xiǎohuì

Drill Four: *Advising about titles.*

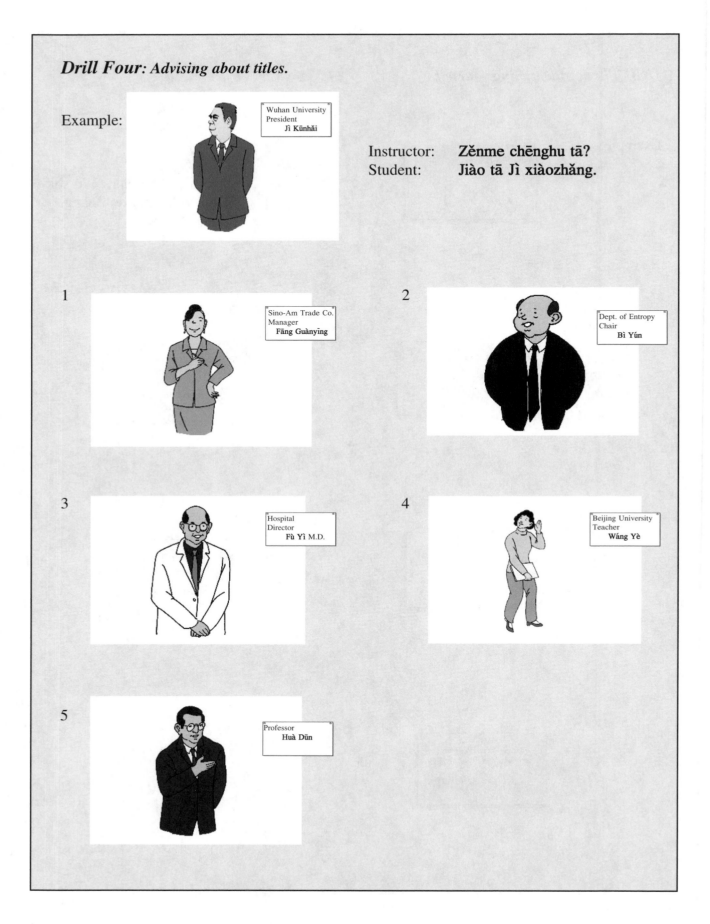

Example:

Wuhan University
President
Jì Kūnhǎi

Instructor: **Zěnme chēnghu tā?**
Student: **Jiào tā Jì xiàozhǎng.**

1

Sino-Am Trade Co.
Manager
Fāng Guànyìng

2

Dept. of Entropy
Chair
Bì Yún

3

Hospital
Director
Fù Yì M.D.

4

Beijing University
Teacher
Wáng Yè

5

Professor
Huà Dūn

Drill Five: Asking the Chinese names of things.

Example:

Instructor: **Yǒu méi-you wèntí?**
Student: **Yǒu wèntí. "Paris" zhōngwén jiào shénme?**

1

2

3

4

5

6

Drill Six: *Noting down the Chinese names.*

Example: Instructor: "Gone with the Wind" zhōngwén zěnme shuō?
          Student: Zhōngwén jiào "Piāo".

1. _____   2. _____

3. _____   4. _____

5. _____

Drill Seven: *Answering questions about names and terms of address.*

Example: Instructor: Tā shi dàxué de xiàozhǎng, yīngwén zěnme chēnghu tā?
          Student: Yīngwén jiào tā "president".

Example: Instructor: "Liánhé Hángkōng Gōngsī" yīngwén jiào shénme?
          Student: Duìbuqǐ. Wǒ bù-dǒng nǐde wèntí.

    1.   2.   3.   4.

    5.   6.   7.   8.

Drill Eight: *Introducing persons.*

Example 1:

Qīnghuá University
Professor
Lín Tōng

Instructor: **Zhèwèi shi......**
Student: **Wǒ gěi nǐmen jièshào yíxià. Zhōu jīnglǐ, zhèwèi shi Qīnghuá Dàxué de Lín Tōng jiàoshòu.**

Example 2:

The University
President
Cén Dǎmíng

Instructor: **Qǐng nǐ gěi wǒmen jièshào......**
Student: **Wǒ gěi nǐmen jièshào yíxià. Zhōu jīnglǐ, zhèwèi shi wǒmen xuéxiào de Cén xiàozhǎng.**

1

The School
Dean
Mǐ Zǐlóng

2 Professor
   Yú Qiú

3 The School
   Wáng Yán
   Student

4 The Company
   Assistant Manager
   Huà Xiǎohuì

Dialogue Comprehension

Zhāng Róng:	Qǐngwèn, nín shi Bái jiàoshòu ma?
Bái Délún:	Wǒ jiùshi.
Zhāng Róng:	Zìwǒ jièshào yíxià. Wǒ shi Qīnghuá Dàxué de Zhāng Róng.
Bái Délún:	Ò, Zhāng jiàoshòu. Huānyíng, huānyíng...... Zhēn duìbuqǐ ya.

UNIT 1 STAGE 10

Self Test

Section A: Answer the following questions about the Chinese you have studied in this course.

Vocabulary: Select and fill in the word that has an opposite meaning from the given word.

bèn	gāoxìng	lǎn
nénggàn	shòu	lǎo
piàoliang	yánzhòng	gāo
xiǎo	rènzhēn	lǐmào
píngjìng	línghuó	

1. dà: ____________

2. jǐnzhāng: ____________

3. nǔlì: ____________

4. niánqīng: ____________

5. wángù: ____________

6. ǎi: ____________

7. nánkàn: ____________

8. wúnéng: ____________

9. cōngming: ____________

10. pàng: ____________

Write in the term of address that is most appropriate for the person described below:

xiáojie	xiānsheng	jiàoshòu
tóngxué	xiàozhǎng	jīnglǐ
tàitai	nǚshì	tóngzhì
xuésheng		

11. a young unmarried woman in Taiwan: _____

12. a foreign man in China: _____

13. a fellow student: _____

14. a married woman outside of China: _____

15. a university professor: _____

16. a university president: _____

17. a business woman: _____

18. the manager in a company: _____

19. a Chinese person addressing another in Mainland China irrespective of age, gender or social status:

    _____

20. a Chinese man outside of China: _____

Jīnglǐ

Grammar: Select an appropriate word from the given list and write it in the space provided:

bú	bǐjiào	dōu	hěn
yě	yǒu	zài	zhēn
hé	de	le	ma
zěnme	zài	yòu	ne

21. Wǒmen dōu hěn hǎo, nǐ _____?

22. Yǐqián xuéshēngmen dōu hěn nǔlì, zuìjìn lǎn _____.

23. Lǎoshī hěn nǔlì, xuésheng _____ hěn nǔlì.

24. Fāng jīnglǐ yòu cōngming _____ nénggàn.

25. Xiǎo Wáng tóngxué _____ gāo.

26. Shèng lǎoshī _____ Huáng lǎoshī dōu gǎnmào le.

27. Qǐng nǐ _____ shuō yíbiàn.

28. Tā shi nèige bǐjiào lǎo _____ rén.

29. Tā _____ shi fùjīnglǐ, tā shi mìshū.

30. Tā shi Fāng jīnglǐ _____?

Function Exercises: What you would say for each of the following situations?

31. Greet Professor Lǐ.

   _____

32. Apologize for failing to meet someone's expectations.

   _____

33. Introduce yourself.

   _____

34. Ask a classmate what the teacher's last name is.

   _____

35. Explain that you do not have any free time.

_____

36. Ask the identity of someone you do not recognize.

_____

37. Ask what the secretary looks like.

_____

38. Explain that the secretary is more intelligent than the manager.

_____

39. Ask what Mr. Huáng, the teacher, is like.

_____

40. State that you have gotten busier lately.

_____

Section B: Listen to the following segments of conversational exchanges and answer the questions as they are asked.

Segment 1   1. When you hear this, the teacher wants you to ...
             a) repeat after her
             b) listen
             c) sit down

Segment 2   2. Where does this encounter probably take place?
             a) Beijing
             b) Taiwan
             c) New York

             3. What is the relationship between these two people?
             a) friends
             b) strangers
             c) colleagues

Segment 3   4. What is being discussed?
             a) someone's name
             b) someone's occupation
             c) someone's physical appearance

5. The person being discussed is
    a) probably Chinese
    b) probably not Chinese
    c) difficult to identify as being Chinese or not

Segment 4   6. When you hear this, the instructor wants you to...
    a) repeat
    b) listen
    c) sit down

Segment 5   7. These two people are...
    a) friends
    b) strangers
    c) relatives

8. Both of these people are...
    a) well
    b) tired
    c) busy

Segment 6   9. When you hear this, the instructor wants you to...
    a) go home
    b) leave class
    c) begin the lesson

Segment 7   10. Overhearing this conversation, you can tell that
    a) the two people know each other
    b) this is their first meeting
    c) the first speaker knows the other man's name

11. This conversation probably takes place in ...
    a) Beijing
    b) Taibei
    c) Hongkong

Segment 8   12. This conversation concerns ...
    a) a man
    b) a woman
    c) two women

13. Zhāng Róng is relatively
    a) plump
    b) thin
    c) familiar

14. The person being pointed out is ...
    a) familiar looking
    b) Zhāng Róng
    c) plump

Segment 9   15. The instructor wants to know ...
    a) if you understand
    b) if you know the answer
    c) if you have a question

16. The instructor is speaking to ...
    a) a class
    b) a single student
    c) fellow workers

Segment 10   17. This question concerns ...
    a) what a person's occupation is
    b) how to address a person
    c) what a person's name is

18. The person asking the question wants to know ...
    a) a Chinese term of address
    b) an English name
    c) a Chinese family name

Segment 11   19. This conversation is between ...
    a) two old friends
    b) two acquaintances
    c) two people who have not previously met

20. The first speaker ...
    a) recognizes the other person, but is not certain of his identity
    b) has no idea to whom she is speaking
    c) is sure of the identity of the other person

21. The person from Qīnghuá University ...
    a) is welcoming the other person
    b) is introducing the other person
    c) is welcomed by the other person

Segment 12   22. The person being talked about ...
    a) is a teacher
    b) is an assistant manager
    c) is a secretary

23. The person asking the questions does not know ...
      a) the person's name or position
      b) the name of the company
      c) the proper term of address

Segment 13   24. The instructor wants you to ...
      a) answer questions
      b) ask questions
      c) leave the class

Segment 14   25. The person asking the questions wants to know ...
      a) how someone looks
      b) how someone feels
      c) what someone knows

26. The person answering the question is ...
      a) not doing well
      b) very comfortable
      c) doing quite well

27. The condition of the person answering the question is ...
      a) the same as fellow students
      b) the same as fellow workers
      c) improving

Segment 15   28. The person asking the questions ...
      a) seems to want information about the company
      b) seems to want to talk to Mr. Huà
      c) is a friend of the person answering the questions

29. Mr. Huà is best described as ...
      a) thin and short
      b) short and fat
      c) familiar looking

Segment 16   30. The instructor wants you to ...
      a) listen again
      b) answer a question
      c) repeat what you have just said

Section A:

Vocabulary:

1. xiǎo	2. píngjìng	3. lǎn	4. lǎo	5. línghuó/kāitong
6. gāo	7. piàoliang	8. nénggàn	9. bèn	10. shòu

11. xiáojie	12. xiānsheng	13. tóngxué	14. tàitai	15. jiàoshòu
16. xiàozhǎng	17. nǔshì	18. jīnglǐ	19. tóngzhì	20. xiānsheng

Grammar:

21. ne	22. le	23. yě	24. yòu	25. zhēn, hěn, bǐjiào
26. hé	27. zài, yě	28. de	29. bù	30. ma

Function Exercises:
31. Lǐ jiàoshòu, nǐ hǎo.
32. Duìbuqǐ.
33. Zìwǒ jièshào yíxià, wǒ shi......
34. Lǎoshī xìng shénme? / Lǎoshī jiào shénme míngzi?
35. Wǒ hěn máng. / Wǒ méi-you kòng.
36. Tā shi shéi?
37. Mìshū zhǎngde zěnmeyàng?
38. Mìshū bǐ jīnglǐ cōngming.
39. Huáng lǎoshī zěnmeyàng?
40. Wǒ zuìjìn máng le.

Section B:

1. b	2. a	3. b	4. a	5. b
6. a	7. a	8. c	9. c	10. b
11. a	12. c	13. a	14. a	15. c
16. a	17. b	18. a	19. c	20. a
21. c	22. b	23. a	24. a	25. b
26. a	27. b	28. b	29. a	30. c

Máng

UNIT 2
Location: People and Activities Associated with Them

U nit Two is designed to give you some basic skills at locating people and mentioning what they do at these locations.

The general procedure is to guide you through authentic conversations in the Chinese context, rehearse your participation in that conversation, and then expand your ability to participate in similar, but different conversations. Your success in learning to perform the Chinese on this audio program will depend on how intensively you work with it. The more you listen and participate using your normal speaking voice, the more you will remember and the better you will perform.

In Unit Two, you will learn to do the following in Mandarin Chinese:

Stage One, *Locating People*: discuss where people are and describe the places.

Stage Two, *Learning People's Origins and Place of Work*: discuss a person's origins, profession and work place.

Stage Three, *Locating the Action*: describe and locate meeting places.

Stage Four, *Discussing Ethnicity and Nationality*: discuss marital status, spouse's profession and work place along with ethnicity and nationality.

Stage Five, *Pronunciation and Romanization: Initials, Medials, and Finals*: pronunciation practice.

Stage Six, *Locating Things around the Office*: locate things in the immediate environment of an office. Ask and answer questions regarding work.

Stage Seven, *Discussing Populations*: talk about and comment on the student enrollments in the university.

Stage Eight, *Getting Lunch on the Train*: sell and buy lunch on a train steaming south from Beijing to Fuzhou.

Stage Nine, *Pronunciation and Romanization: Tones, Initials, Medials, and Finals*: pronunciation practice.

Stage Ten, *Self Test*: test your command of the Chinese you have studied.

Locating People

Dialogue Setting

Sino-American Trade Co., Washington, DC

The following exchange occurs in the Washington office of the Sino-American Trade Company between two co-workers. The assistant manager, Hua Xiaohui, is interested in the whereabouts of Ms. Fang, the manager of the company. He directs his question to the secretary, Wang Liyu, who seems to know everything.

Huà Xiǎohuì: Fāng jīnglǐ xiànzài zài nǎr?
Wáng Lìyù: Zài Běijīng.

Huà Xiǎohuì: Zài Běijīng (de) nǎr?
Wáng Lìyù: Zhōngguó Guójì Màoyì Zhōngxīn.
             Nǐ zhīdao nèige dìfang ma?
Huà Xiǎohuì: Zhīdao. Nèige dìfang de shèbèi
             tǐng hǎo.

Dialogue Information:

* Asking where the manager, Fang, is: **Fāng jīnglǐ xiànzài zài nǎr?**
                                              Fāng jīnglǐ xiànzài zài nǎli?

* locating people and things: **zài**

* Asking if Prof. Huang is around: **Huáng lǎoshī zài bú-zai?**
                                              Huáng lǎoshī zài ma?

* Stating that she's not here: **Tā bú-zài.**

*

ZÀI	Place name: Běijīng; Shànghǎi; Xiānggǎng; Jiùjīnshān (Sānfānshì); Niǔyuē
DÀO	Place word: nǎr; nǎli
	Place: jiā; gōngchǎng; fànguǎn
	Noun + loc: shān-shang; chéng-li

(The shaded area includes similar items to be covered later.)

* Stating that (Ms. Fang is) in Beijing: **Zài Běijīng.**

* Asking where in Beijing: **Zài Běijīng nǎr?**
                                            Zài Běijīng nǎli?
                                            Zài Běijīng de nǎr?
                                            Zài Běijīng de nǎli?

* Stating that (she is at) the China
International Trade Center: **(zài) Zhōngguó Guójì Màoyì Zhōngxīn**

* the general term for "place":   **dìfang**

* that place: **nèige dìfang**

* Asking if you know anything
about that place: **Nǐ zhīdao nèige dìfang ma?**

* know: **zhīdao**

* the general word for "equipment": **shèbèi**

* the equipment in that place: **nèige dìfang de shèbèi**

* Commenting that the equipment there
  is very good: **Nèige dìfang de shèbèi tǐng hǎo.**

Vocabulary (Shēngcí)

1. Place Names (dìmíng)
   Běijīng
   Shànghǎi
   Xiānggǎng
   Jiùjīnshān (Sānfānshì)
   Niǔyuē
   Zhījiāgē
   Dōngjīng
   Lúndūn
   Bālí
   Huáshèngdùn
   Zhōngguó Guójì Màoyì Zhōngxīn
   Guójì Dà Fàndiàn
   Shǒudū Jùchǎng

2. Question Words (yíwèncí)
   nǎr
   nǎli

3. Nouns (míngcí)
   dìfang
   shèbèi

4. State Verbs (zhuàngtài dòngcí)
   zài
   rènshi
   xǐhuan

5. Adverb (fùcí)
   tǐng

6. Phrase (cízǔ)
   shénme dìfang

Tīng

Shuō

Drill One: Locating people and organizations. *Review the following place names and the images we use to represent them for this drill:*

Běijīng

Tiān Tán, where dynastic rulers in China worshipped heaven. One of the most famous attractions in Beijing.

Shànghǎi

Dōngfāng Míngzhū Tǎ, the Oriental Pearl broadcasting and television tower has become the new symbol of Shanghai.

Xiānggǎng

Diànchē, the double-deck tram, is one of the famous sights of Hong Kong.

Huáshèngdùn

Guóhuì Dàshà, built, burnt, rebuilt, extended, and restored ever since 1793, is one of the most famous attractions in Washington, D.C.

Lúndūn

Dà Běn Zhōng, built in 1858/9, is one of the most famous attractions in London.

Zhījiāgē

Xī'ěrsī Dàshà, built in 1973 as the world's tallest building, is a major feature of the Chicago skyline.

Jiùjīnshān (Sānfānshì)

Jīnménqiáo, built in 1937, is one of the tourist attractions in San Francisco.

Niǔyuē

Zìyóu Nǚshén, a gift from France in 1886, is a symbol of freedom, democracy and international friendship.

Bālí

Āifēi'ěr Tiětǎ, built in 1889, is an enduring symbol of the city of Paris.

When asked about the location of people or organizations, answer according to the picture. In the example, you will be asked about Qinghua University.

Example:

Instructor: **Qīnghuá Dàxué zài nǎr?**
Student: **Zài Běijīng.**

1

2

3

4

5

6

7

8

9

10

Drill Two: *Getting further information on the location. Review one more place name for this and the following drills:*

Dōngjīng

Huánggōng, the Imperial Palace where the emperor resides, is in the center of Tokyo.

Example: Instructor: **Shǒudū Jùchǎng zài Běijīng.**
          Student: **Zài Běijīng nǎr?**

1.   2.   3.   4.   5.

Drill Three: *Correcting a misunderstanding about locations.*

Example:

Instructor: **Fāng jīnglǐ zài Niǔyuē ba.**
Student: **Bú-zài Niǔyuē. Fāng jīnglǐ zài Běijīng.**

1

2

3

4

5

6

7

8

9

10

Drill Four: *Making conclusions about past locations.*

Example 1: Instructor: **Xiànzài Fāng jīnglǐ zài Shànghǎi le.**
          Student: **Yǐqián tā bú-zài Shànghǎi.**

Example 2: Instructor: **Xiànzài nèige xuéyuàn zài Huáshèngdùn le.**
          Student: **Yǐqián nèige xuéyuàn bú-zài Huáshèngdùn.**

          1.   2.   3.   4.   5.

Zuìjìn zěnmeyàng ne?

Drill Five: *Answering questions about the location of people and things.*

Example:

Instructor: **Nǐ zhīdao wǒmende shèbèi xiànzài zài nǎr?**

Student: **Zhīdao. Xiànzài wǒmende shèbèi zài Xiānggǎng.**

1

2

3

4

5

Bù-shūfu

Drill Six: *Confirming a previous state. Review the following state verbs for this drill:*

jiào	to be called something
rènshi	to recognize
shì/shi	to be
xǐhuan	to like
xìng	to have the family name of _____
yǒu	to have, possess
zài	to exist at someplace

Example: Instructor: **Xiànzài wǒ xǐhuan Běijīng le.**
Student: **Yǐqián nǐ bù-xǐhuan Běijīng ma?**

1. 2. 3. 4. 5.

6. 7. 8. 9.

Drill Seven: *Confirming that you know people.*

Example:

Instructor: **Nǐ rènshi Wáng Lìyù ma?**
Student: **Rènshi. Wáng Lìyù tǐng nénggàn.**

Shū

1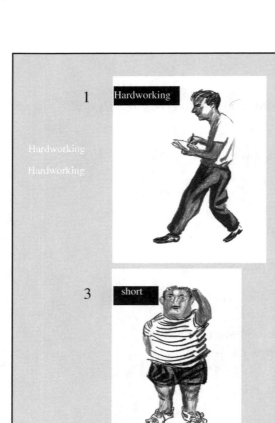
Hardworking

Hardworking
Hardworking

2 Stubborn
Never!

3 short

4 Ugly

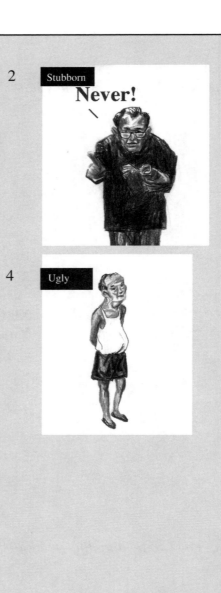

5 Petty

Drill Eight: Stating your likes and dislikes.

Example:

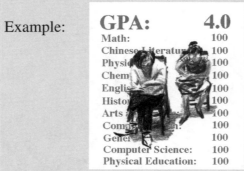

GPA: **4.0**
Math: 100
Chinese Literature 100
Physic 100
Chem 100
Englis 100
Histor 100
Arts 100
Comp 100
Gener 100
Computer Science: 100
Physical Education: 100

Student: **Lǎoshī, nǐ xǐhuan bù-xǐhuan tóngxuémen?**

Instructor: **Xǐhuan. Tāmen dōu tǐng cōngming.**

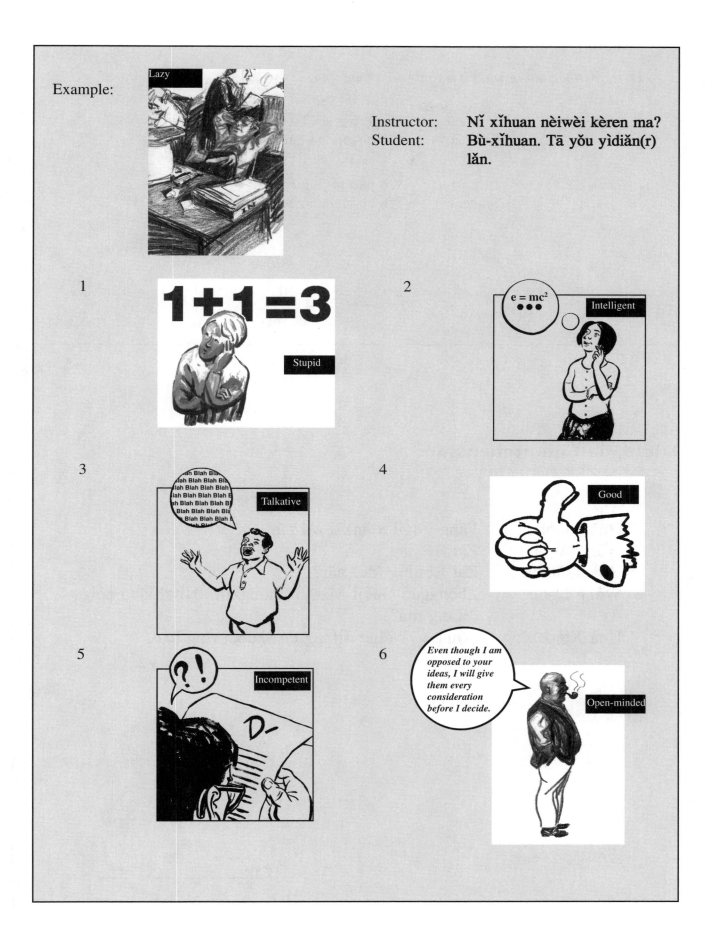

Example:

Instructor: **Nǐ xǐhuan nèiwèi kèren ma?**
Student: **Bù-xǐhuan. Tā yǒu yìdiǎn(r) lǎn.**

Drill Nine: *Stating what it is that you do not know.*

Example 1:   Instructor: **Nèige rén shì bu-shi Cuī Jiàn?**
                               Student: **Wǒ bù-zhīdao nèige rén shi shéi.**

Example 2:   Instructor: **Wǒ jiào tā jīnglǐ ma?**
                               Student: **Wǒ bù-zhīdao zěnme chēnghu tā.**

1.   2.   3.   4.   5.   6

7.   8.   9.   10.   11.   12.

Dialogue Comprehension

Huà Xiǎohuì: **Fāng jīnglǐ xiànzài zài nǎr?**
Wáng Lìyù: **Zài Běijīng.**
Huà Xiǎohuì: **Zài Běijīng (de) nǎr?**
Wáng Lìyù: **Zhōngguó Guójì Màoyì Zhōngxīn. Nǐ zhīdao nèige**
                             dìfang ma?
Huà Xiǎohuì: **Zhīdao. Nèige dìfang de shèbèi tǐng hǎo.**

Lèi le

Learning People's Origins and Place of Work

Dialogue Setting

Chinese Visitor to American Campus

The following exchange occurs on an American campus. Ouyang Li, a graduate student, is getting to know Professor Zhang, whom he has been assigned to look after while she is a visiting researcher on his campus.

Ōuyáng Lǐ: Nín shi nǎr (de) rén? Shì Běijīngrén ba?
Zhāng Róng: Bú-shì. Wǒ jiā zài Qīngdǎo. Wǒ shi zài Běijīng zuò yánjiū gōngzuò.

Ōuyáng Lǐ: Zài Běijīng nǎr gōngzuò?
Zhāng Róng: (Zài) Qīnghuá Dàxué.

Dialogue Information:

* Asking the question "where":	**Năr?**
	Năli?
	Shénme dìfang?
	Něige dìfang?
	Năge dìfang?
* Asking a person's country:	**něiguó**
	năguó
	něige guójiā
	năge guójiā
* Asking where Prof. Zhāng is from:	**Nín shi năr (de) rén?**
* Assuming that (she) is a person from Beijing:	**Shì Běijīngrén ba?**
* Telling that (I) am not (a person from Beijing):	**Bú-shì.**
* My hometown is Qīngdăo:	**Wŏ jiā zài Qīngdăo.**
* do work:	**zuò gōngzuò**
* do research work:	**zuò yánjiū gōngzuò**
* Stating that I conduct research in Běijīng:	**Wŏ shi zài Běijīng zuò yánjiū gōngzuò.**
* Asking where in Běijīng:	**Zài Běijīng năr?**
* Asking where you work in Běijīng:	**Zài Běijīng năr gōngzuò?**
* Telling that (I work in) Qīnghuá University:	**(Zài) Qīnghuá Dàxué.**

Shuō

Vocabulary (Shēngcí)

1. Place Names (dìmíng)
Àodàlìyà
Jiānádà
Měiguó
Rìběn
Yīngguó
Zhōngguó
Gēlúnbù
Guǎngzhōu
Luòshānjī
Qīngdǎo
Wǔhàn
Jìnán Dàxué
Fùdàn Dàxué

2. Question Words (yíwèncí)
nǎguó
něiguó

3. Places (dìdiǎn)
yīyuàn
gōngchǎng
shāngdiàn
jiā

4. Nouns (míngcí)
guǎnlǐ
línshígōng
jiāoshū
jiàoxué
kuàijì
shèjì
yánjiū
yīwù
gōngzuò
guójiā

5. Verbs (dòngcí)
gōngzuò
jiāoshū
shèjì
yánjiū
zuò

6. Phrase (cízǔ)
zuò gōngzuò

7. Marker (qiángdiào)
shì

Dú

Xiě

DRILLS

Drill One: Identifying nationalities.

Example:

Instructor: **Qǐngwèn, nín shi něiguó rén?**

Student: **Wǒ shi Àodàlìyàrén.**

1

2

3

4

5

6

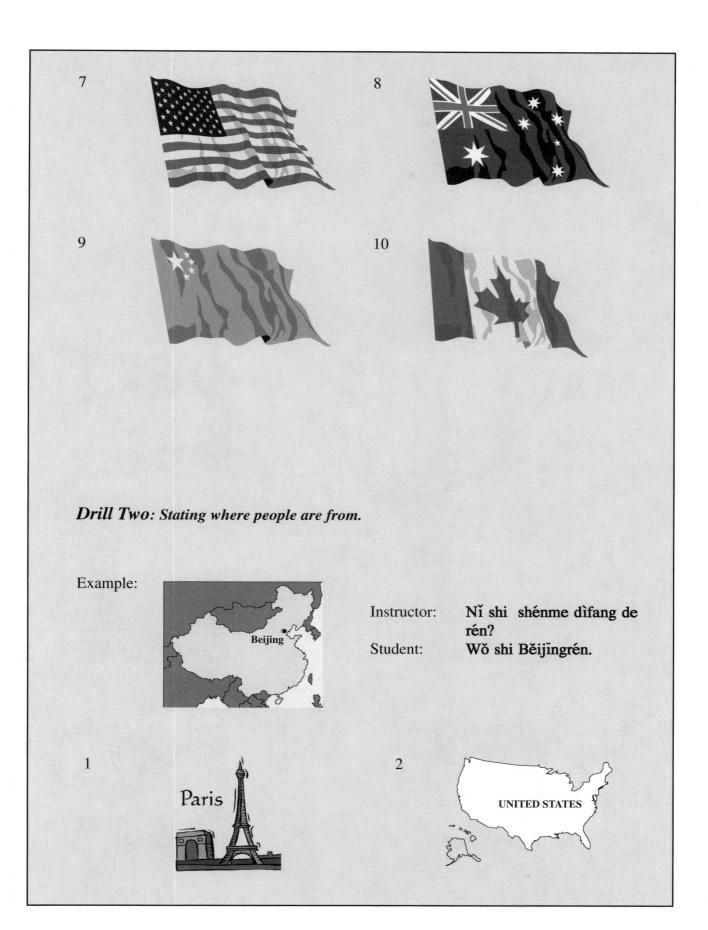

Drill Two: *Stating where people are from.*

Example:

Beijing

Instructor: **Nǐ shi shénme dìfang de rén?**

Student: **Wǒ shi Běijīngrén.**

1 Paris

2 UNITED STATES

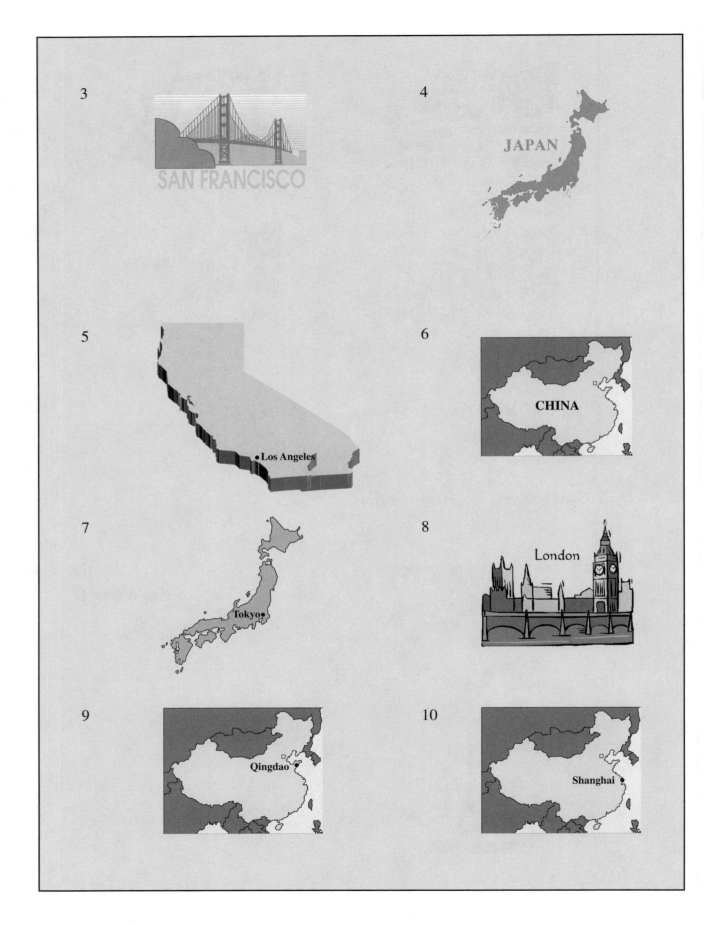

3

4

JAPAN

5

● Los Angeles

6

CHINA

7

Tokyo●

8

London

9

Qingdao ●

10

Shanghai ●

Drill Three: *Correcting a geographical identity.*

Example:

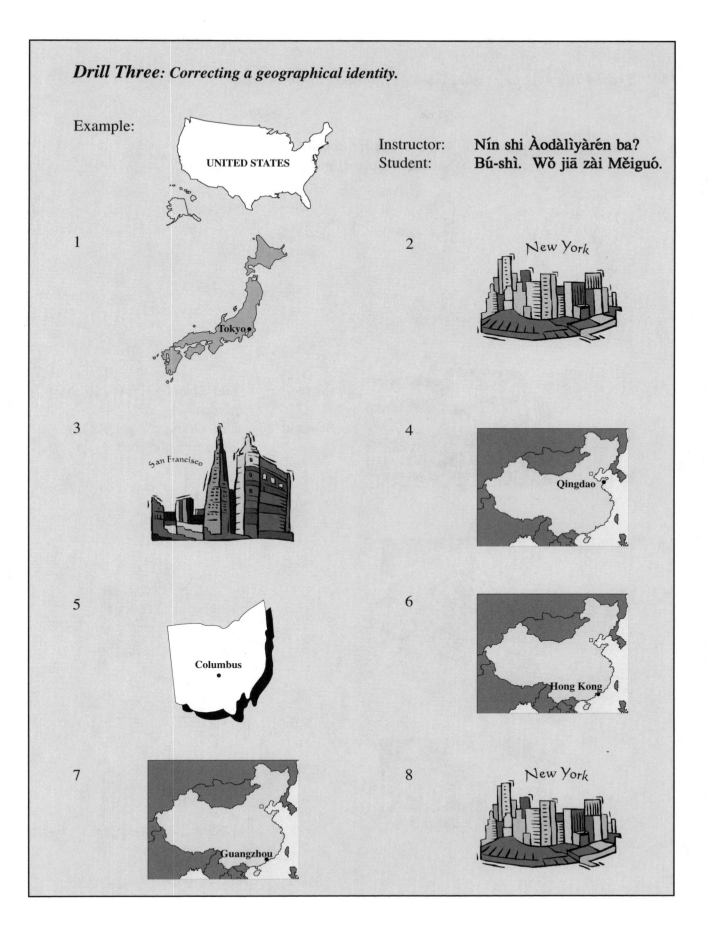

UNITED STATES

Instructor: **Nín shi Àodàlìyàrén ba?**
Student: **Bú-shì. Wǒ jiā zài Měiguó.**

1

Tokyo

2

New York

3

San Francisco

4

Qingdao

5

Columbus

6

Hong Kong

7

Guangzhou

8

New York

Drill Four: Getting information about where people work.

Example: Instructor: **Wǒ zuò kuàijì gōngzuò.**
                 Student: **Nǐ zài shénme dìfang zuò kuàijì gōngzuò?**

1.	2.	3.	4
5.	6.	7.	8.
9.	10.		

Drill Five: Explaining where people work.

Example:

                        Instructor: **Lǎo Zhāng zài nǎr zuò shèjì gōngzuò?**
                        Student: **Lǎo Zhāng zài gōngchǎng zuò shèjì gōngzuò.**

1

2

3

4

5

6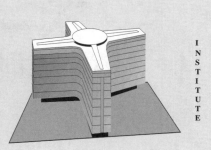

INSTITUTE

Drill Six*: Explaining what kind of work people do.*

Example:

Instructor: **Nǐ zài dàxué zuò shénme gōngzuò?**
Student: **Zuò kuàijì gōngzuò.**

1

2

3

4

5

Drill Seven: Correcting misunderstandings about places of employment.

Example:

UNIVERSITY

Instructor: **Lǎo Huán zài gōngsī zuò shèjì gōngzuò.**

Student: **Bù, Lǎo Huán shì zài dàxué zuò shèjì gōngzuò.**

Xiǎng wèntí

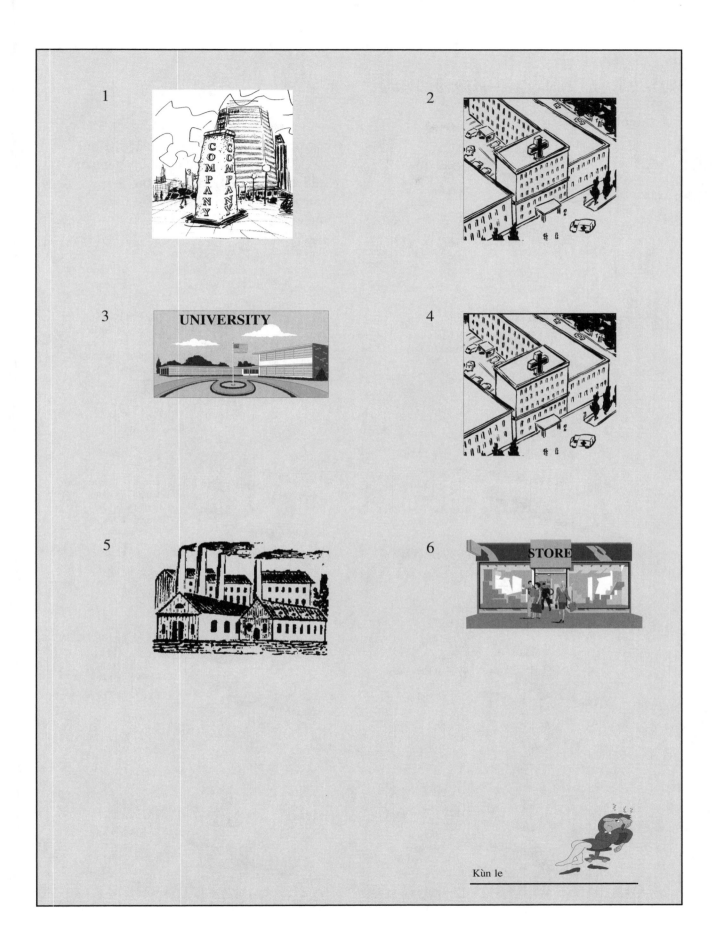

1

2

3 UNIVERSITY

4

5

6 STORE

Kùn le

Drill Eight: *Giving more detailed locations.*

Example:

Zhìmíng Xǔ
Designer
Jinan University
Guangzhou

Instructor: **Xǔ Zhìmíng zài shěnme dìfang zuò shèjì gōngzuò?**
Student: **Zài Guǎngzhōu.**
Instructor: **Zài Guǎngzhōu nǎr?**
Student: **Jìnán Dàxué.**

1

Xīng Liú
Instructor
Wuhan University
Wuhan

2

Zhōngmín Hú
Dept. of Physics
Beijing University
Beijing

3

Lìyù Wáng
Secretary
Sino-Am Trade Co.
Washington

4

Guànyīng Zhào
MD
Shanghai University
Shanghai

5

Bīn Xiè
Prof. of Chemistry
Fudan University
Shanghai

6

Tiānwèn Jiǎn
Prof. of Math
UCLA
Los Angeles

7

Hàn Lín
Manager
JC Company
Tokyo, Japan

8

Lìwěi Wáng
Manager
Star Company
Qingdao, China

Drill Nine: *Geography test.*

Example:

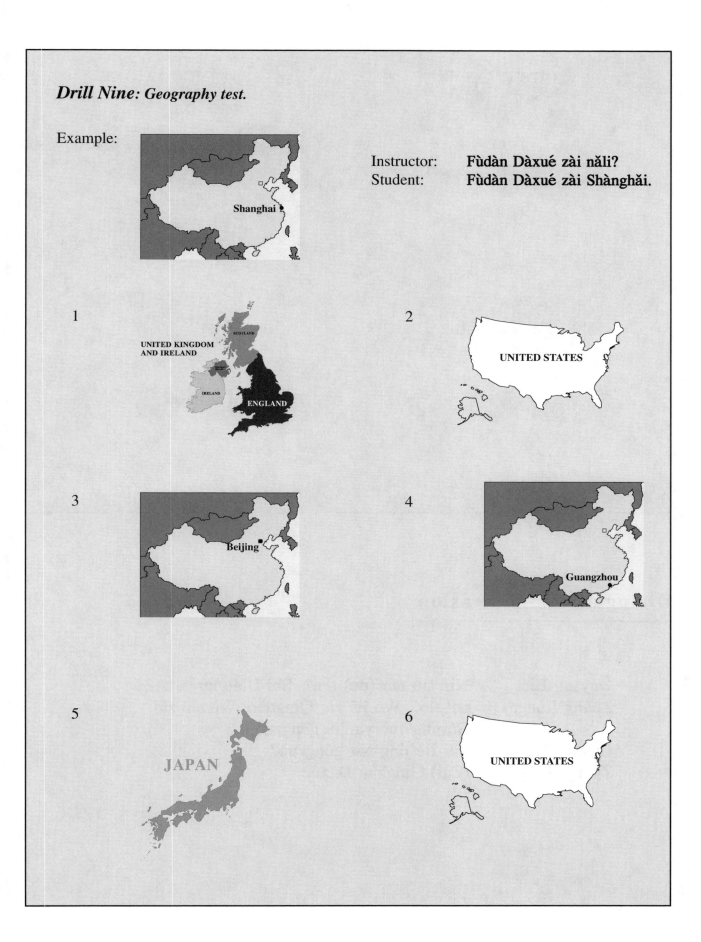

Instructor: **Fùdàn Dàxué zài nǎli?**
Student: **Fùdàn Dàxué zài Shànghǎi.**

1

2

3

4

5

6

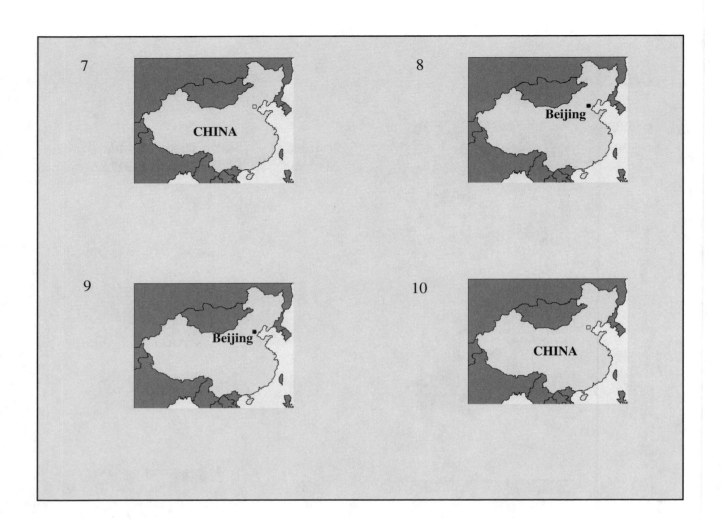

Dialogue Comprehension

Ōuyáng Lǐ: Nín shi nǎr (de) rén? Shì Běijīngrén ba?
Zhāng Róng: Bú-shì. Wǒ jiā zài Qīngdǎo. Wǒ shi zài
Běijīng zuò yánjiū gōngzuò.
Ōuyáng Lǐ: Zài Běijīng nǎr gōngzuò?
Zhāng Róng: (Zài) Qīnghuá Dàxué.

Locating the Action

Dialogue Setting

Sino-American Trade Co., Beijing Office

The following conversation takes place as Sheng Ying is accompanying her boss to a meeting with the head of a factory. They are to meet him at the entry to the Friendship Store, a large department store catering to foreigners where many Chinese export items are on display. Sheng Ying's boss, Fang Guanying (Gwen Fountain), is fresh from the main office in the U.S. Sheng Ying is not too familiar with Fang who has recently been assigned to head the Sino-Am Trading Company by the multinational corporate entity that owns it.

Shèng Yīng: Fāng jīnglǐ, nín kàn Běijīng zěnmeyàng?

Fāng jīnglǐ: Bú-cuò. Jiē-shang dōu hěn rènao.

Fāng jīnglǐ: Zánmen zài nǎr jiàn Lǚ chǎngzhǎng?

Shèng Yīng: Tā shuō zài Yǒuyì Shāngdiàn de dàménkǒu(r) děng wǒmen.

Dialogue Information:

* Asking what someone thinks: **Nín kàn zěnmeyàng?**

* Asking what someone thinks about Beijing: **Nín kàn Běijīng zěnmeyàng?**

* Giving a positive response: **Bú-cuò.**

* lively and bustling: **rènao**

* on the street(s):   **zài jiē-shang**

* Commenting that the streets are full of activity: **Zài jiē-shang dōu hěn rènao.**
                                                         Jiē-shang dōu hěn rènao.

* Asking where we are to meet Mr Lü: **Zánmen zài năr jiàn Lǚ chǎngzhǎng?**

* the title and term of address for someone who
  is the head of a factory: **chǎngzhǎng**
  dean of school   **yuànzhǎng**
  principal, president   **xiàozhǎng**

* Telling that he told me that he would meet us at
  the main entrance to the Friendship Store: **Tā shuō zài Yǒuyì Shāngdiàn de dàménkǒu(r) děng wǒmen.**

* door, entrance or gate: **ménkǒu**
                                                         ménkǒu(r)

* main entrance to some place: **dà ménkǒu**
                                                        dà ménkǒu(r)

* the main entrance to the Friendship Store: **Yǒuyì Shāngdiàn de dàménkǒu(r)**

* Requesting someone to wait a bit: **Qǐng nǐ děng yíxià.**

* Telling that this waiting is going to occur at the
  main entrance to the Friendship Store: **Zài Yǒuyì Shāngdiàn de dàménkǒu(r) děng wǒmen.**

Vocabulary (Shēngcí)

1. Place Words (noun +locative) (fāngwèicí)
   jiē-shang
   hǎi-biān(r)
   chéng-lǐ
   chéng-wài
   shān-xià
   ménkǒu
   lùkǒu
   chuāngkǒu

2. Place Words (verb + locative) (fāngwèicí)
   jiǎnpiàokǒu
   rùkǒu
   chūkǒu

3. Adverbs (fùcí)
   tài
   dàochù

4. Adjectives (xíngróngcí)
   rènao
   bú-cuò
   chǎo
   ānjìng

   měi
   gānjìng
   zāng
   hǎowán(r)
   yōngjǐ
   pǔtōng
   yǒu yìsi
   méi(-yǒu) yìsi

5. Verbs (dòngcí)
   děng
   jiàn
   jiǎnpiào

6. Phrase (cízǔ)
   Nǐ kàn zěnmeyàng?

7. Term of Address (chēnghu)
   chǎngzhǎng

8. Nouns (míngcí)
   chéng
   chǎngzhǎng

Dǎ diànhuà

Dú shū

DRILLS

Drill One: *Getting an opinion about a place.*

Example:　　Instructor:　**Zhège dìfang shi Běijīng.**
　　　　　　Student:　　**Nǐ kàn Běijīng zěnmeyàng?**

1.　　　　2.　　　　3.　　　　4.　　　　5.

6.　　　　7.　　　　8.　　　　9.　　　　10.

Drill Two: *Giving a positive opinion about places. Review the reasons for liking places and the icons for these reasons.*

ānjìng　　　　quiet, peaceful

gānjìng　　　　clean

hǎowán(r)　　　　fun, entertaining

yǒu yìsi

As for points of interest, there are too many ...

interesting, amusing

měi

beautiful

rènao

lively, bustling

hǎo

good

When asked what you think about a city, answer according to the picture. In the example, you will be asked what you think about Paris.

Example:

Instructor: **Nǐ kàn Bālí zěnmeyàng?**
Student: **Bú-cuò. Jiē-shang dōu hěn rènao.**

9

10

Drill Three: *Giving a negative opinion about places. Review the reasons for disliking places and the icons for these reasons.*

chǎo   noisy

pǔtōng   Nothing special here.   common

zāng   dirty

yōngjǐ   crowded

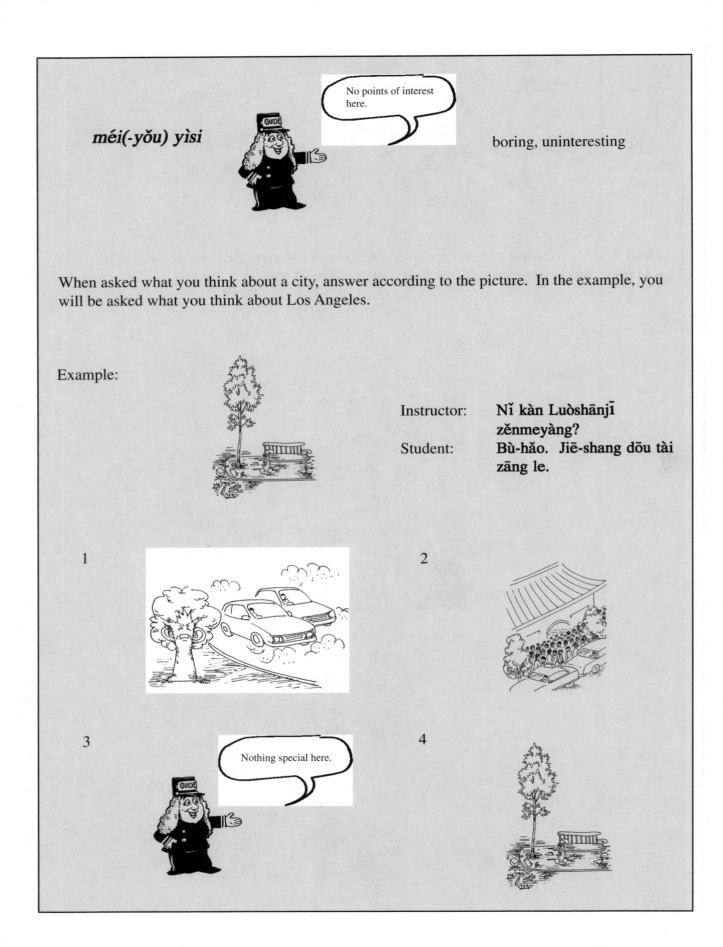

méi(-yǒu) yìsi

boring, uninteresting

When asked what you think about a city, answer according to the picture. In the example, you will be asked what you think about Los Angeles.

Example:

Instructor: **Nǐ kàn Luòshānjī zěnmeyàng?**

Student: **Bù-hǎo. Jiē-shang dōu tài zāng le.**

1

2

3

4

Hǎi-biān(r)

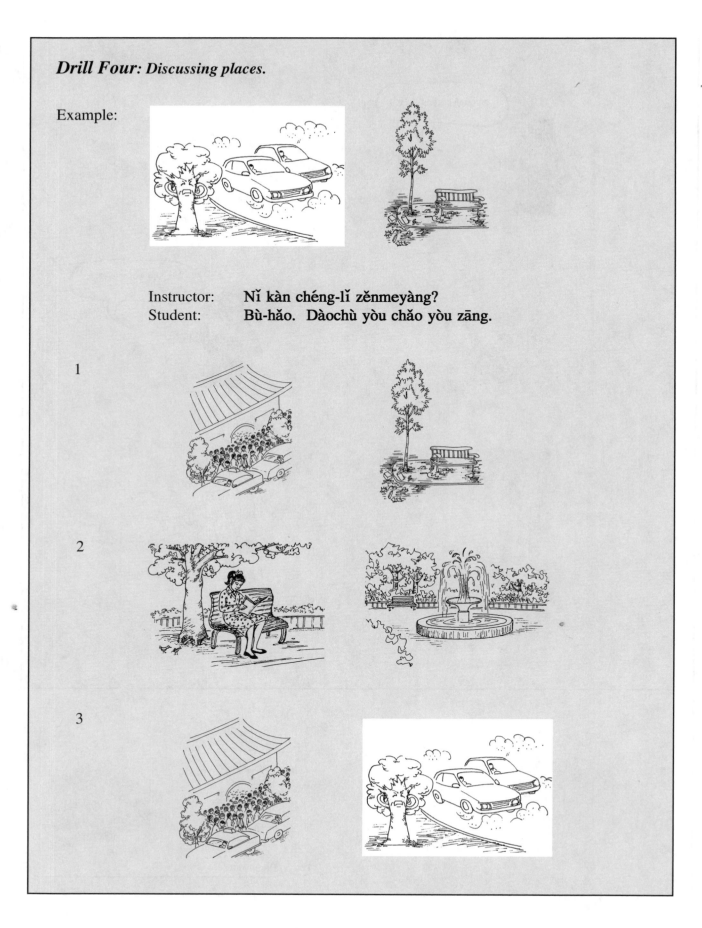

Drill Four: *Discussing places.*

Example:

Instructor: **Nǐ kàn chéng-lǐ zěnmeyàng?**
Student: **Bù-hǎo. Dàochù yòu chǎo yòu zāng.**

1

2

3

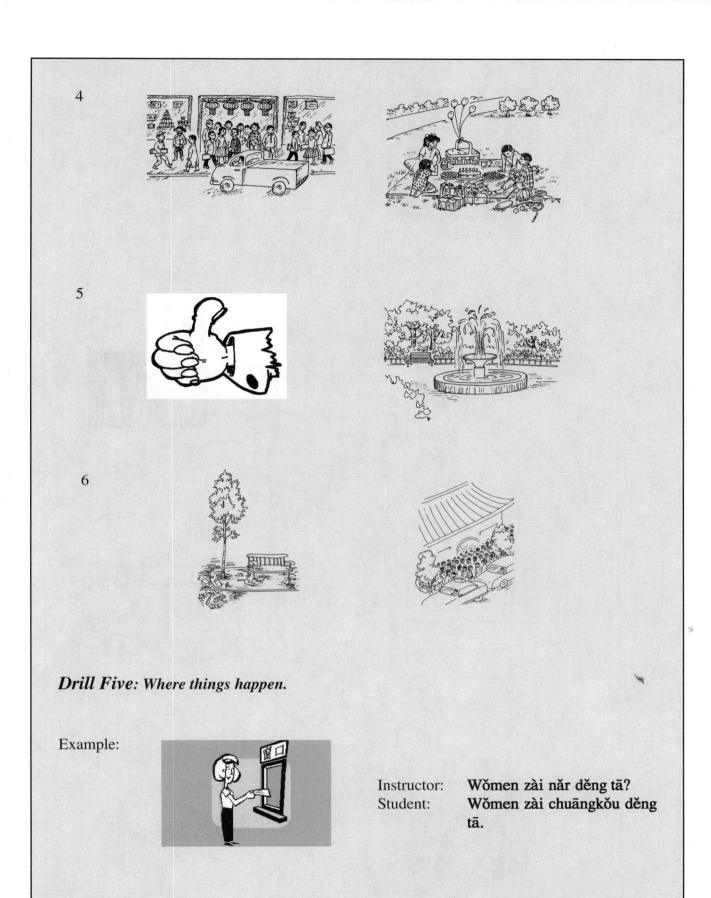

4

5

6

Drill Five: *Where things happen.*

Example:

Instructor: **Wǒmen zài nǎr děng tā?**
Student: **Wǒmen zài chuāngkǒu děng tā.**

1

2 出口

3 Ticket Gate

4 **Friendship Store**

5 入口

6

7 jiē-shang

8 Ticket Gate

9

10

Drill Six: *Telling where things really happen.*

Example:

Instructor: **Nǐ zài jiē-shang děng Xiǎo Wáng ba?**

Student: **Wǒ bú-zài jiē-shang děng Xiǎo Wáng. Wǒ shi zài hǎi-biān(r) děng tā.**

1

2

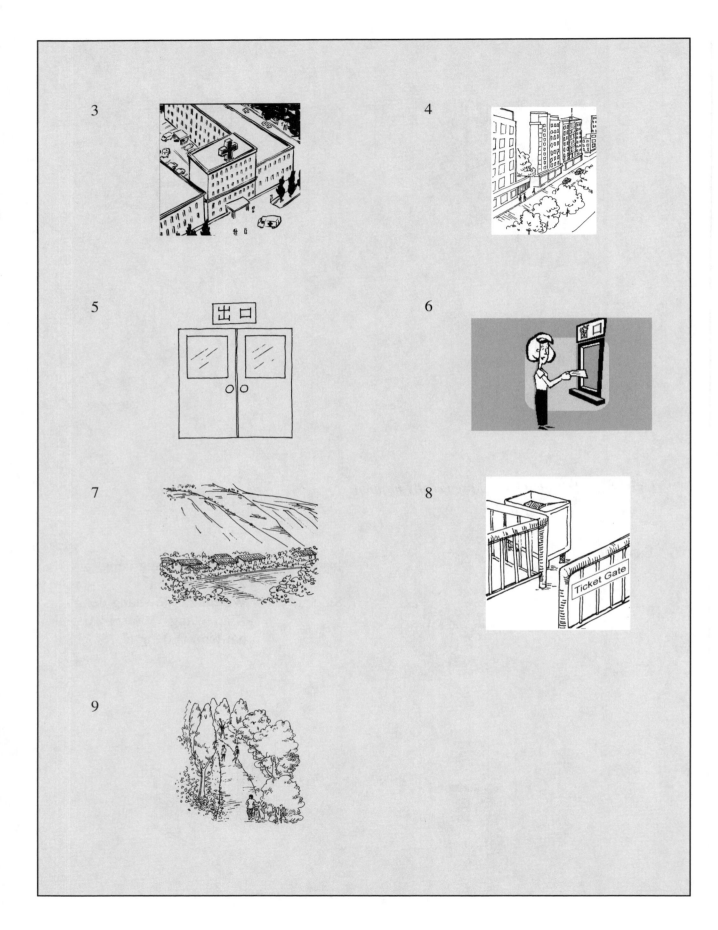

3

4

5

出口

6

7

8

Ticket Gate

9

Drill Seven: *Comparing places.*

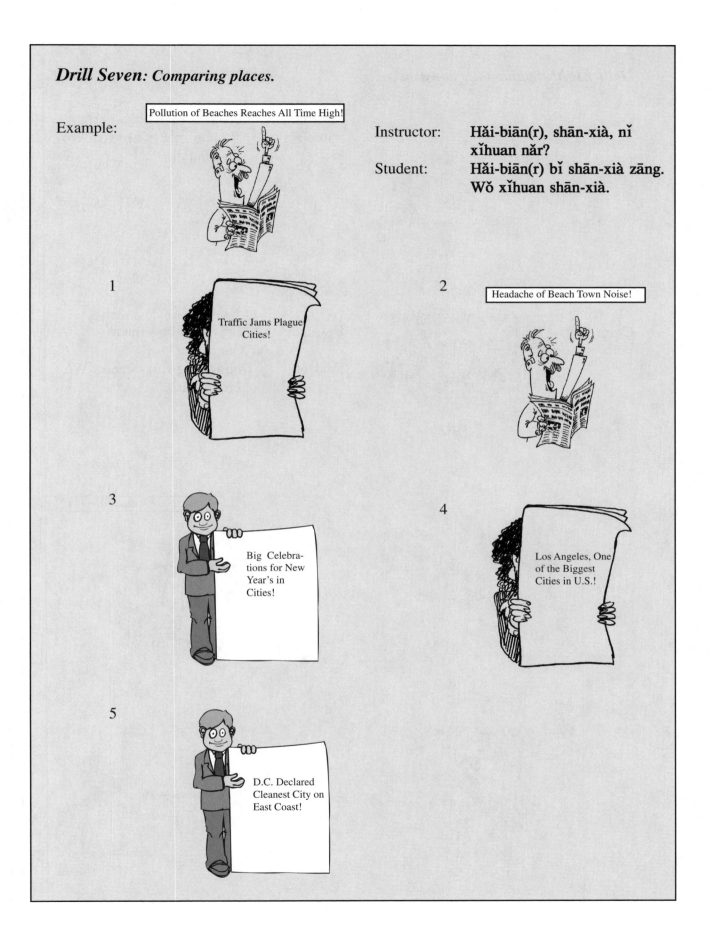

Example:

Pollution of Beaches Reaches All Time High!

Instructor: Hǎi-biān(r), shān-xià, nǐ xǐhuan nǎr?

Student: Hǎi-biān(r) bǐ shān-xià zāng. Wǒ xǐhuan shān-xià.

1

Traffic Jams Plague Cities!

2

Headache of Beach Town Noise!

3

Big Celebrations for New Year's in Cities!

4

Los Angeles, One of the Biggest Cities in U.S.!

5

D.C. Declared Cleanest City on East Coast!

Drill Eight: *Stating likes and dislikes.*

Example 1:

Instructor: **Nǐ xǐhuan Wǔhàn ma?**
Student: **Wǔhàn méi(yǒu)-yìsi. Wǒ bù-xǐhuan.**

Example 2:

Instructor: **Nǐ xǐhuan-bu-xǐhuan Xiānggǎng?**
Student: **Xiānggǎng tǐng rènao. Wǒ hěn xǐhuan.**

1

2

Tourists Crowded Beach Towns!

3

4

5

Drill Nine: *Discussing people.*

Example:

Mr. Luó, the director, is competent.

Instructor: **Wáng chǎngzhǎng, Luó chǎngzhǎng, nǐ xǐhuan nǎge?**

Student: **Luó chǎngzhǎng bǐjiào nénggàn. Wǒ xǐhuan tā.**

1

Prof. Huáng is stubborn.

2

Mr. Lín, the manager, is petty.

3

Bái Tiān is smart.

4

The President of the Normal Universiy is too talkative.

Dialogue Comprehension

Shèng Yīng:	Fāng jīnglǐ, nín kàn Běijīng zěnmeyàng?
Fāng jīnglǐ:	Bú-cuò. Jiē-shang dōu hěn rènao. Zánmen zài nǎr jiàn Lǚ chǎngzhǎng?
Shèng Yīng:	Tā shuō zài Yǒuyì Shāngdiàn de dàménkǒu(r) děng wǒmen.

Xià=kè le

Discussing Ethinicity and Nationality

Chinese Visitor to American Campus

Dialogue Setting

Here, Professor Zhang is getting to know more about Ouyang Li, who is a Chinese-American graduate student in the East Asian Department. Although he is ethnically Chinese, Ouyang is culturally American and has learned most of his Chinese in school. Although Zhang inadvertently asks personal questions that Ouyang is not always comfortable with, in this conversation he does not hesitate to discuss certain aspects of his private life. This conversation takes place on campus near Professor Zhang's office.

Zhāng Róng: Nǐ jié=hūn le méi-you?
Ōuyáng Lǐ: Yǐjing jié-guò hūn le. Wǒ qīzi zài lǐbiān. Tā shi zài dàxué zuò mìshū gōngzuò.

Zhāng Róng: Nǐ fūren yě shì měijí huáyì ma?
Ōuyáng Lǐ: Bú-shì. Tā fùqin shi Rìběnrén, mǔqin shi Měiguó yóutàirén.

Dialogue Information:

* Asking whether someone married:

         Nǐ jié=hūn le ma?
         Nǐ jié=hūn le méi-you?

* Telling that I have not married:

         Wǒ méi-you jié=hūn.
         Wǒ méi jié=hūn.

* Asking if Ms. Fang is an American:

         Fāng nǚshì shì bú-shi Měiguórén?
         Fāng nǚshì shì Měiguórén bú-shi?

* Informing that (I'm) married:

         Jié=hūn le./Jiē=hūn le.

* Asking what you did:

         Nǐ gàn shénme le?

* Replying that (I) attended class:

         Shàng=kè le.

* Telling that (I'm) already married:

         Yǐjing jié-guò hūn le.

* Affirming that (I) attended that class:

         Shàng-guò kè le.

* Affirming that (I) answered those questions:

         Huídá-guò wèntí le.

* Affirming that (I) answered the questions:

         Huídá-guò le.

* Telling that my wife is inside the building:

         Wǒ qīzi zài lǐbiān(r).
         Wǒ tàitai zài lǐbiān(r).

* locating something inside the factory:

         zài gōngchǎng lǐbiān(r)

* Emphasizing that his wife works as a secretary *at the university*:

         Tā shi zài dàxué zuò mìshū gōngzuò.
         Shi zài dàxué zuò mìshū gōngzuò.

* Asking Ouyang if his wife is also Chinese American:

         Nǐ fūren yě shì měijí huáyì ma?

* Chinese American:

         měijí huáyì

* Chinese people:

         huárén

* North China: **Huáběi**

* Overseas Chinese   **huáqiáo**

* Chinese language: **huáyǔ**

* Japanese Chinese: **rìjí huáyì**

* father   **fùqin**

* mother   **mǔqin**

* parents: **fùmǔ**

* Japanese: **Rìběnrén**

* Informing that her father is a Japanese: **Tā fùqin shi Rìběnrén.**

* American Jew: **Měiguó yóutàirén**

* Informing that her mother is an American Jew: **Tā mǔqin shi Měiguó yóutàirén.**

Xióngmāo

Vocabulary (Shēngcí)

1. Phrases (cízǔ)
   Jié=hūn le méi-you?
   Hái méi-you jié=hūn.
   Jié=hūn le.
   Gàn shénme?

2. Verb (dòngcí)
   jié=hūn

3. Sentence Particle (jùzi zhùcí)
   le

4. Adverbs (fùcí)
   hái
   yǐjing

5. Grammatical Marker (yǔfǎ biāojì)
   méi-you
   méi-
   V-guò X le

6. Place Words [noun + biān(r)] (fāngwèicí)
   pángbiān(r)
   shēnbiān(r)
   lǐbiān(r)
   wàibiān(r)
   shàngbiān(r)
   xiàbiān(r)
   qiánbiān(r)
   hòubiān(r)

7. Significant Others (duìxiàng)
   qīzi
   fūren
   àiren
   nàkǒuzi/nèikǒuzi
   zhàngfu
   xiānsheng
   duìxiàng

8. Parents (fùmǔ)
   fùqin
   bà(ba)
   diē
   mǔqin
   mā(ma)
   niáng
   fùmǔ

9. Terms of Address (chēnghu)
   bà(ba)
   diē
   mā(ma)
   niáng

10. Nationality (guójí)
    měijí
    rìjí

11. Ethnicity (zhǒngzú)
    huáyì
    huáqiáo
    huárén
    Rìběnrén
    yóutàirén
    hēirén

12. Nouns (míngcí)
    huáyǔ
    Huáběi

Wǒ de Zhōngwén shū hěn duō!

DRILLS

Drill One: Passing on greetings to your parents. Look at the images we use to represent urban and rustic.

chéngshì   urban

xiāngxia   rustic

When you see the image that represents a rustic setting, use the terms **Diē** or **Niáng**. When you see the icon that represents an urban setting, respond with **Bà(ba)** and/or **Mā(ma)**. In the example, you will be asked to use an urban term to address your mother.

Example:

Instructor: **Wèn nǐ mǔqin hǎo.**
Student: **Māma, Wéi lǎoshī wèn nǐ hǎo.**

1

2

3

4

5

Drill Two: *Explaining that it has been done.*

Example: Instructor: **Fāng jīnglǐ jiàn kèren le méi-you?**
             Student: **Fāng jīnglǐ yǐjing jiàn-guò kèren le.**

1.   2.   3.   4.   5.

6.   7.   8.   9.   10.

Drill Three: *Explaining what you have done.*

Example:

Instructor: **Nǐ gàn shénme ne?**
Student: **Wǒ tīng zhōngwén ne.**

Example:

Instructor: **Nǐ gàn shénme le?**
Student: **Wǒ zuò shèjì gōngzuò le.**

1

2

Dú=shū

Drill Four: *Positive answers.*

Example: Instructor: **Nǐ yǒu duìxiàng méi-you?**
           Student: **Yǒu.**

1.   2.   3.   4.   5.

6.   7.   8.   9.   10.

Drill Five: *It hasn't happened yet.*

Example: Instructor: **Nǐ jié=hūn le méi-you?**
           Student: **Wǒ hái méi-you jié=hūn.**

1.   2.   3.   4.   5.

6.   7.   8.   9.   10.

11.   12.   13.

Drill Six: *Continuing on.*

Example: Instructor: **Yǐqián nǐ zuò guǎnlǐ gōngzuò, xiànzài ne?**
           Student: **Xiànzài wǒ hái zuò guǎnlǐ gōngzuò.**

1.   2.   3.   4.   5.

6.   7.   8.   9.   10.

11.

Jié=hūn

Drill Seven: *Where is Huà Dōu? Look at the icon of Huà Dōu and review the following locations.*

Huà Dōu

pángbiān(r)    on the side of, beside

lǐbiān(r)   inside

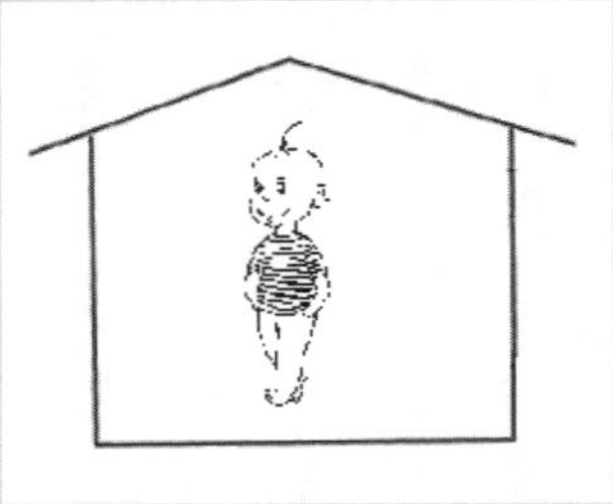

wàibiān(r)   outside

hòubiān(r)   behind

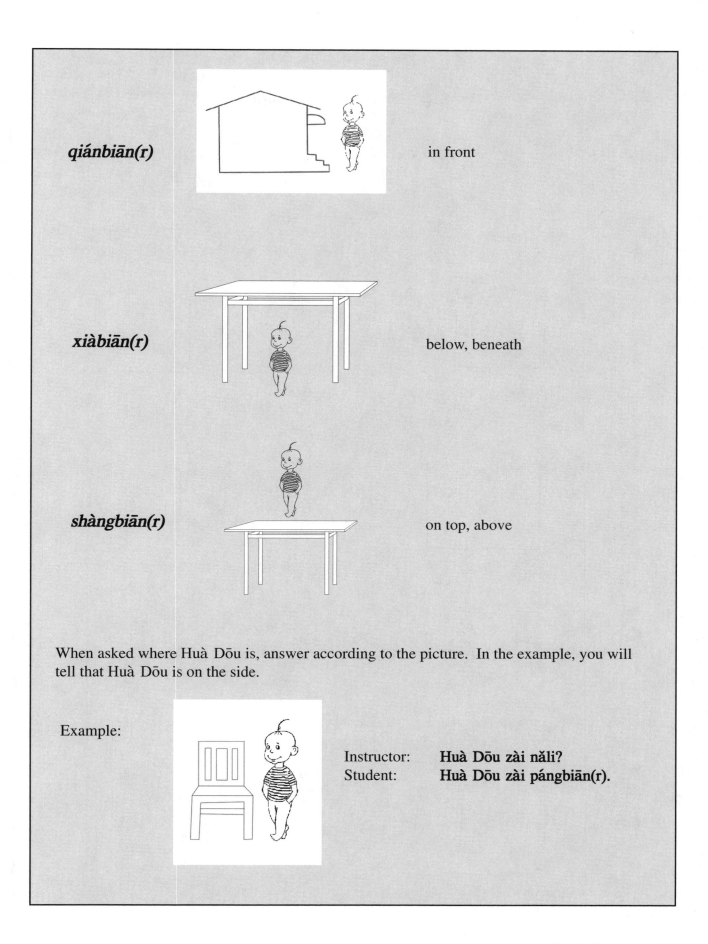

qiánbiān(r)   in front

xiàbiān(r)   below, beneath

shàngbiān(r)   on top, above

When asked where Huà Dōu is, answer according to the picture. In the example, you will tell that Huà Dōu is on the side.

Example:

Instructor: **Huà Dōu zài nǎli?**
Student: **Huà Dōu zài pángbiān(r).**

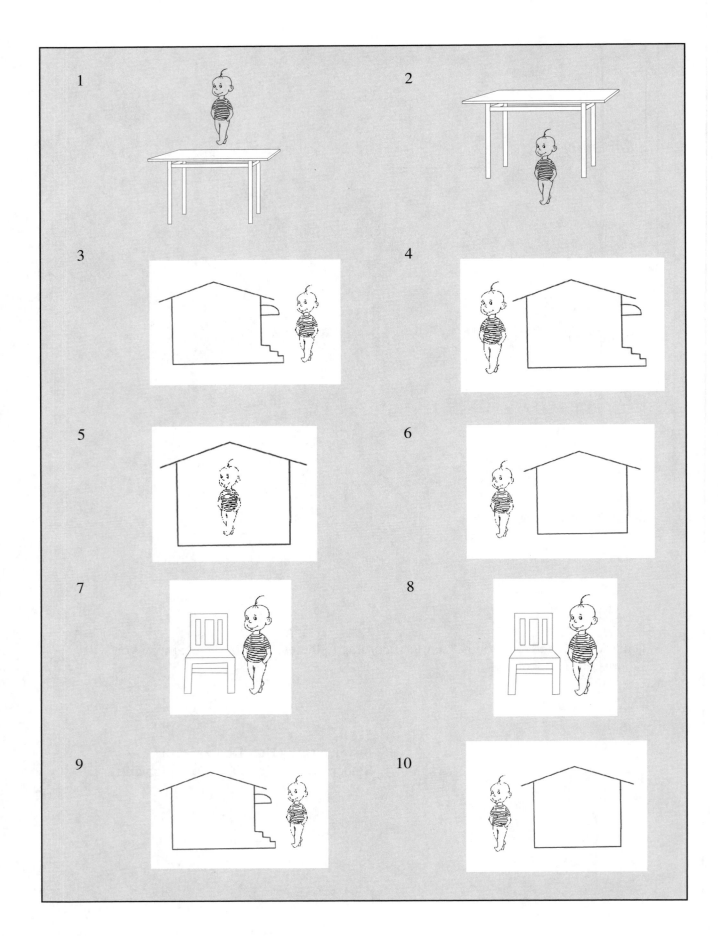

11

12

Drill Eight: *Locating family members (asking males).*

Example:

Instructor: **Nǐ fūren zài nǎli?**
Student: **Wǒ nèikǒuzi zài Àodàlìyà.**

1

2

3

4

5

6

7

Drill Nine: *Locating family members (female perspective).*

Example:

Instructor: **Nǐ zhàngfu zài nǎge guójiā?**
Student: **Wǒ nèikǒuzi zài Yīngguó.**

1

2

3

4

5

6

7

Drill Ten: *Erroneous assumptions.*

Example: Instructor: **Nǐ fūren zài nàge gōngchǎng gōngzuò ba?**
         Student: **Bù. Wǒ qīzi bú-zài nàr gōngzuò.**

1.   2.   3.   4.   5.

6.   7.

Dialogue Comprehension

Zhāng Róng:	Nǐ jié=hūn le méi-you?
Ōuyáng Lǐ:	Yǐjing jié-guò hūn le. Wǒ qīzi zài lǐbiān(r).
	Tā shi zài dàxué zuò mìshū gōngzuò.
Zhāng Róng:	Nǐ fūren yě shì měijí huáyì ma?
Ōuyáng Lǐ:	Bú-shi. Tā fùqin shi Rìběnrén, mǔqin shi
	Měiguó yóutàirén.

Àodàlìyà

Pronunciation and Romanization: Initials, Medials, and Finals

In this stage, we will practice distinguishing initials. In Chinese, there are only 21 initials. In Chinese primary schools where children are expected to memorize them, they are usually grouped according to the positions of tongue and lips:

b p m f
d t n l
g k h
j q x
z c s
zh ch sh r

| j | q | x |

| zè | cè | sè |

| zh | sh | ch | r |

Starting from these approximations, we will work with these Chinese sounds by contrasting words that differ *only* by these sounds. Let's start with what might be the most difficult sounds for speakers of English—the retroflex initials:

zhózi  roller

chózi  silk

zh-	like *"ds"* in *hands* , with a curl, no voicing, no aspiration	
ch-	like *"ts"* in *its*, with a curl, no voicing, and strong aspiration	

The two initials, *sh-* and *r-* can be identified in the following two words:

shìzi  persimmon

rìzi 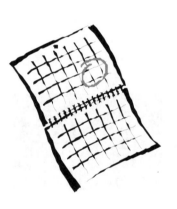 day

sh-	like the *sh-* in <u>*shrimp*</u>, with the strong curl of the tongue
r-	like the *wr-* in <u>*wren*</u>, with the strong curl and (sometimes) a slight buzz

The intials *j-*, *q-*, *x-* are only followed by the high vowels –*i*- and umlaut –*u*-.

jīzi  small machine

qīzi  wife

xízi  mat

ji-	sounds like the *jee-* in *jeep*, with the tip of the tongue touching the lower teeth and no voicing.
qi-	sounds like the *chee-* of *cheese*, the tip of the tongue touching the lower teeth and with strong aspiration
xi-	sounds closest to the *see-* of *seep*, with the tip of the tongue touching the lower teeth and the air flowing out.

Practice these initials by repeating after your instructor a couple of times:

$j\bar{\imath}zi$ small machine

$q\bar{\imath}zi$ wife

$x\acute{\imath}zi$ mat

Three other initials, z-, c-, and s-, can be heard and contrasted in the following three words.

zuòzi  pedestal

cuózi  dwarf

suǒzi  lock

Listen again and repeat after the instructor.

Two labial initials, *b-* and *p-,* sound close to their English equivalents, with one important exception—they are both aspirated. Listen carefully to these two words:

bāozi

stuffed steamed bun

páozi

gown

The only differences in these two words are tones and the strong aspiration on the *p-*. Listen again and repeat after the instructor.

Now, listen to two other words whose pronunciations differ only by aspiration:

dízi

flute

tízi

hoof

The position and manner of articulation of *t-* are the same as those of *d-*. The only difference is that it is strongly aspirated. Listen again and repeat after the instructor.

Now, listen to these three with initials that are formed in the back of your mouth—*g-, k-,* and *h-:*

gēzi    pigeon

kézi    hard shell

hézi    box

The *g-* and the *k-* are the most difficult to distinguish. If you have any problem here, listen a few times until you hear the aspiration on the *k-.*

Another set of labial initials, *m-* and *f-*, have the same pronunciation as their English equivalents.

mèizi  younger sister

fēizi  imperial concubine

Listen again and repeat after the instructor.

Now, Listen to the following two words:

nǎozi 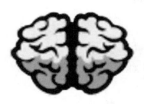 brain

lǎozi  father

The initial *n-* in *nǎozi* is usually pronounced just like the "n" in "not". The initial *l-* is like the "l" in "lout". Listen again and repeat after the instructor.

DRILLS

Drill One: **Distinguishing initials.** **When you hear a word, identify it by choosing the appropriate illustration.**

Example: Cue: **Shìzi.**

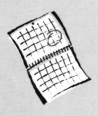

1

2

3

4

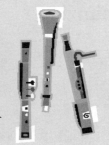

5

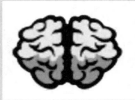

6
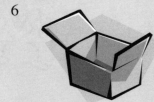

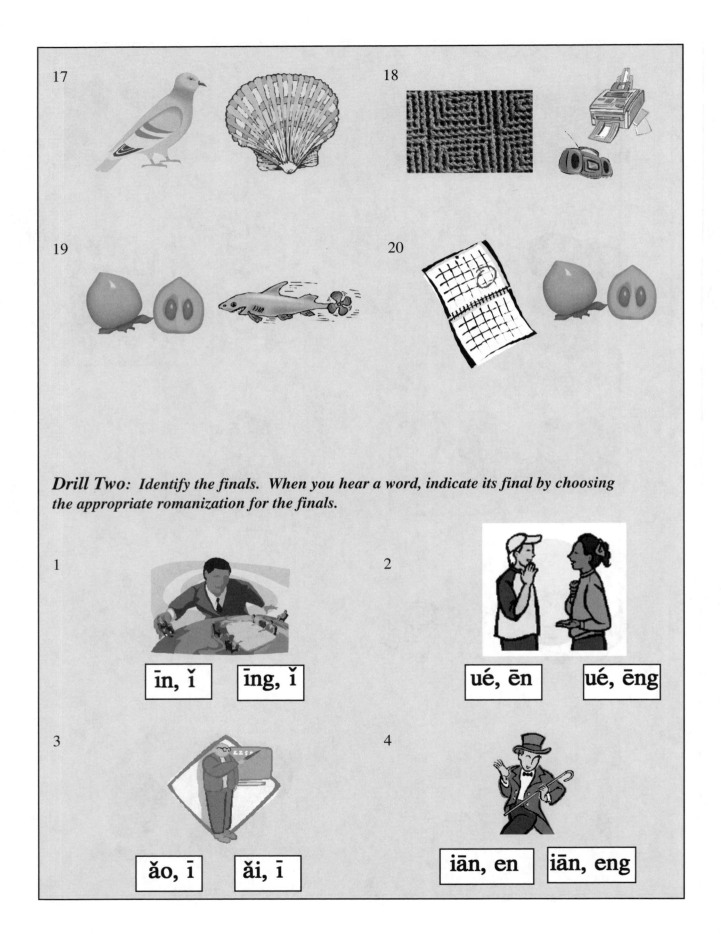

17

18

19

20

Drill Two: *Identify the finals. When you hear a word, indicate its final by choosing the appropriate romanization for the finals.*

1

| īn, ǐ | īng, ǐ |

2

| ué, ēn | ué, ēng |

3

| ǎo, ī | ǎi, ī |

4

| iān, en | iān, eng |

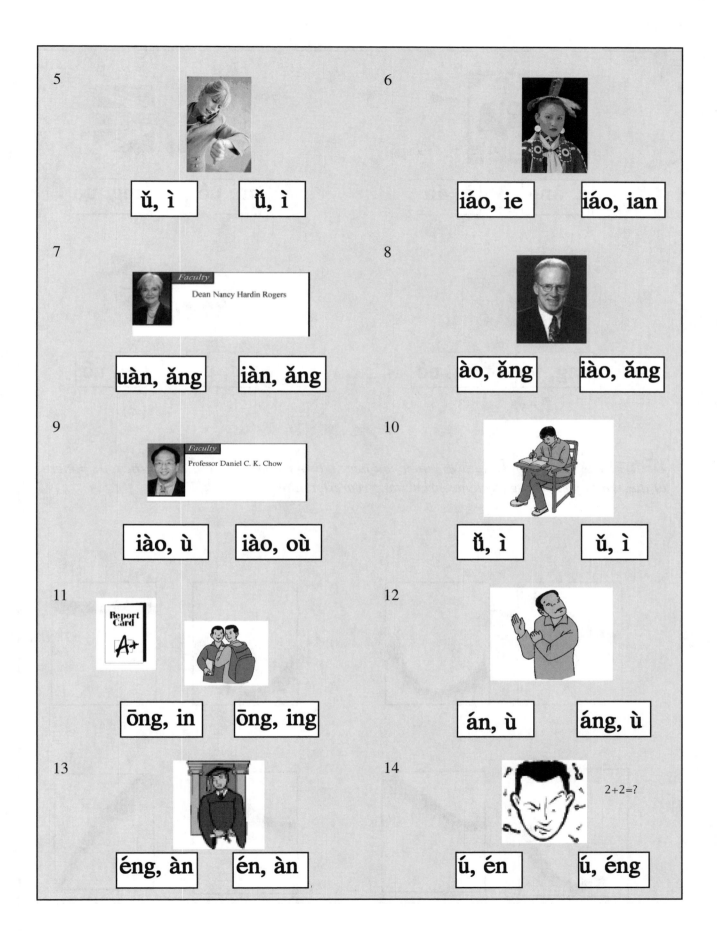

5   ǔ, ì   ǚ, ì

6   iáo, ie   iáo, ian

7   uàn, ăng   iàn, ăng

8   ào, ăng   iào, ăng

9   iào, ù   iào, où

10   ǚ, ì   ǔ, ì

11   ōng, in   ōng, ing

12   án, ù   áng, ù

13   éng, àn   én, àn

14   ú, én   ú, éng

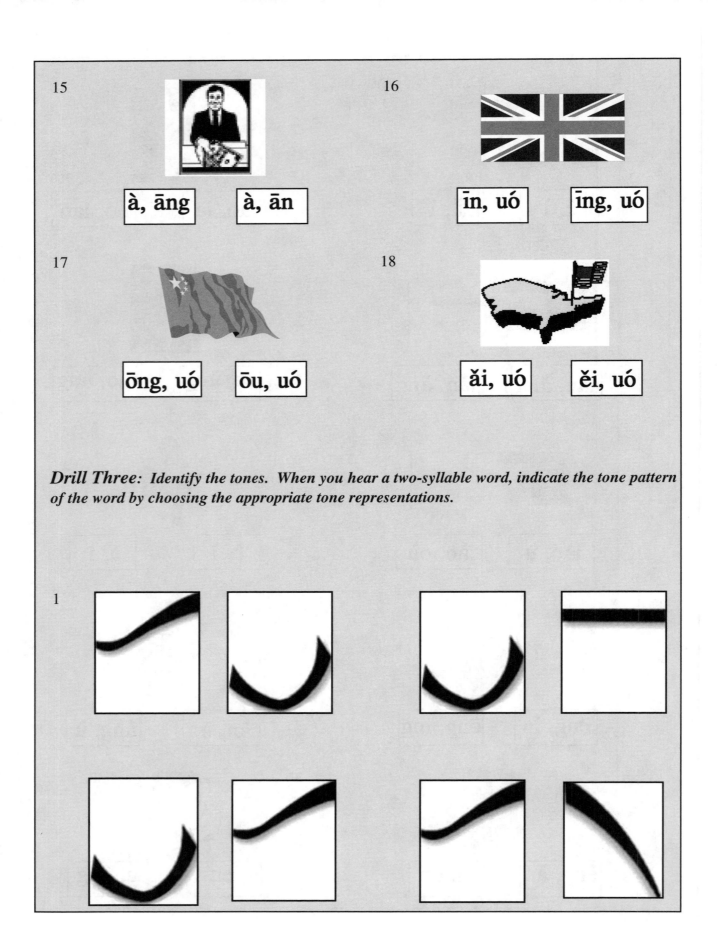

15

à, āng   à, ān

16

īn, uó   īng, uó

17

ōng, uó   ōu, uó

18

ǎi, uó   ěi, uó

Drill Three: *Identify the tones. When you hear a two-syllable word, indicate the tone pattern of the word by choosing the appropriate tone representations.*

1

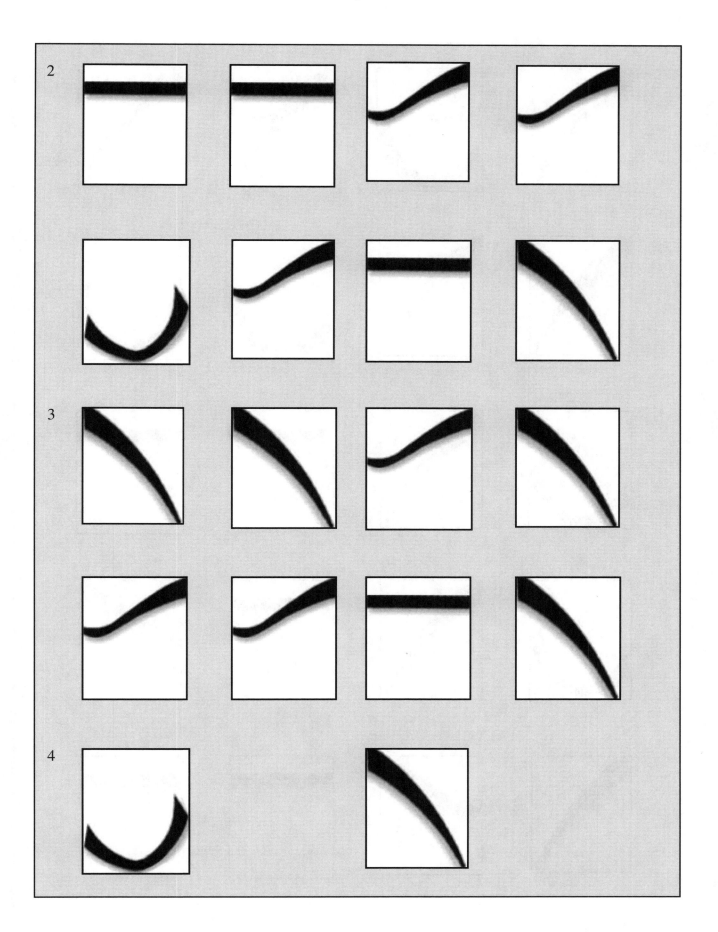

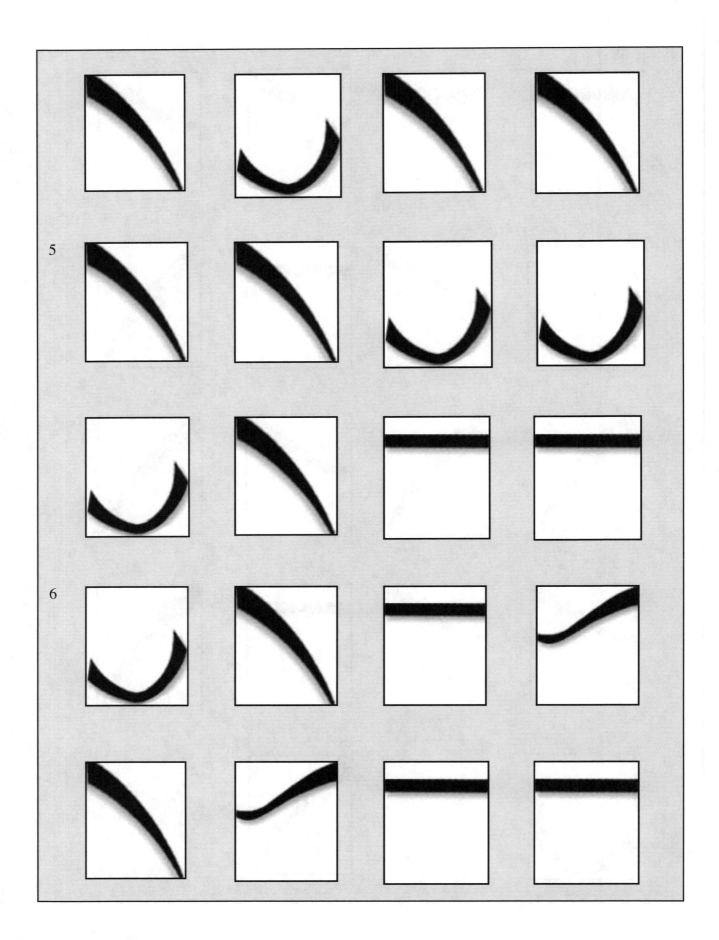

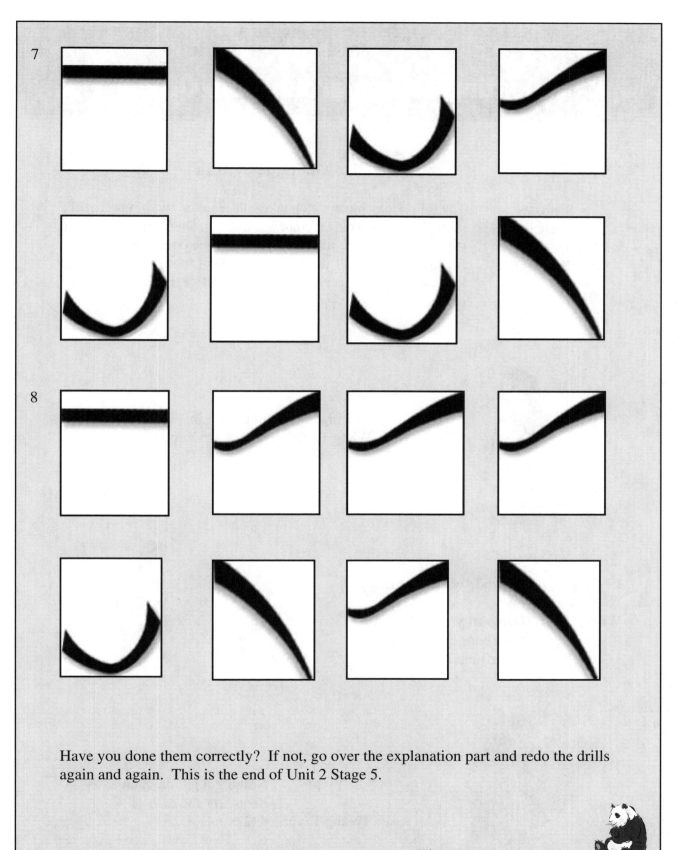

7

8

Have you done them correctly? If not, go over the explanation part and redo the drills again and again. This is the end of Unit 2 Stage 5.

Xióngmāo

Locating Things around the Office

Dialogue Setting

Sino-American Trade Co., Washington, DC

The following conversation takes place in the Washington office of the Sino-Am Trade Company. Li Ping, a new member on the staff, is learning the fundamentals of office operations. She has finished a letter and wants to know what to do with it. Wang Liyu, who knows everything about the office, is showing her the ropes.

Lǐ Píng: Zhèifēng xìn zěnme bàn?
Wáng Lìyù: Fā chuánzhēn bei.

Lǐ Píng: Zài zhèr yǒu chuánzhēnjī ma?
Wáng Lìyù: Dāngrán yǒu. Zài Bái xiānsheng nàr yǒu yìtái. Yòng nèitái fā ba.

Lǐ Píng: Nèige gōngsī de chuánzhēn hàomǎ(r) shi......?
Wáng Lìyù: 432-5104.

Dialogue Information:

* Asking about a course of action: **Zěnme bàn?**

* this letter: **zhèifēng xìn**

* Asking what to do with the letter: **Zhèifēng xìn zěnme bàn?**

* fax: **chuánzhēn**

* Telling someone to send the letter by fax: **Fā chuánzhēn bei.**

* Asking if there is a fax machine here: **Zài zhèr yǒu chuánzhēnjī ma?**

* Asking if there is one here: **Zài zhèr yǒu ma?**

* Stating the obvious existence of an inquired
  object: **Dāngrán yǒu.**

* Suggesting that (someone) sit here with me: **Zuò zài wǒ zhèr ba.**

* Locating Xiao Wang with mother: **Xiǎo Wáng zài tā māma nàr.**

* Locating Xiao Fang next to my wife: **Xiǎo Fāng zài wǒ tàitai shēnbiān(r).**

* Locating (something) in the vicinity of Mr. Bai: **Zài Bái xiānsheng nàr.**

* Indicating there is one fax machine: **Yǒu yìtái chuánzhēnjī.**

* Locating one (fax machine, computer etc.) in
  the vicinity of Mr. Bai: **Zài Bái xiānsheng nàr yǒu yìtái.**

* Telling that there is a fax machine over where
  Mr. Bai is: **Zài Bái xiānsheng nàr yǒu yìtái chuánzhēnjī.**

* Suggesting to use that machine to send (the fax): **Yòng nàtái fā ba.**

* use a fax machine: **yòng chuánzhēnjī**

Dǎ diànhuà

* make a phone call:	**dǎ diànhuà**
* send a telegram:	**dǎ diànbào**
* send a fax:	**fā chuánzhēn**
* Suggesting to use that machine to send the fax:	**Yòng nàtái fā chuánzhēn ba.** **Yòng nàtái chuánzhēnjī fā ba.**
* Asking what the (fax, telephone) number is:	**Hàomǎ(r) shi duōshao?**
* Asking what the company's fax number is:	**Nèige gōngsī de chuánzhēn hàomǎ(r) shi......?**
* zero:	**líng**
* one:	**yī** **yāo**
* two:	**èr**
* three:	**sān**
* four:	**sì**
* five:	**wǔ**

Fā chuánzhēn

Vocabulary (Shēngcí)

1. Placewords (fāngwèicí)
   nàr
   nàlǐ
   zhèr
   zhèlǐ

2. Verbs (dòngcí)
   fā
   dǎ
   jì
   tōngzhī
   gàosu
   xiě
   yǒu
   yòng

3. Instrumental Co-verb (liándòngcí)
   yòng

4. Nouns (míngcí)
   chuánzhēn
   chuánzhēnjī
   diànhuà
   diànnǎo
   xìn
   bǐ
   hàomǎ(r)
   shùzì

5. Measures (liàngcí)
   -fēng
   -tái

6. Sentence Particle (jùzi zhùcí)
   bei

7. Adverb (fùcí)
   dāngrán

8. Serial Numbers (xùhào shùcí)
   líng
   yī/yāo
   èr
   sān
   sì
   wǔ
   liù
   qī
   bā
   jiǔ
   shí

9. Serial Number Suffix (xùhào hòuzhuì)
   hào

10. Phrases (cízǔ)
    Zěnme bàn?
    Diànhuà hàomǎ(r) (shi) duōshao?

Pǎo

DRILLS

Drill One: *Identifying numbers.*

0 零	1 一	2 二
3 三	4 四	5 五
6 六	7 七	8 八
9 九	10 十	

Example:

Instructor: **Zhè shi shénme shùzì?**
Student: **Wǔ.**

1

2

3

4

5

6

7

8

9

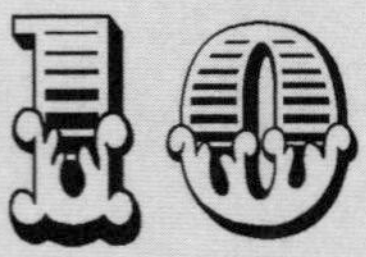

10

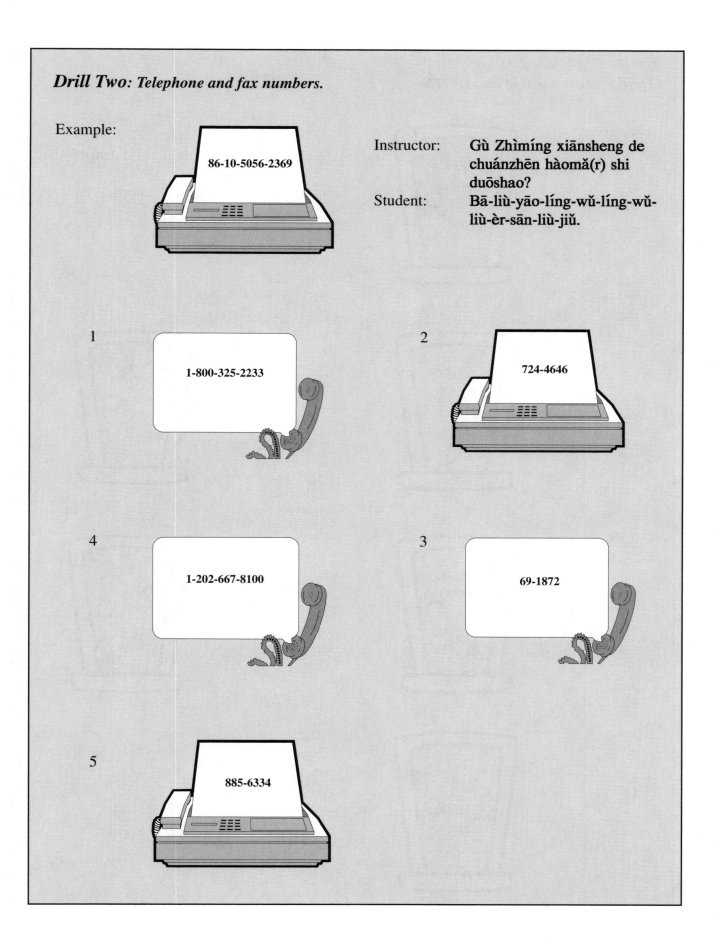

Drill Two: *Telephone and fax numbers.*

Example:

86-10-5056-2369

Instructor: **Gù Zhìmíng xiānsheng de chuánzhēn hàomǎ(r) shi duōshao?**
Student: **Bā-liù-yāo-líng-wǔ-líng-wǔ-liù-èr-sān-liù-jiǔ.**

1

1-800-325-2233

2

724-4646

4

1-202-667-8100

3

69-1872

5

885-6334

Drill Three: Finding the right room.

Example:

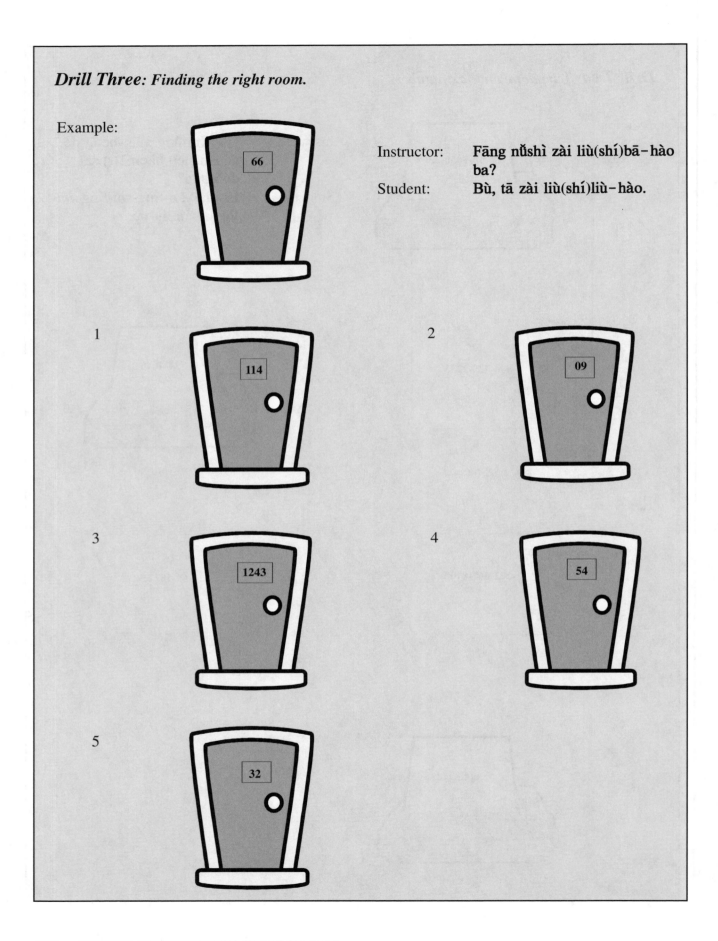

66

Instructor: **Fāng nǚshì zài liù(shí)bā–hào ba?**

Student: **Bù, tā zài liù(shí)liù–hào.**

1

114

2

09

3

1243

4

54

5

32

Drill Four: *Asking how to do something.*

Example:	Instructor:	**Zánmen tōngzhī Huà xiānsheng ba.**
	Student:	**Zánmen zěnme tōngzhī tā?**

1.   2.   3.   4.   5.   6.

7.   8.   9.   10.   11.

Drill Five: *Explaining how to do things. Review the following means of accomplishing the tasks.*

yòng chuánzhēnjī  use a fax machine

yòng diànhuà  use a telephone

xiě xìn  write a letter

fā chuánzhēn  send a fax

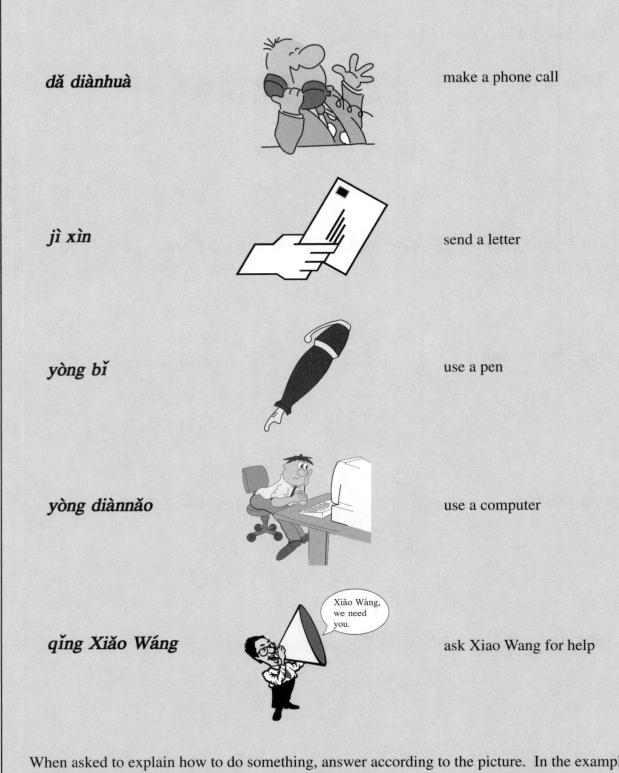

dǎ diànhuà   make a phone call

jì xìn   send a letter

yòng bǐ   use a pen

yòng diànnǎo   use a computer

Xiǎo Wáng, we need you.

qǐng Xiǎo Wáng   ask Xiao Wang for help

When asked to explain how to do something, answer according to the picture. In the example, you will be asked how to inform Lao Li, who is in Japan.

Example:

Instructor: **Zánmen zěnme tōngzhī Lǎo Lǐ? Tā xiànzài zài Rìběn.**
Student: **Fā chuánzhēn bei.**

1

2

3

4

5

6

7

8

Xiǎo Wáng, we need you.

9

10

Drill Six: Pointing out where one is.

Example 1:

Instructor: **Zhèr yǒu kuàijì ma?**
Student: **Dāngrán yǒu. Hòu-biān(r) jiù yǒu yíwèi.**

Example 2:

Huáng Zhìgāng
Director

Instructor: **Zhèr yǒu bǐ méi-you?**
Student: **Dāngrán yǒu. Huáng xiānsheng nàr jiù yǒu yìzhī.**

1

2

3

4

5

Drill Seven: *Locate a specified object.*

Example:

Instructor: **Nǐ zhīdao wǒde bǐ zài nǎr ma?**

Student: **Zhīdao. Nǐde bǐ zài Bái xiānsheng nàr.**

Mr. Bái

1

2

Drill Eight: *Reaffirming possession.*

Example: Instructor: **Wǒde bǐ zài lǐbiān(r).**
             Student: **Ò, lǐbiān(r) de nèizhī bǐ jiùshi nǐde.**

1.   2.   3.   4.   5.

Drill Nine: *Correcting attributions of possessions.*

Example:

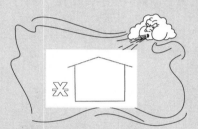

Instructor: **Wǒmen de diànhuà zài lǐbiān(r).**
Student: **Lǐbiān(r) de diànhuà bú-shì nǐmen de. Nǐmen de diànhuà zài wàibiān(r).**

1

2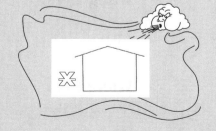

3

4

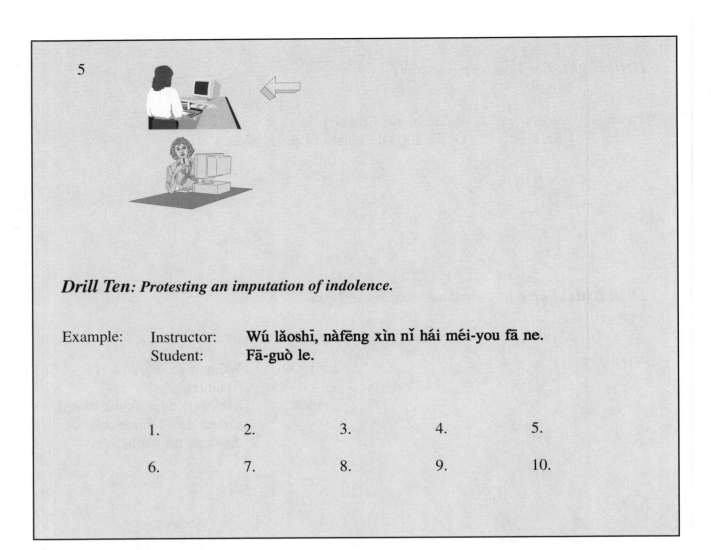

5

Drill Ten: *Protesting an imputation of indolence.*

Example:　Instructor:　**Wú lǎoshī, nàfēng xìn nǐ hái méi-you fā ne.**
　　　　　　Student:　　**Fā-guò le.**

1.　　　2.　　　3.　　　4.　　　5.

6.　　　7.　　　8.　　　9.　　　10.

Dialogue Comprehension

Lǐ Píng:	Zhèifēng xìn zěnme bàn?
Wáng Lìyù:	Fā chuánzhēn bei.
Lǐ Píng:	Zài zhèr yǒu chuánzhēnjī ma?
Wáng Lìyù:	Dāngrán yǒu. Zài Bái xiānsheng nàr yǒu yìtái. Yòng nèitái fā ba.
Lǐ Píng:	Nèige gōngsī de chuánzhēn hàomǎ(r) shì......?
Wáng Lìyù:	432-5104.

Discussing Populations

Dialogue Setting

Chinese Visitor to American Campus

The following exchange occurs on an American campus. While being shown around campus by graduate-student guide Ouyang Li, Zhang Rong is getting a sense of the scale of the university where she will spend the next year or so. The conversation begins with Zhang Rong's comment on the size of the place and a question about the student population.

Zhāng Róng: Nǐmen zhèr dàxué zhēn dà. Yǒu duōshao xuésheng?

Ōuyáng Lǐ: Chàbuduō sìwàn. Dànshì zài yánjiūshēngyuàn zhǐ yǒu qīqiānge yánjiūshēng.

Zhāng Róng: Hái bù-shǎo a!

Ōuyáng Lǐ: En.

Dialogue Information:

* Commenting about the large scale of the university:

Nǐmen zhèr dàxué zhēn dà.

* Visitor refers to the people of the host-organization:

nǐmen zhèr

* Commenting on the large scale of the university or universities:

Dàxué zhēn dà.

* Asking how many students there are:

Duōshao xuésheng?

* Asking how many students there are here:

Zài zhèr yǒu duōshao xuésheng?

* Asking how many students there are (here):

Yǒu duōshao xuésheng?

* approximate or almost:

chàbuduō

* Approximately forty thousand:

Chàbuduō sìwàn.

* Stating that you understand almost everything:

Chàbuduō dōu dǒng le.

* hundred:

bǎi

* thousand:

qiān

* ten thousand:

wàn

* forty thousand:

sìwàn.

* graduate student:

yánjiūshēng

* graduate school:

yánjiūshēngyuàn

* seven thousand graduate students:

qīqiānge yánjiūshēng

* Stating that there are only seven thousand graduate students in the Graduate School:

Zài yánjiūshēngyuàn zhǐ yǒu qīqiānge yánjiūshēng.

* Contrasting the 7000 graduate students in the Graduate School (to the 40,000 undergraduates): **Dànshì zài yánjiūshēngyuàn zhǐ yǒu qīqiānge yánjiūshēng.**

* Remarking that (7000 graduate students are centainly) not a few: **Hái bù-shǎo a!**

* Grunting an agreement as a response: **En.**

Vocabulary (Shēngcí)

1. Phrases (cízǔ)
   <u>X</u> de shì zěnmeyàng le?
   chàbuduō

2. Adverbs (fùcí)
   chàbuduō
   zhǐ

3. Places (dìdiǎn)
   bàngōngshì
   yánjiūshēngyuàn

4. Nouns (míngcí)
   yánjiūshēng
   gōngrén

5. Verbs (dòngcí)
   xūyào
   chà

6. Adjectives (xíngróngcí)
   duō
   shǎo
   chà

7. Question Words (yíwèncí)
   jǐ + <u>measure</u>
   duōshao

8. Numbers (shùcí)
   yī + <u>measure</u>
   liǎng + <u>measure</u>
   bǎi
   qiān
   wàn

9. Measure (liàngcí)
   -jiān

Wǒ zhīdao!

Wǒ huì shuō zhōngwén.

Drill One: *Counting to ninety-nine.*

Example:

Instructor: **Nàge shùzì shi liùshíjiǔ ma?**

Student: **Bú-shì. Shì liùshíwǔ.**

1

2

3

4

5

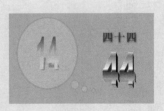

6

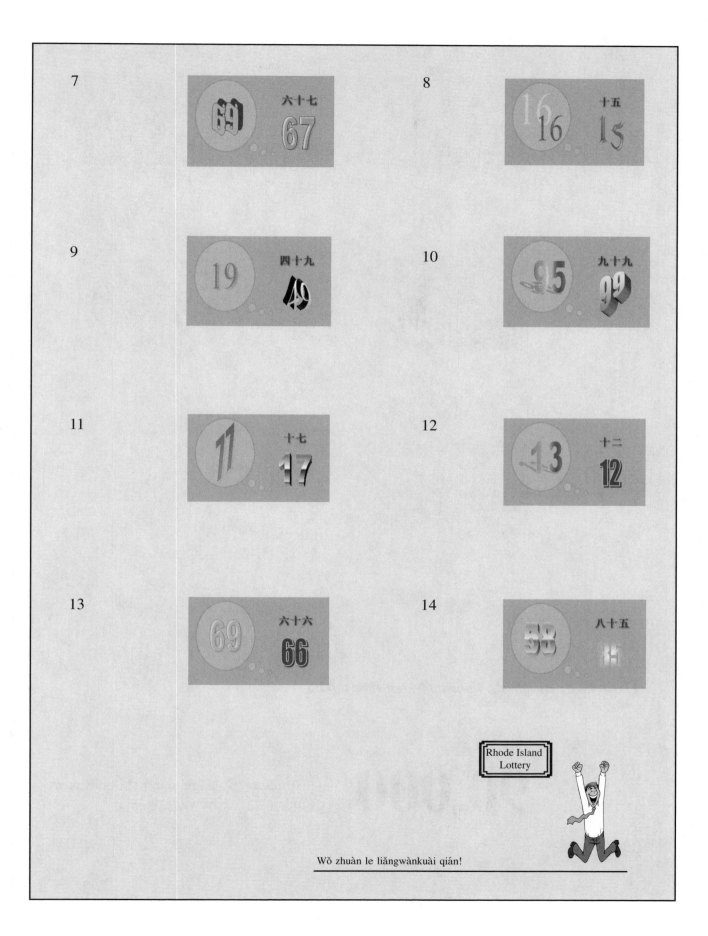

7

8

9

10

11

12

13

14

Rhode Island
Lottery

Wǒ zhuàn le liǎngwànkuài qián!

15  16

17  18

19

Drill Two: *Hundreds, thousands, ten-thousands.*

Example:

90,000

Instructor: **Nàge shùzì shi duōshao?**
Student: **Jiǔwàn.**

1	**500**	2	**8,000**
3	**6,000**	4	**200**
5	**50,000**	6	**700**
7	**60,000**	8	**4,000**
9	**1,000**	10	**700**

Drill Three: *Asking about small amounts.*

Example: Instructor: **Wǒmen bàngōngshì xūyào diànnǎo.**
          Student: **Xūyào jǐtái?**

          1.   2.   3.   4.

          5.   6.   7.   8.

Drill Four: *Asking about the extent of the need.*

Example: Instructor: **Wǒmen bàngōngshì de mìshu tài shǎo le.**
             Student: **Nǐmen hái chà jǐge?**

1.   2.   3.
4.   5.   6.

Drill Five: *Asking about large amounts.*

Example: Instructor: **Zuìjìn wǒmen gōngchǎng de gōngrén tài shǎo le.**
             Student: **Nǐmen gōngchǎng yǒu duōshao gōngrén?**

1.   2.   3.   4.   5.

6.   7.   8.   9.   10.

Drill Six: *Counting things.*

Example:

             Instructor: **Zài zhège gōngsī yǒu jǐge**
                             zuò yīwù gōngzuò de rén?
             Student: **Yǒu liǎngge rén zuò yīwù**
                             gōngzuò.

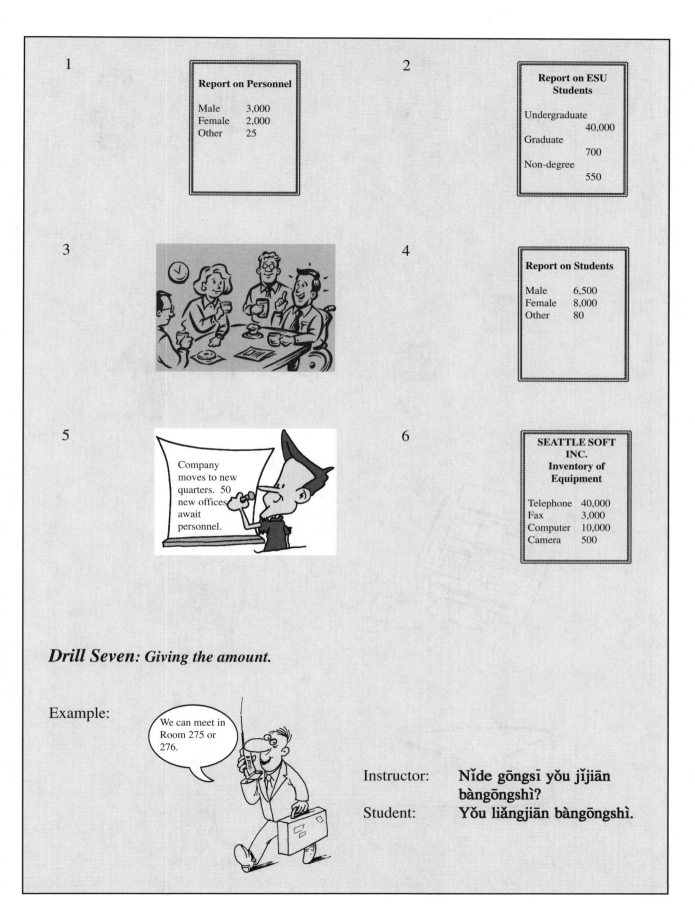

1

Report on Personnel	
Male	3,000
Female	2,000
Other	25

2

Report on ESU Students

Undergraduate	40,000
Graduate	700
Non-degree	550

3

4

Report on Students	
Male	6,500
Female	8,000
Other	80

5

Company moves to new quarters. 50 new offices await personnel.

6

SEATTLE SOFT INC.
Inventory of Equipment

Telephone	40,000
Fax	3,000
Computer	10,000
Camera	500

Drill Seven: *Giving the amount.*

Example:

We can meet in Room 275 or 276.

Instructor: **Nǐde gōngsī yǒu jǐjiān bàngōngshì?**

Student: **Yǒu liǎngjiān bàngōngshì.**

Drill Eight: *Coming up short.*

Example: Instructor: **Wǒmen bàngōngshì xūyào bātái diànnǎo.**
                Student: **Duìbuqǐ, wǒ zhǐ yǒu qītái.**

1.   2.   3.   4.   5.   6.

Drill Nine: *Reporting contrary information.*

Example:

Instructor: **Línshígōng de shì zěnmeyàng le?**

Student: **Wǒmen bàngōngshì xūyào liǎngge xuésheng zuò línshígōng, dànshì tā nàr zhǐ yǒu yíge.**

1

2

3

4

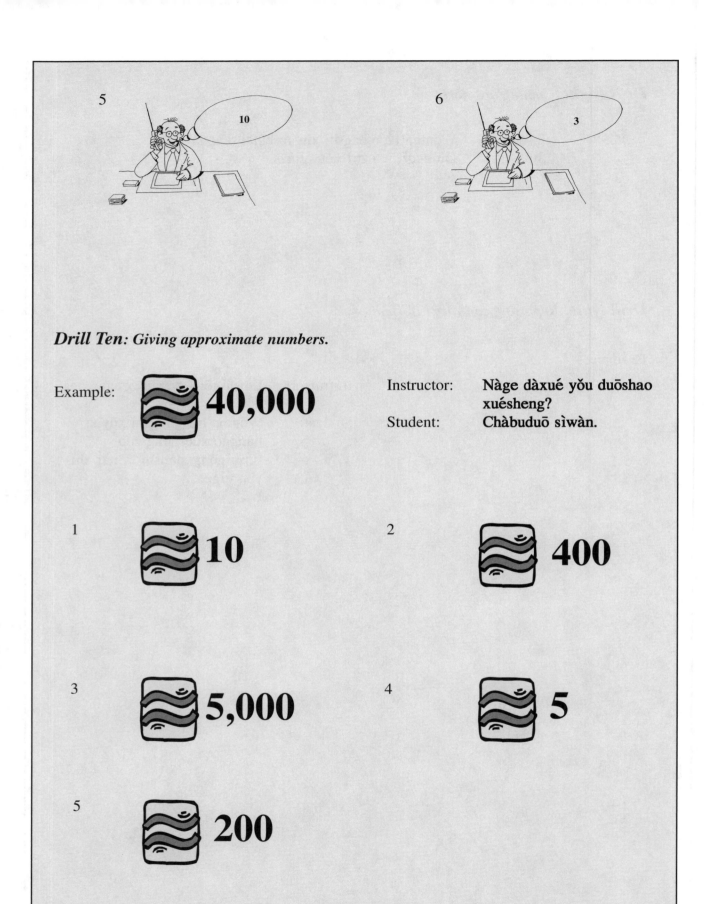

Drill Ten: *Giving approximate numbers.*

Example:

40,000

Instructor: **Nàge dàxué yǒu duōshao xuésheng?**

Student: **Chàbuduō sìwàn.**

1

10

2

400

3

5,000

4

5

5

200

Drill Eleven: *Comparing quantities.*

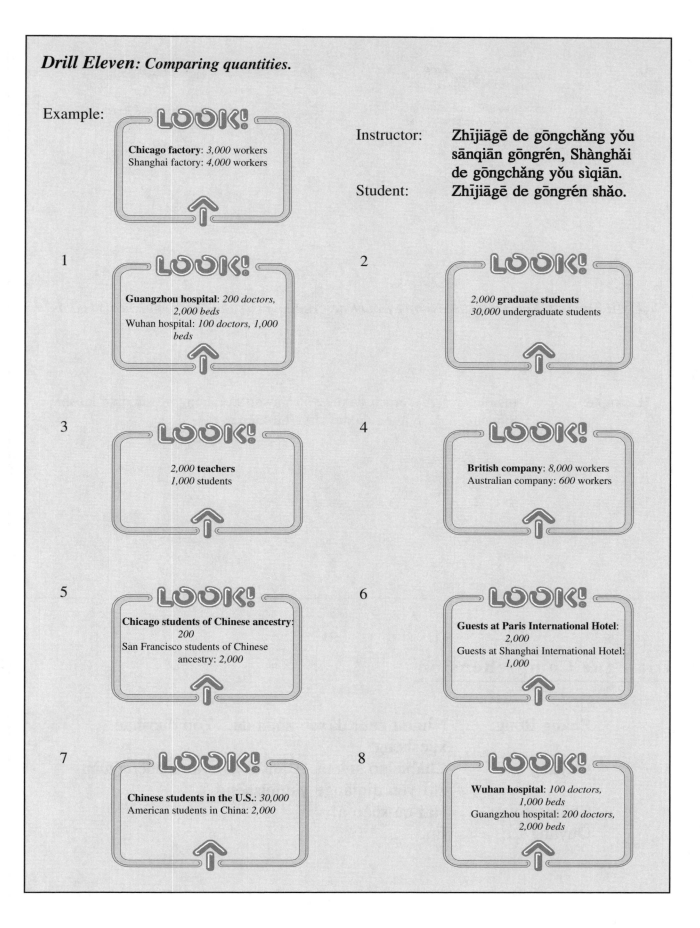

Example:

LOOK!

Chicago factory: *3,000* workers
Shanghai factory: *4,000* workers

Instructor: **Zhījiāgē de gōngchǎng yǒu sānqiān gōngrén, Shànghǎi de gōngchǎng yǒu sìqiān.**
Student: **Zhījiāgē de gōngrén shǎo.**

1

LOOK!

Guangzhou hospital: *200 doctors, 2,000 beds*
Wuhan hospital: *100 doctors, 1,000 beds*

2

LOOK!

2,000 **graduate students**
30,000 undergraduate students

3

LOOK!

2,000 **teachers**
1,000 students

4

LOOK!

British company: *8,000* workers
Australian company: *600* workers

5

LOOK!

Chicago students of Chinese ancestry: *200*
San Francisco students of Chinese ancestry: *2,000*

6

LOOK!

Guests at Paris International Hotel: *2,000*
Guests at Shanghai International Hotel: *1,000*

7

LOOK!

Chinese students in the U.S.: *30,000*
American students in China: *2,000*

8

LOOK!

Wuhan hospital: *100 doctors, 1,000 beds*
Guangzhou hospital: *200 doctors, 2,000 beds*

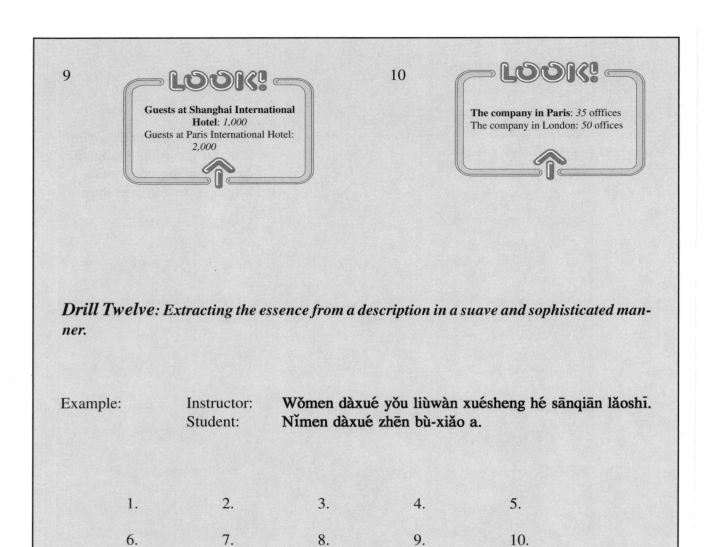

Drill Twelve: *Extracting the essence from a description in a suave and sophisticated manner.*

| Example: | Instructor: | **Wǒmen dàxué yǒu liùwàn xuésheng hé sānqiān lǎoshī.** |
| | Student: | **Nǐmen dàxué zhēn bù-xiǎo a.** |

| 1. | 2. | 3. | 4. | 5. |
| 6. | 7. | 8. | 9. | 10. |

Dialogue Comprehension

Zhāng Róng:	Nǐmen zhèr dàxué zhēn dà. Yǒu duōshao xuésheng?
Ōuyáng Lǐ:	Chàbuduō sìwàn. Dànshì zài yánjiūshēngyuàn zhǐ yǒu qīqiānge yánjiūshēng.
Zhāng Róng:	Hái bù-shǎo a!
Ōuyáng Lǐ:	En.

Gettting Lunch on the Train

Dialogue Setting

Train Trip to Fuzhou

The following conversation takes place on a Chinese train that is steaming south from Beijing to Fuzhou. It's lunch time and the food service attendant is pushing a cart full of lunch boxes down the aisle, serving lunch to the passengers who have purchased meal tickets earlier. Some of the travellers haven't purchased the meal tickets and either go hungry, buy whatever box lunches are leftover, or buy food at the train stations they pass through. Some of the travellers will do both. As the attendant passes out the boxes, she tells the next set of passengers that she is selling food.

Wǒ zhèr liǎngfèn(r).

Mǎi-le cānquàn(r) de lǚkè, qǐng ná fàn le. Nín yào jǐfèn(r)?

Èi, gěi wǒ yìfèn(r). Wǒ gěi qián.

Shīfu, wǒ zhèr yìfèn(r).

Hǎo, qián zhènghǎo. Mài fàn le! Mài fàn le!

Dialogue Information:

* service attendant in the dining car:

cānchē fúwùyuán

* a meal ticket:

cānquàn(r)

* to buy a meal ticket:

mǎi cānquàn(r)

* a person who is buying or has bought a meal ticket:

mǎi cānquàn(r) de rén

* a person who has bought a meal ticket:

mǎi-le cānquàn(r) de rén

* Calling to the passengers who have purchased meal tickets:

Mǎi-le cānquàn(r) de lǚkè.

* Requesting someone to take the food:

Qǐng ná fàn.

* Requesting people *to start* taking the food:

Qǐng ná fàn le.

* Announcing that the passengers who have already purchased meal tickets should start taking the food:

Mǎi-le cānquàn(r) de lǚkè, qǐng ná fàn le.

* Asking how many portions one wants:

Nín yào jǐfèn(r)?

* Telling that I want two portions:

Wǒ zhèr liǎngfèn(r).

* Addressing the attendant and telling her that you want one portion:

Shīfu, wǒ zhèr yífèn(r).

* Telling the attendent to give you one portion:

Èi, gěi wǒ yífèn(r).

* Requesting or politely telling the attendent to give you one portion:

Shīfu, qǐng nín gěi wǒ yífèn(r).

* Telling someone that you are paying:

Wǒ gěi qián.

* Accepting the money and remarking that one is giving just the right amount:

Hǎo, qián zhènghǎo.

* Announcing to a new group that she is selling food:

Mài fàn le!

Vocabulary (Shēngcí)

1. Phrases (cízǔ)
   Xièxie.
   Qián zhènghǎo.

2. Term of Address (chēnghu)
   shīfu

3. Places (dìdiǎn)
   cānchē
   shūdiàn
   wénjùdiàn
   yóujú/yóudiànjú

4. Verbs (dòngcí)
   chī
   gěi
   hē
   kàn
   mǎi
   mài
   ná
   yào

5. Co-verb (liándòngcí)
   gěi

6. Measures (liàngcí)
   -bēi
   -běn
   -dùn
   -fèn
   -gè
   -guàn
   -kuài
   -píng

   -xiē
   -zhāng
   -zhī

7. Nouns (míngcí)
   qián
   fàn
   héfàn
   cānquàn(r)
   qìshuǐ
   chá
   lǚkè
   fúwùyuán
   xìnzhǐ
   xìnfēng
   yuánzhūbǐ
   qiānbǐ
   běnzi
   yóupiào
   jìniàn yóupiào
   míngxìnpiàn(r)
   bāoguǒ
   shū
   bàozhǐ
   zázhì
   dōngxi
   piào

8. Sentence Particle (jùzi zhùcí)
   le

9. Grammatical Marker (yǔfǎ biāojì)
   le

Wǒ hē liǎngbēi!

Vocabulary Check-out

Write down the Chinese equivalents of the following categories of words. Don't forget to mark the tones.

1)   Things to eat (chī de dōngxi)

         box lunch   ____
         food   ____
         rice   ____

2)   Things sold at a bookstore (zài shūdiàn-li mài de dōngxi)

         books   ____
         magazines   ____
         newspapers   ____
         post cards   ____

3)   Things purchased at a ticket window (zài chuāngkǒu mǎi de dōngxi)

         tickets   ____
         food coupons   ____

4)   Things you can post (zài yóujú jì de dōngxi)

         letters   ____
         packages   ____
         post cards   ____

5)   Things sold at a stationery shop (zài wénjùdiàn mài de dōngxi)

         notebooks   ____
         letter paper   ____
         envelopes   ____
         writing implements   ____
         ball-point pens   ____
         pencils   ____
         post cards   ____

6)   Things sold at the post office (zài yóujú mài de dōngxi)

         postage stamps   ____
         commemorative stamps   ____
         post cards   ____
         envelopes   ____

7) Things you drink (hē de dōngxi)

tea   _____
soda   _____

8) People in the dining car (zài cānchē-li de rén)

passengers   _____
attendants   _____

9) Something you need in all these places
and to do all these things (xūyào de dōngxi)

money   _____

10) Place where food is sold (mài fàn de dìfang)

dining car   _____

11) Things you read (kàn de dōngxi)

newspapers   _____
magazines   _____
books   _____
letters   _____

[score: _____ x 33.3 = _____%]

Respond that you want two of the following items by using an appropriate measure.

1. Jìniàn yóupiào, nǐ yào duōshao?   _____
2. Qìshuǐ, nǐ yào duōshao?   _____
3. Shū, nǐ yào duōshao?   _____
4. Fàn, nǐ yào duōshao?   _____
5. Xìnzhǐ, nǐ yào duōshao?   _____
6. Chá, nǐ yào duōshao?   _____
7. Bàngōngshì, nǐ yào duōshao?   _____
8. Qiānbǐ, nǐ yào duōshao?   _____
9. Cānquàn(r), nǐ yào duōshao?   _____
10. Xìnfēng, nǐ yào duōshao?   _____

[score: _____ x 10 = _____%]

DRILLS

Drill One: *Offering to do something for someone.*

Example: Instructor: **Fāng jīnglǐ yào wǒ jì zhèxiē xìn.**
          Student: **Wǒ gěi nǐ jì ba.**

    1.   2.   3.   4.

    5.   6.   7.

Drill Two: *Denying that you did it.*

Example:

    Instructor: **Nǐ mǎi míngxìnpiàn(r) le ba.**
    Student: **Méi-you. Wǒ mǎi-le bǐ.**

1

2

3

4

5

I informed the managers!

6

7

8

9

Drill Three: *Deciding whether or not to act.*

Example 1:

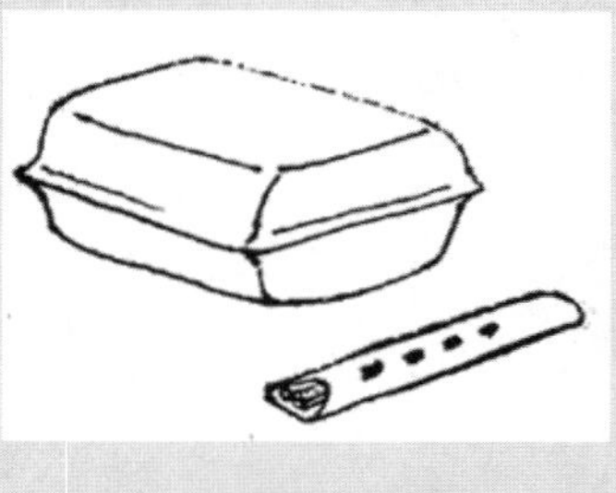

Instructor: **Măi-le héfàn de rén qǐng ná chá le.**
Student: **Wǒmen mǎi-le héfàn. Ná ba.**

Āiyā, tài nán le!

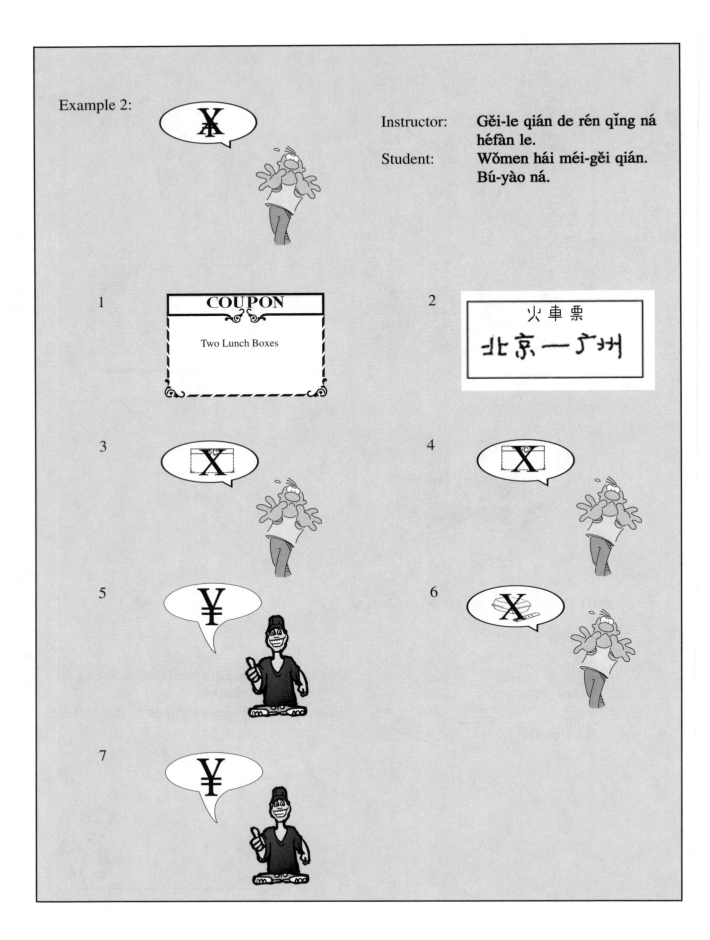

Example 2:

Instructor: Gěi-le qián de rén qǐng ná héfàn le.

Student: Wǒmen hái méi-gěi qián. Bú-yào ná.

1

COUPON

Two Lunch Boxes

2

火車票
北京—广州

3

4

5

6

7

Drill Four: *Revealing your purchases. Review places where you can purchase certain products.*

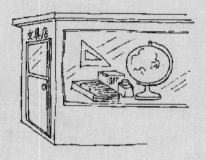

shūdiàn   a book store

wénjùdiàn   a stationery store

yóu(zhèng)jú   a post office

**yóujú de wài-
biān(r)**   outside a post office

zài jiē-shang 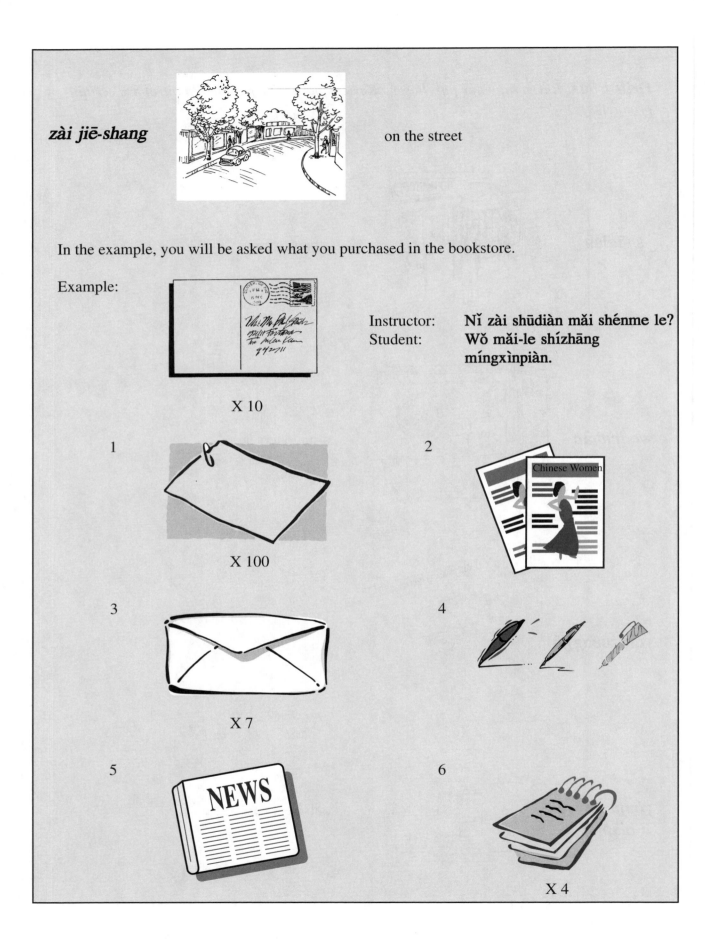 on the street

In the example, you will be asked what you purchased in the bookstore.

Example:

X 10

Instructor: **Nǐ zài shūdiàn mǎi shénme le?**
Student: **Wǒ mǎi-le shízhāng míngxìnpiàn.**

1

X 100

2

Chinese Women

3

X 7

4

5

NEWS

6

X 4

7

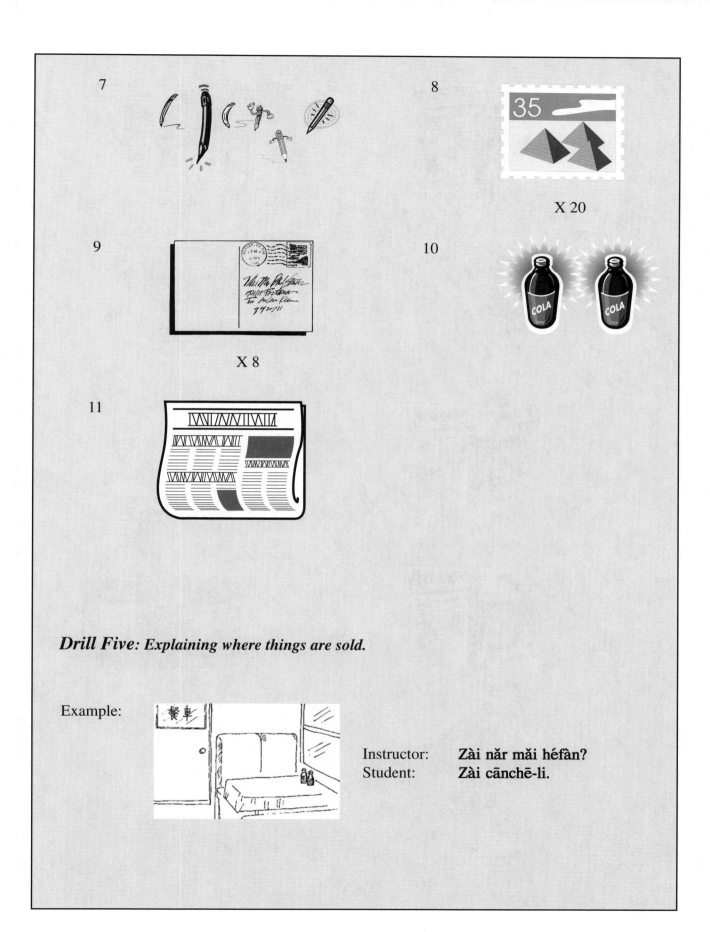

8

X 20

9

X 8

10

11

Drill Five: *Explaining where things are sold.*

Example:

| | Instructor: | **Zài nǎr mǎi héfàn?** |
| | Student: | **Zài cānchē-li.** |

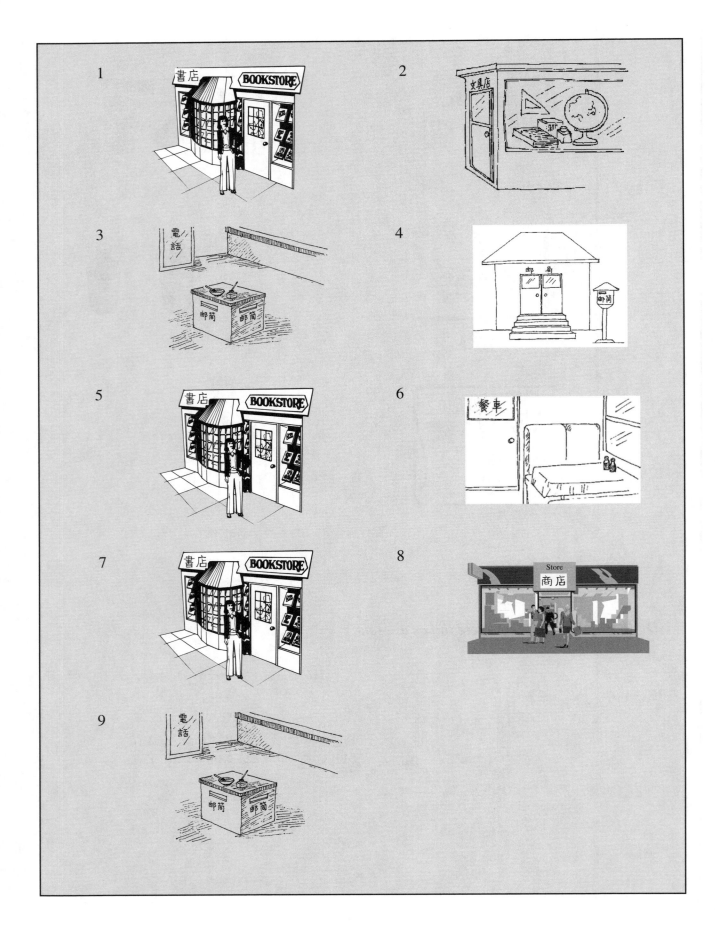

Drill Six: Negative answers.

Example: Instructor: **Lǎo Huáng yòng qiānbǐ xiě xìn.**
             Student: **Lǎo Huáng bú-yòng qiānbǐ xiě xìn.**

1.   2.   3.   4.   5.

6.   7.   8.   9.   10.

Dialogue Comprehension

Cānchē Fúwùyuán:	Mǎi-le cānquàn(r) de lǚkè, qǐng ná fàn le. Nín yào jǐfèn(r)?
Lǚkè Jiǎ:	Wǒ zhèr liǎngfèn(r).
Lǚkè Yǐ:	Shīfu, wǒ zhèr yífèn(r).
Lǚkè Bǐng:	Èi, gěi wǒ yífèn(r). Wǒ gěi qián.
Cānchē Fúwùyuán:	Hǎo, qián zhènghǎo. Mài fàn le! Mài fàn le!

Yóupiào

UNIT 2 STAGE 9
Pronunciation and Romanization: Tones, Initials, Medials, and Finals

In this stage, we want to give you the opportunity to practice with words that combine the five tones of Mandarin. We will choose our target words and expressions based on the assumption that "everybody's gotta be some place." And, when we are there, then we have to eat. So, we will focus this practice session on words that refer to places and on things you can eat or drink.

Since we will include all the two-syllable combinations in this stage, you might want to revisit this stage periodically in your course of study to review and re-practice the tones.

When compared to native speakers of Mandarin, we foreign learners of the language tend to have a much smaller high-low range for the tones of the language. For example, a non-native speaker of the language would be likely to pronounce Bèngbù, the name of a city in Anhui, with a slight falling tone:

Bèngbù

b			b	
	e			u
		n		
			g	

A native speaker will have a longer vowel and a longer high-to-low falling tone.

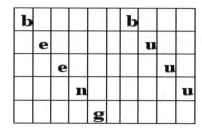

Often we non-natives make the mistake of starting too low, thereby not leaving ourselves with enough space to fall. With this in mind, do not hesitate to "exaggerate" your pronunciation in this practice session.

We start with the falling tone, which observation has shown is the most difficult for learners of Mandarin as a foreign language to perform well. We will simply give you a number of words and expressions that combine the falling tone with the four tonal possibilities.

The first combination is falling followed by high-level.

Sìchuān

Repeat this after the model, making sure to begin *sì* at a high enough point to allow the desired drop.

Xiāngjiāo

Another important province in China is Zhejiang. A coastal province just south of Shanghai known for its elegant cities, Zhejiang has a population of over 46 million. The first syllable begins with your tongue curled back toward your soft pallet and no aspiration or voicing.

zhè   the name of the river

The second syllable is the morpheme meaning "big river." It begins with the tip of your tongue behind your lower teeth and no aspiration or voicing.

jiāng

Now, repeat the name of this province after your instructor.

Zhèjiāng

Other falling tone/high-level tone combinations refer to edibles:

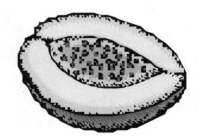

mùguā

This consists of *mù*, the morpheme for "wood," and *guā*, the morpheme for "mellon." Repeat the word for "papaya" after your instructor.

The word for bread is composed of the morphemes for "wheat" and "bun." Repeat the word for bread after your instructor:

miànbāo

To practice a falling tone/neutral tone combination, let's listen to a word for "stomach" or "belly." The initial is "*d*," a voiceless, non-aspirated consonant.

dùzi

Repeat the word for "belly" after your instructor.

If you want to express "hunger," you can simply say your *dùzi* is hungry:

Dùzi è le.

Now, we will practice falling tones followed by rising tones. Again, if you feel that you are exaggerating the tones in this session, you are probably doing it right.

The first place we want to focus your attention on is Seoul, the capital of South Korea. The syllables that make up this name are *hàn,* the name of a river and (incidentally) the name of the majority ethnic group in China, and *chéng,* a morpheme with the meaning of "a walled city."

Hànchéng

Repeat after your instructor, making sure that you begin the rising tone low enough to allow a distinctive rise.

Another important city in China is *Tàiyuán,* the capital city of Shanxi province that claims a historical pedigree of 2400 years. The first syllable of this name is *tài,* meaning "ultimate, great." The second syllable is a morpheme, *yuán,* for "plain."

Tàiyuán

Tàiyuán

Repeat the name of this city after your instructor.

Our consumables for this tone combination are two liquids that are quintessentially Chinese. The first is "soy sauce" and the second is "green tea."

jiàngyóu

The first morpheme, or syllable, is *jiàng,* meaning a "paste made from fermented grains and legumes" or "jam." Remember to begin this syllable with the tip of your tongue behind your lower teeth. The second morpheme is *yóu,* meaning 'oil." Practice this by repeating after your instructor.

"Green tea" is a term made from "green" and "tea." *lǜ,* green, is formed in the same way you would say *lì* (*lì* with a falling tone), except that your lips are pursed in what we refer to as the semi-chaste kiss formation. Tea is *chá,* made with your tongue curled and with a strong aspiration.

lǜchá

Practice the word for green tea by repeating after your instructor.

You can order a cup of green tea by saying to the waiter:

Qǐng lái yìbēi lùchá.

When you eat in China, you can ask for chopsticks with yet another falling tone/neutral tone combination. Namely, *kuàizi.*

kuàizi

Practice referring to these necessary implements by repeating after your instructor.

In China you will always be provided with *kuàizi.* However, if you want to ask for a pair of *kuàizi* in a Chinese restaurant outside of China, you can say.

Qǐng gěi wǒ
yìshuāng kuàizi.

The low-rising tone is best performed by making sure your beginning pitch is low enough and that your rising vowel is long enough.

We will begin our practice of the falling tone/low rising tone combinations by focusing on two spectacular cities—Shanghai and Dali.

Shanghai is one of the great cities in the world. The largest city in China, Shanghai is the financial and cultural center for much of China. It is quickly developing as an international city with a truly cosmopolitan flavor. The first syllable of this name is *shàng,* meaning "on" or "above." The second syllable is *hǎi,* meaning "sea."

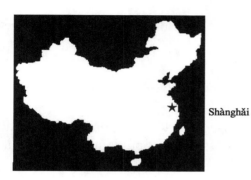

Shànghǎi

Repeat after your instructor to practice this city name.

A favorite destination for visitors in China is the city of Dàlǐ, located in the Bai Autonomous Region in Yunnan Province. Dàlǐ is an ancient center of religion and music and retains the flavor of that cultural heritage. Many visitors, especially younger ones, tarry in Dàlǐ longer than they had planned to.

Dàlǐ

Practice this city name by repeating after your instructor.

If you spend anytime living in China, you will have to purchase rice. In the restaurant, you order *mǐfàn*, or cooked rice, but if you are buying a bag of rice at the grocery store or the stall of the grains merchant, you order *dàmǐ* (literally, great rice).

Practice this falling tone/low rising tone combination for rice grain by repeating after your instructor:

dàmǐ

In the American Midwest another grain, corn, is important. This falling tone/low rising combination is made from the morphemes for "jade" and "rice." *Yù*, the word for jade, is pronounced with your lips pursed. *Mǐ* is simply a low rising tone version of your favorite object.

Practice this combination by repeating after your instructor:

yùmǐ

Another falling tone/neutral tone combination is the word for "chestnut." This word will come in handy when you want to buy roasted chestnuts from a vendor on a wintry Beijing street corner. It will also come in handy later, when we want you to distinguish it from other words that differ only by tone.

Repeat the word for "chestnut" after your instructor:

lìzi

To practice words with two sequenced falling tones, we look to the area between the Yellow River and the Yangzi River in Eastern China to the province of *Ānhuī*, where *Bèngbù*, a city of about one half million, is located on the banks of the Huai River.

Practice this placename by repeating after your instructor:

Bèngbù

Another city name that has this pattern of two falling tone syllables is the hometown of Chiang Kaishek, the former president of the Republic of China. This city of less than one half million persons is known for its garment industry and peaches. So, when you are asked about the birth place of Chiang Kaishek, be sure to say the *Fènghuà* with clear and distinct falling tones, just as your instructor and model do here:

Practice this placename by repeating after your instructor:

Fènghuà

Moving on to edibles, one of the most important ingredients in cuisines around the world is garlic, and the various cuisines of China are no exception. The word for "garlic" is *dàsuàn*. *Dàsuàn* is composed of the morpheme for "great," *dà* and the morpheme for "garlic," *suàn*.

Repeat this word after your instructor:

dàsuàn

Another important consumable with two falling tone syllables is the word for mung bean. Mung beans are the main source of the bean sprouts that enhance so many entrees and salads. The word for mung bean is *lùdòu*. *Lù*, meaning green, is pronounced like *lì*, except your lips are rounded. *Dòu* means "bean."

Repeat the word for *mung bean* after your instructor:

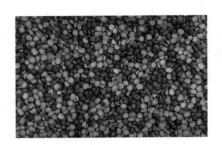

lùdòu

We will conclude our work with another falling tone/neutral tone combination. This is the word for "rabbit," which is *tùzi*, if you see the creature in the garden.

Repeat the word after your instructor:

tùzi

If you happen to see the creature in a stew, then the word would be

tùròu

a two falling tone combination of the morphemes for "rabbit," *tù*, and the morpheme for "meat," *ròu*. We won't ask you to repeat this expression because Peter Rabbit in a pot is just too horrible an illustration for our gentle profession.

Now, let's practice words with an initial low-rising tone. When practicing the low-rising syllables, be sure you begin low enough and end high enough to perform this tone well.

Low-rising/high-level combinations are our starting point. The first two words are hugely important Chinese cities and, therefore, your pronunciation should be perfect.

Běijīng is formed from the morphemes for "north," *běi*, and "capital," *jīng*.

Běijīng

Repeat the name of the capital of China, until you sound as if you had been hearing it mentioned all your life. American news readers like to pronounce this with the "*j*" sounding like the "*j*" in "bonjour." But contrary to the ideas of our media elites, not all foreign languages sound like French. Remember that the second syllable, the morpheme for "capital," *jīng*, is a hard consonant, pronounced with the tip of your tongue behind your lower teeth.

Our second city, *Guǎngzhōu*, is the place where the economic miracle of modern China first took off. It is the capital of Guangdong Province and is also known as *Yángchéng* or Goat City.

Repeat this city name after your instructor:

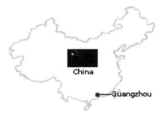

Guǎngzhōu

Kǎoyā is a low-rising/high-level combination that refers to a food that is associated with Beijing and is world renowned. *Kǎo* means to "roast, bake, or toast," and *yā* refers to "duck." Usually, if you order *kǎoyā* in a restaurant in the United States, you have to order a day or so in advance, and it is well worth your wait. In Beijing, however, you can find many restaurants specializing in *kǎoyā* that will accommodate your appetite right away.

Repeat the expression for *roast duck* after the Beijing native that happens to be your instructor for this session:

kǎoyā

If you have a lesser appetite, we have another low-rising/high-level combination that refers to "crackers and cookies." *Bǐnggān* is formed with the morphemes *bǐng*, meaning "cake-shaped," and *gān*, meaning "dry, dried."

Repeat referring to this confection after your instructor:

bǐnggān

A low-rising/neutral tone combination is the word for "plum." The morpheme for "plum," *lǐ*, plus *zi* refers to the fruit. *Lǐ* by itself is the popular family name.

Repeat the word for *plum* after the instructor.

lǐzi

For an example of a low-rising/rising tone combination, we will introduce you to a major city in Northeast China. *Shěnyáng*, is the capital of Liáoníng Province. The old Manchu capital, *Shěnyáng* is a major center of commerce, science and culture for Northeast China.

Repeat this city name after your instructor:

Shěnyáng

Another low-rising/rising tone combination name for a famous place is *Jiǔlóng*, the part of the Hong Kong Special Administrative Region that is on the Mainland directly across the bay from Hong Kong island. On the maps you will see this called Kowloon. This place name is composed of, *jiǔ*, the morpheme for "nine," and *lóng*, the morpheme for "dragon."

Repeat the name for this busy district after your instructor:

Jiǔlóng

If we want to practice this low-rising/rising tone combination with something we can eat, strawberries come to mind. The word is *căoméi*. *Căo* is the morpheme for "grass," and *méi* the morpheme for "edible berry."

Get this word down perfect in time for the season by repeating after your instructor:

căoméi

If you are daring enough, or young enough, to take your strawberries with cream, you can get that with another low-rising/rising tone. *Năiyóu* is composed of the morphemes for "milk," *năi*, and "oil" or "grease," *yóu*.

Practice getting the cream for your *năiyóu* by repeating after your instructor:

năiyóu

Next we will practice combinations consisting of two low-rising tones. The interesting thing about two or more low-rising tones in a row is they do not occur. Only the last tone is low-rising, the syllable or syllables before it turn into rising tones. This applies to both multi-syllable words and to strings of words in expressions or sentences. Thus, when things are going well for you, you combine three low-rising tone words into a sentence of two rising tone words and one low-rising tone word:

Wŏ hĕn hăo.

The first place we will practice is *Běihǎi*, a resort city of less than half a million people on the Guangxi coast. There is also a famous park in Beijing with this name:

Běihǎi Gōngyuán

Běi is the morpheme for "north," and *hǎi* is the morpheme for "ocean" or "sea." Repeat this exotic placename after your instructor:

Běihǎi

Another interesting placename that fits this pattern is the name of a town in the mountains of southern *Yúnnán* Province. *Pǔ'ěr,* usually spelled p- u- e- r- h on the maps, is famous for one of the distinct kinds of teas. Produced by a fermentation process and often sold in hard bricks, this tea is renowned for both its distinct earthy flavor and its health benefits.

Practice celebrating the hometown of this concoction by repeating this placename after your instructor:

Pǔ'ěr

In case you want to try the tea, here you can get the correct pronunciation from your instructor:

Pǔ'ěr chá

A commonly consumed grain in northern China is millet. As contrasted with *dàmǐ* (literally *great rice*), the word for *"millet"* is *xiǎomǐ*. *Xiǎo* is the morpheme for *"small"* or *"minor,"* and *mǐ* is the morpheme for *"rice."* *Xiǎomǐ* is often consumed in a porridge.

Repeat after your instructor so that you are able to make yourself clear to your neighborhood grain merchant.

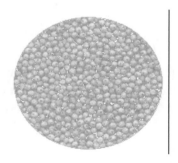

xiǎomǐ

Cǎoméi

If you are more likely to purchase foods in restaurants, you might want to pay special attention to the combination of two low-rising tones for "boiled dumpling." The word is *shuǐjiǎo.* *Shuǐ* is the morpheme for "water" and *jiǎo* is the morpheme for "dumpling."

Repeat the word for this gustatory delight after your hungry instructor:

shuǐjiǎo

If you are looking for dumplings that may be steamed or fried as well as boiled, you can use this term formed with a low-rising/neutral tone combination.

jiǎozi

This may be one of the most important words you learn in this course.

To practice combinations of low-rising/falling tones, we ask you to look to the capital of *Húběi* Province. *Wǔhàn* is formed from the morpheme *wǔ* meaning "martial" and the designation of the majority ethnic group in China, *hàn.* *Wǔhàn,* the birthplace of the 1911 Revolution, is located on the confluence of the Yangzi River and Han River. With an urban population of over four and a half million, *Wǔhàn* is a major center of education, commerce, and culture for Central China.

Practice this placename by repeating after your instructor.

Wǔhàn

Another city that permits us to practice this pattern is *Bǎodìng*. *Bǎo* means to "protect" and *dìng* means "fixed" or "stable." It is 137 kilometers south of Beijing and was the administrative center of Hebei Province until the last century.

Repeat the name of this city of over 500,000 after your instructor:

Bǎodìng

Even though a good number of Chinese are lactose intolerant, the food we choose to practice this tonal combination is the word for "cheese." *Nǎilào* is composed of the morphemes for "milk" and "cheese." In recent decades *nǎilào* has become a popular item in Chinese supermarkets for those who have no problem with milk products.

Repeat after your instructor so you can find out who moved your cheese... if you need to.

nǎilào

Another low-rising/falling tone combination is one of the words for "potato." *Tǔdòu* is formed from the morpheme for "dirt," *tǔ*, and the morpheme for "bean," *dòu*.

Repeat the word for the "earth bean" or "potato."

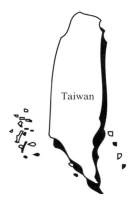

tǔdòu

We can practice rising tone/high level tone combinations by focusing on the island province of *Táiwān*. *Tái* is a morpheme for "platform" and *wān* is a morpheme with the sense of "bay."

Repeat this well known placename following your instructor:

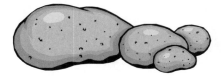

Táiwān

Shīzi

Another place name is *Nánchāng*, the capital of Jiangxi Province. *Nánchāng* is formed from the morpheme *nán* meaning "south" and *chāng* meaning "prosperous." For many centuries, it was a storage and distribution center for the famous porcelain from nearby *Jǐngdézhèn*. It is also known as a heroic city because of the Nanchang Uprising on August 1, 1927. Today, the anniversary of the uprising is celebrated each year in China as the day the People's Liberation Army was founded.

Practice this placename by repeating after your instructor:

Nánchāng

A rising tone/high-level tone combination referring to "onion" is our next example. The large, white, yellow, and purple onions you buy in an American supermarket are called *yángcōng*. *Yáng* means "foreign" and *cōng* is the morpheme for "shallot."

Learn how to call for this basic vegetable by repeating after your instructor:

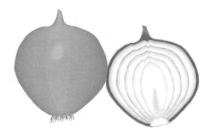

yángcōng

Another key vegetable is the cucumber. In Chinese this is *huánggūa*. *Huáng* is the morpheme for "yellow" and *guā* is the morpheme for "melon."

Learn to call for the "yellow melon" or "cucumber" by repeating after your instructor:

huánggūa

A rising tone/neutral tone combination is the word for "pear," *lízi*.

Learn to get the right fruit by repeating after your instructor:

lízi

One of the most popular tourist destinations in China is the Southwestern province of *Yúnnán*. We will use this placename to practice the two rising tone combination. *Yún* is the morpheme for "cloud" and *nán* is the morpheme for "south."

Repeat the name of this province after your instructor:

Yúnnán

Another placename with two rising tone syllables is *Liáoníng,* a province in Northeastern China. *Liáo* is the morpheme for "far" or "distant" and *níng* means "peace."

Practice this two rising tone combination by repeating after your instructor:

Liáoníng

You have already been introduced to two general kinds of tea: *Pǔěr chá* and *lǜchá.* To practice another two rising tones combination, another general type of tea will be our example. It is *hóngchá,* the term for "black tea." *Hóng* is the morpheme for "red" and *chá* is the morpheme for "tea."

Practice ordering "black tea" by repeating after your instructor:

hóngchá

With a more hearty appetite, you might want the word for a beefsteak. The word is *niúpái. Niú* is the morpheme for "cow" and *pái* refers to a "plank" or "raft."

niúpái

Here is the chance to learn to take a break from all that healthful Chinese food and go for the cholesterol by repeating after your instructor.

To practice the rising tone/low-rising tone combination, we direct your attention to the largest city on *Táiwān.* This is *Táiběi. Tái* is the morpheme for "platform" and *běi* is the morpheme for "north."

Repeat this city located, where else, in the north of Taiwan.

Táiběi

The South China Sea, the part of the Pacific Ocean bordered by South China, Vietnam, and The Philippines. *Nánhǎi* is composed of *nán,* meaning "south," and *hǎi,* meaning "sea" or "ocean."

Repeat after your instructor the name of this exotic clime:

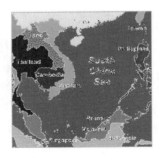

Nánhǎi

For food examples of rising and low-rising tone combinations, we can get pretty basic. The word for cows milk and the word for apple. Cows milk is composed of the morpheme for "cow," *niú,* and the morpheme for "milk," *nǎi.*

Repeat this word after your instructor:

niúnǎi

Apple is composed of the morpheme for "duckweed," *píng,* and the morpheme for "fruit," *guǒ.*

Repeat the word for "apple" after the instructor:

píngguǒ

Another rising tone/neutral tone combination is the word for "eggplant," *qiézi*. Begin this word with the tip of your tongue behind your lower teeth as you repeat after your instructor.

qiézi

This is the word Chinese say when having their pictures taken, the equivalent of Americans saying "cheese."

To practice a rising tone/falling tone combination, we can look toward Sichuan, where *Chóngqìng*, located on the confluence of the Yangzi and Jialing Rivers, used to be the largest city. *Chóngqìng* is now the fourth National Municipality, after Beijing, Shanghai, and Tianjin. *Chóng* is a morpheme meaning "to repeat." *Qìng* is a morpheme meaning "to celebrate."

Repeat the name of this important city after your instructor:

Chóngqìng

Another important placename with this rising tone/falling tone combination is the province of *Fújiàn*. Across the Taiwan Straits from Taiwan, *Fújiàn*, with a population of approximately thirty million, is the original home of millions of Chinese who have immigrated to other countries. Despite having so many of its people seek their fortunes abroad, *Fújiàn* is one of the most prosperous and scenic regions of China.

Practice the name of this province by repeating after your instructor.

Fújiàn

For edible examples of rising tone/falling tone combinations, we will go vegetarian: the word for "celery" is *qíncài*. *Qín* is the morpheme for "celery" and *cài* is the morpheme for "vegetable."

Practice saying the name of this crunchy treat, being sure that you produce enough aspiration on each syllable.

qíncài

One of the great contributions of Chinese cuisine has been the ability to make cabbage delicious. Chinese cabbage is generally referred to as *báicài*. *Bái* is the morpheme for "white" and, as just mentioned, *cài* is "vegetable."

Repeat after your instructor to make sure your pronunciation of this crucial ingredient is perfect.

báicài

The morpheme *cài* is also used as a general term for "food." For example, "Chinese food" is often called:

Zhōngguó cài

To practice two high-level tone combinations, we will choose two important placenames. The first is *Shāndōng*, the province that occupies the peninsula that juts out toward Korea across the Yellow Sea. As the home of Confucius and the locale of the novel *Men of the Marshes, Shāndōng* has longstanding claims as the source of many Chinese traditions.

Repeat this important placename after your instructor:

Shāndōng

Tiānjīn is another National Municipality, located on the shores of the *Bóhǎi, Tiānjīn* is located 76 miles (120 kilometers) from Beijing.

Repeat the name of this major city after your instructor:

Tiānjīn

Things you can eat that are represented by two high-level tone combinations include bananas and another version of *jiǎozi*. Banana is *xiāngjiāo*. *Xiāng* is the morpheme for "fragrant" and *jiāo* is the morpheme for "raw hemp." Both of these syllables begin with the tip of your tongue behind your lower teeth.

Repeat the name of this universally prized fruit after your instructor:

xiāngjiāo

The type of *jiǎozi* we are going to practice is what appears on menus as "potstickers." This is a literal translation of *guōtiē*. These are lightly fried dumplings, best eaten with a sauce of soy sauce, vinegar, and pepper oil.

Practice mentioning this dish by repeating after your instructor:

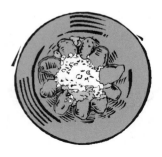 guōtiē

A legendary tourist city in Yunnan is our example of a high-level tone/rising tone combination. *Kūnmíng* is located on a plateau over one mile above sea level and is famous for its year-round good weather in addition to its scenic attractions.

Practice saying this placename which is also the capital of Yunnan Province.

 Kūnmíng

The second example of a high-level/rising tone combination is a much less well known agriculture center in Zhejiang Province. *Jīnhuá* is formed from *jīn*, the morpheme for "gold," and *huá*, a morpheme that busily refers to "ornate," "splendorous," "prosperous," and "China."

On the chance that you might be inspecting the agricultural centers of Zhejiang, practice this placename by repeating after your instructor:

 Jīnhuá

A useful ingredient in Chinese cooking is a good example for a high-level tone/rising tone combination. This is *xiāngyóu,* an ingredient consisting mostly of sesame oil. *Xiāng* is a morpheme meaning "fragrant" and *yóu* means "oil."

Repeat asking for this ingredient after your instructor:

xiāngyóu

If you want to ask specifically for sesame oil, you can use a three syllable word that contains a high-level tone, a neutral tone, and a rising tone, *zhīmayóu.* *Zhīma* is sesame.

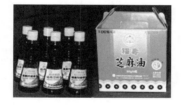

zhīmayóu

The second edible that is a high-level/rising tone combination is a critter that has dined on a few species itself. That is a "shark," or *shāyú.* *Shā* is the morpheme for "shark" and *yú* is the morpheme for "fish." When you repeat this fish, remember that *shā* is pronounced with your tongue strongly curled back, and *yú* is pronounced as if you are saying *yí,* the number one before a falling tone measure, except your mouth is rounded.

If you do not eat *shāyú,* you might want to still repeat this after your instructor in case you find yourself on a beach in China and you want to know when someone is shouting an identification of the species.

shāyú

We can practice high-level and rising tone in combination with a neutral tone with the name of a well-known Chinese dish that is essentially a big meatball. That is *shīzitóu*. *Shīzi* is the word for "lion" and *tóu* is the morpheme for "head."

shīzi

Repeat this dish after your instructor:

shīzitóu

We have two famous seaports to help us practice high-level/low-rising tone combinations, Hong Kong and Tsingtao.

Xiānggǎng

Qīngdǎo

The Mandarin name of Hong Kong is *Xiānggǎng*. *Xiāng* is the morpheme for "fragrant" and *gǎng* is the morpheme for "harbor." Repeat this name for the Hong Kong Special Administrative Region after your instructor:

Xiānggǎng

If you drink beer in Chinese restaurants, you might have encountered Tsingtao Beer. The *pīnyīn* spelling of this city name is q-i-n-g-d-a-o. And the word for "beer" is *píjiǔ*.

Qīngdǎo píjiǔ

In addition to beer, this biggest city in Shandong is known for its unique German architecture and pleasant weather.

Repeat this city name after your instructor:

Qīngdǎo

If you want to try the beer the next time you patronize a Chinese restaurant, you might want to practice ordering the beverage by repeating after your instructor:

Qīngdǎo píjiǔ

Many people like to have spring rolls with their beer or tea. Spring rolls are called *chūnjuǎn*. *Chūn* is the morpheme for "Spring" and *juǎn* means "to roll up" or "rolled up objects." *Chūn* is pronounced with your tongue strongly curled backwards and *juǎn* begins with the tip of your tongue behind your lower teeth.

Repeat this staple of American Chinese restaurants after your instructor:

chūnjuǎn

Another example of a high-level/low-rising tone combination is another standard fare — the sesame griddle cake. This is called *shāobǐng*. *Shāo* is the morpheme for "baking" or "roasting," *and bǐng* is something that has the shape of a cake.

Repeat after your instructor:

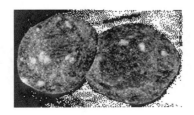

shāobǐng

To practice high-level/falling tone combinations, we will go west. First to *Gānsù*, a province that lies along the upper reaches of the Yellow River through which the Silk Road passed. *Gānsù* has historically been the crossroads of cultures from across Asia.

Repeat this placename after your instructor.

Gānsù

Another western placename is *Xīzàng*. This is the Mandarin name for Tibet. *Xī* is the morpheme for "west" and *zàng* is the morpheme for "repository" or "storehouse." Known as the "roof of the world," the population of *Xīzàng* is a little over a couple of million people, the great majority of whom are *Zàngzú*, or Tibetan.

Repeat the name of the home of the *Zàngzú* after your instructor:

Xīzàng

When selecting food terms to practice the high-level/falling tone combination, we decided to go basic. First the breakfast staple for hundreds of millions of Chinese is a dish that is rendered into English as "conjee," "porridge," or "gruel." This is pronounced *xīfàn*. *Xī* is the morpheme for "sparse" and *fàn* is the term for "cooked rice." *Xīfàn* is made from either rice or millet. If you want millet gruel, it would best to ask for:

xiǎomǐ xīfàn

Practice getting your breakfast in China by repeating after your instructor:

xīfàn

There are gourmets who hold that the genius of Chinese cuisine lies in the treatment of vegetables, or *shūcài*. Of course, there are more physicians who hold this view. Whether you are motivated by taste or the fear of a premature diet-induced death, you should be able to call for vegetables when your Chinese hosts overdo the heavy protein by treating you to over generous portions of meat, poultry, insects, and seafood.

Repeat this important word after your instructor:

shūcài

In case you are hungry for edible arachnids, we have a final high-level/neutral tone combination for you. Whether you like your scorpions deep fried or kicking fresh, you will need the word *xiēzi* to order them.

Repeat the name of this delicacy after your hungry instructor:

xiēzi

DRILLS

Drill One: *Identify the tones. When you hear a two-syllable word, identify it by choosing the appropriate tone pattern.*

Example: Cue: **Bèngbù.**

| **Bèngbù** | **Bēngbù** | **Běngbù** |

✓

1

| **Bèngbù** | **Bēngbù** | **Běngbù** |

2

| **Sǐchuān** | **Sìchuān** | **Sīchuān** |

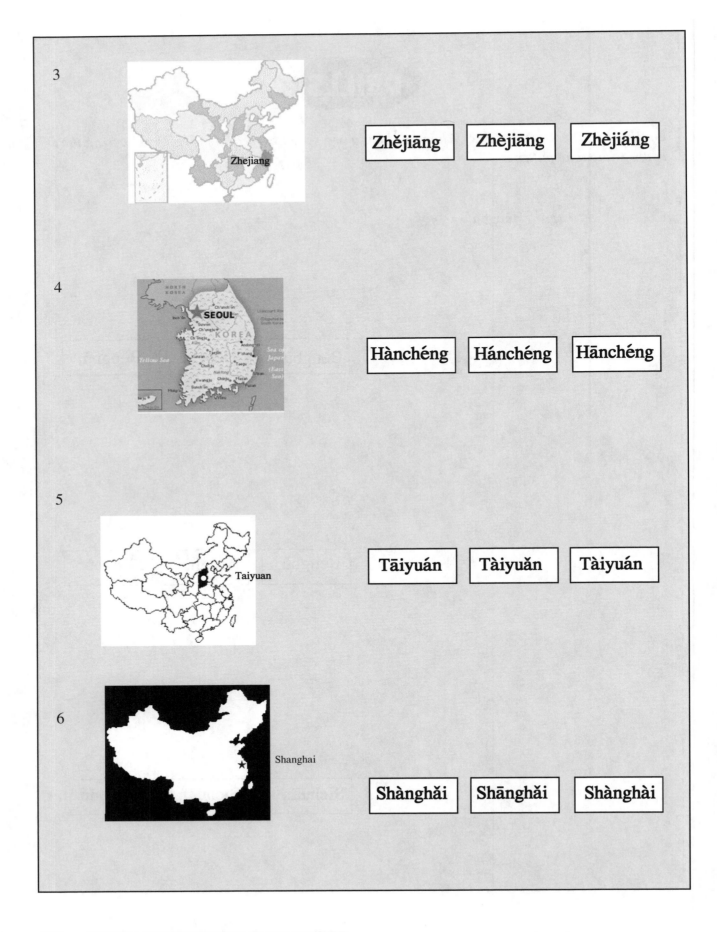

3

Zhějiāng   Zhèjiāng   Zhèjiáng

4

Hànchéng   Hánchéng   Hānchéng

5

Tāiyuán   Tàiyuǎn   Tàiyuán

6

Shànghǎi   Shānghǎi   Shànghài

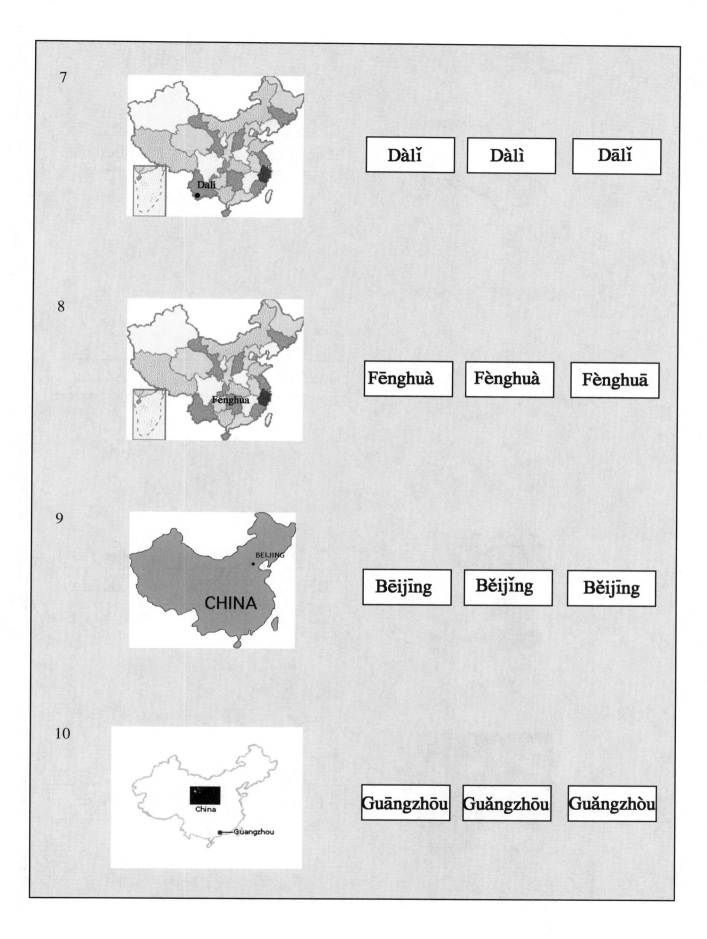

7

Dàlǐ   Dàlì   Dālǐ

8

Fēnghuà   Fènghuà   Fènghuā

9

Bēijīng   Běijǐng   Běijīng

10

Guāngzhōu   Guǎngzhōu   Guǎngzhòu

11

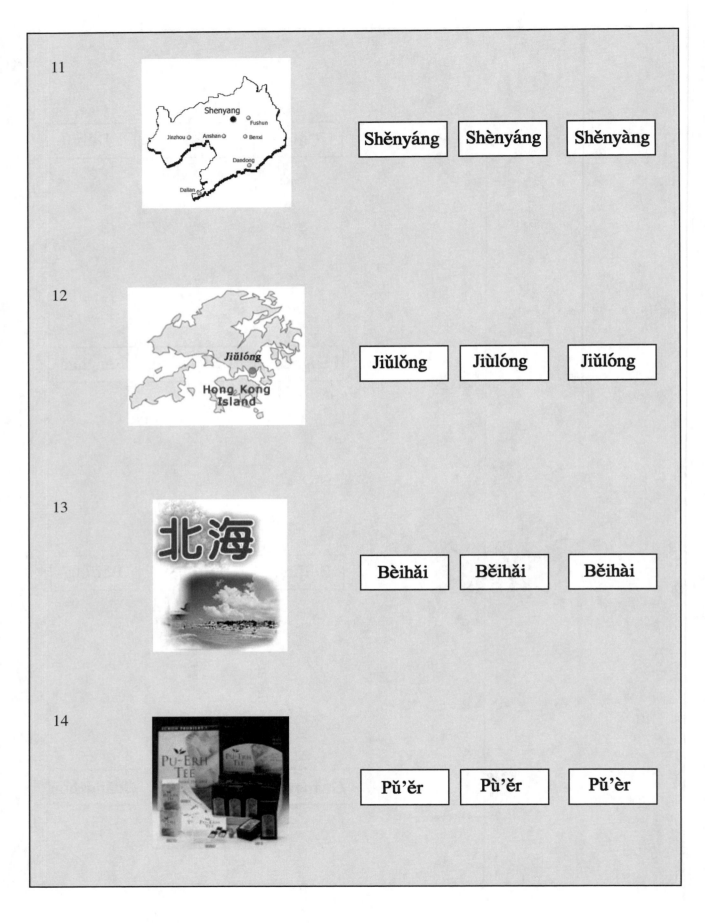

| Shěnyáng | Shènyáng | Shěnyàng |

12

| Jiǔlǒng | Jiùlóng | Jiǔlóng |

13

| Bèihǎi | Běihǎi | Běihài |

14

| Pǔ'ěr | Pù'ěr | Pǔ'èr |

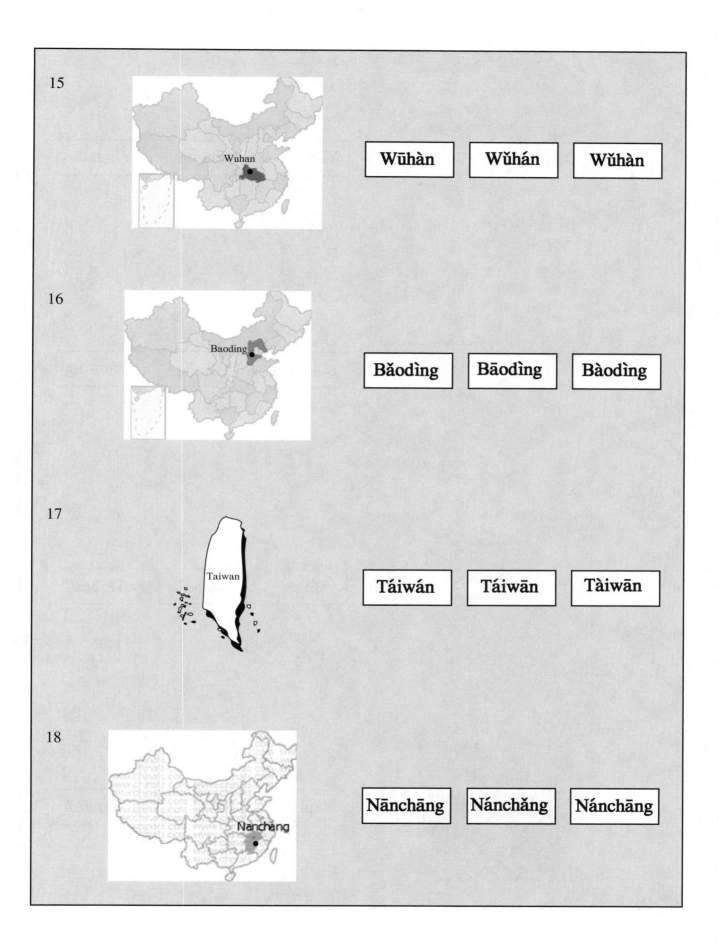

15

Wūhàn | Wǔhán | Wǔhàn

16

Bǎodìng | Bāodìng | Bàodìng

17

Táiwán | Táiwān | Tàiwān

18

Nānchāng | Nánchǎng | Nánchāng

19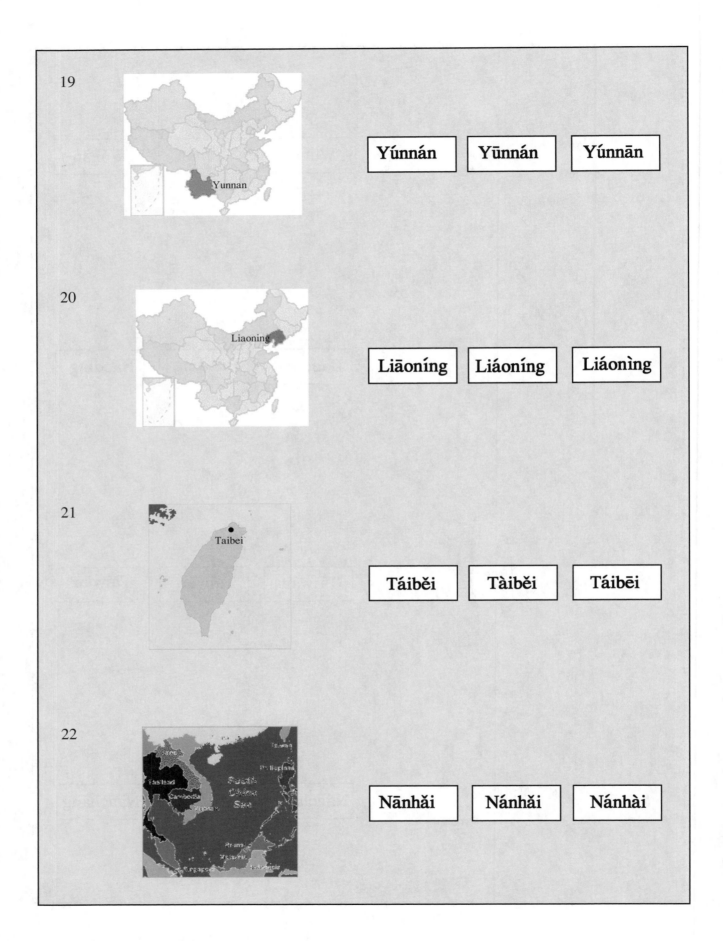

Yúnnán   **Yūnnán**   **Yúnnān**

20

Liāoníng   **Liáoníng**   **Liáonìng**

21

Táiběi   **Tàiběi**   **Táibēi**

22

Nānhǎi   **Nánhǎi**   **Nánhài**

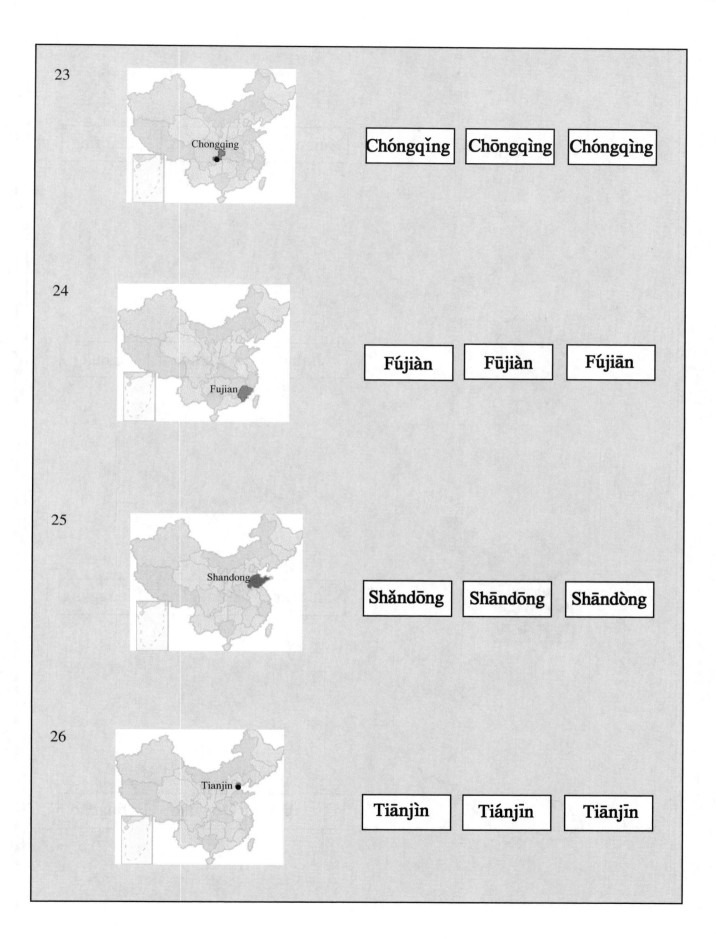

23

Chongqing

Chóngqǐng Chōngqìng Chóngqìng

24

Fujian

Fújiàn Fūjiàn Fújiān

25

Shandong

Shǎndōng Shāndōng Shāndòng

26

Tianjin

Tiānjìn Tiánjīn Tiānjīn

27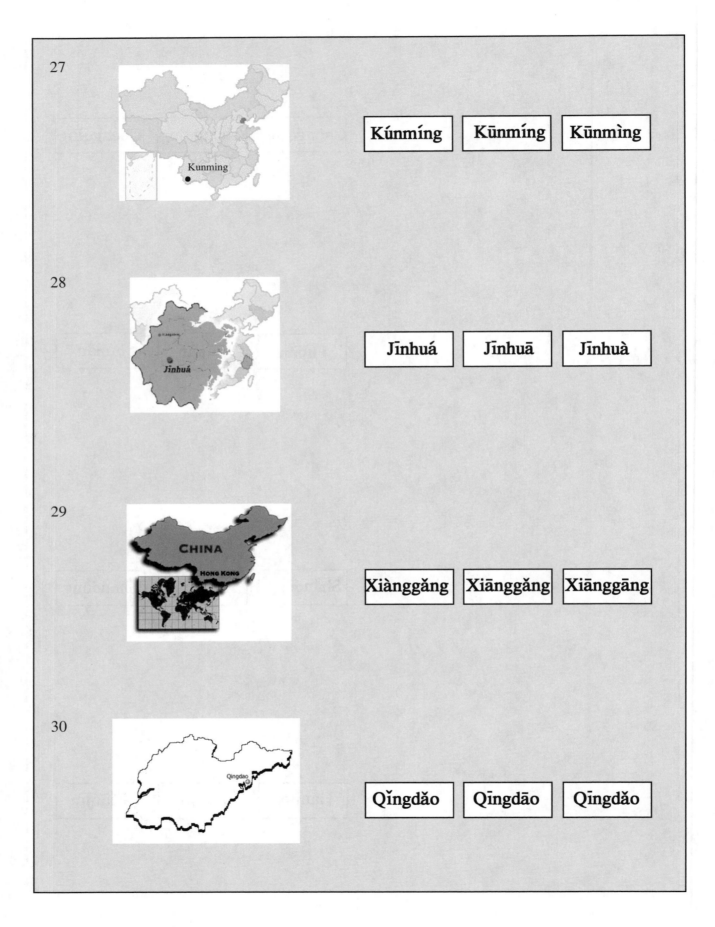

| Kúnmíng | Kūnmíng | Kūnmìng |

28

| Jǐnhuá | Jǐnhuā | Jǐnhuà |

29

| Xiànggǎng | Xiānggǎng | Xiānggāng |

30

| Qǐngdǎo | Qīngdāo | Qīngdǎo |

31

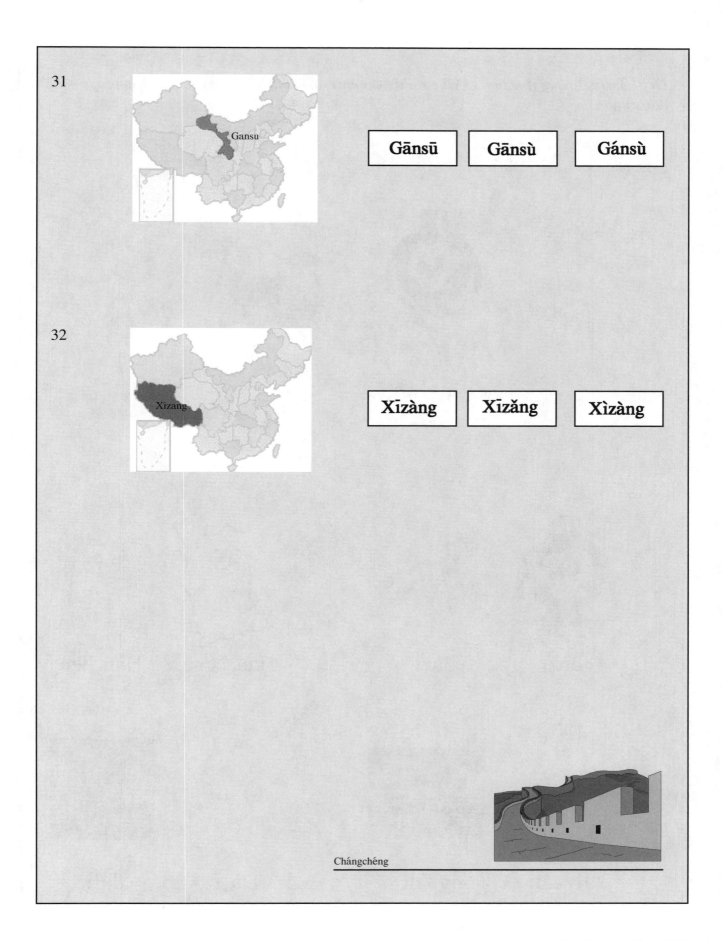

| Gānsū | Gānsù | Gánsù |

32

| Xīzàng | Xīzǎng | Xìzàng |

Chángchéng

Drill Two: *Identifying tones. **When you hear a word, identify it by choosing the appropriate illustration.***

Example: Cue: **Dùzi.**

dùzi   dúzi

1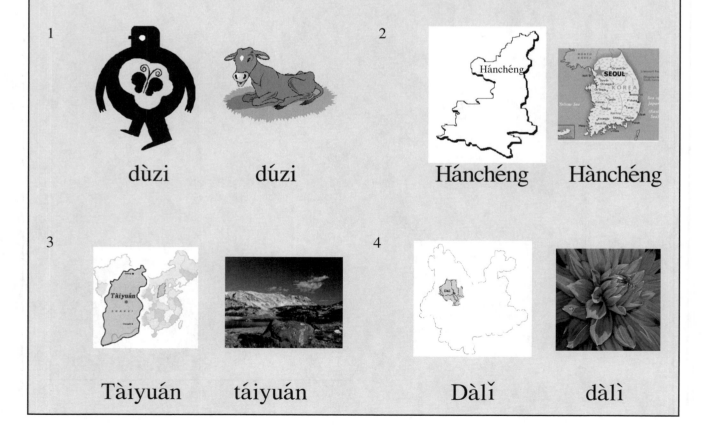

dùzi   dúzi

2

Hánchéng   Hànchéng

3

Tàiyuán   táiyuán

4

Dàlǐ   dàlì

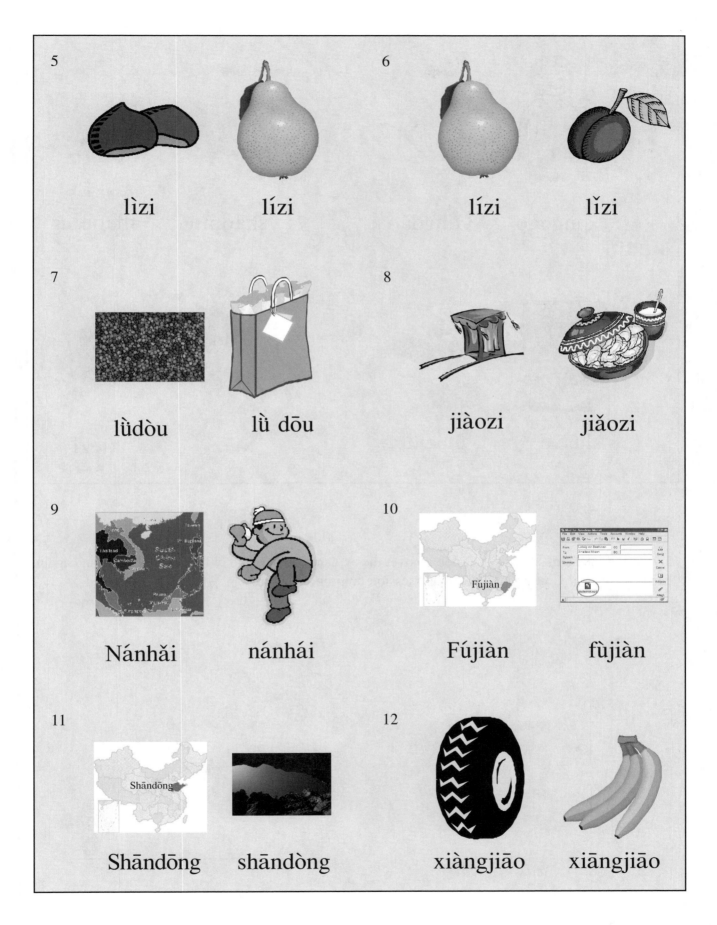

5   lìzi   lízi

6   lízi   lǐzi

7   lǜdòu   lǜ dōu

8   jiàozi   jiǎozi

9   Nánhǎi   nánhái

10   Fújiàn   fùjiàn

11   Shāndōng   shāndòng

12   xiàngjiāo   xiāngjiāo

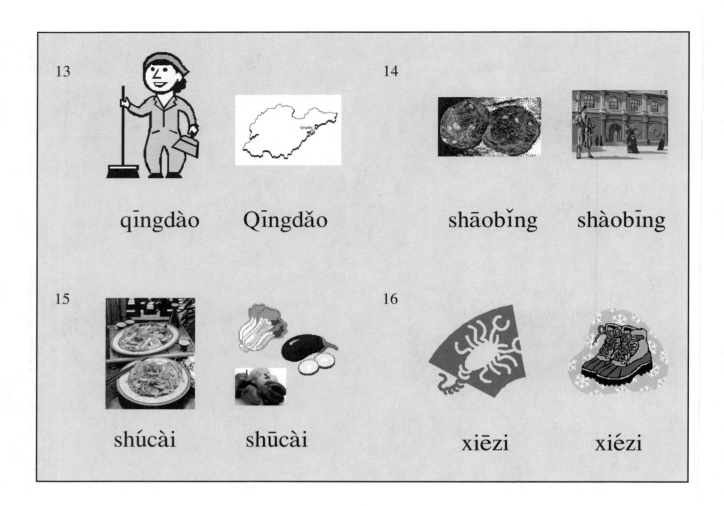

13   qīngdào   Qīngdǎo

14   shāobǐng   shàobīng

15   shúcài   shūcài

16   xiēzi   xiézi

Have you done them correctly? If not, go over the explanation part and redo the drills again and again. This is the end of Unit 2 Stage 9, the last session on pronunciation.

Nánhái

In this Stage you can check out your command of the vocabulary, patterns, and situations encountered in Unit Two.   Listening to the audio program, give responses to all the following items. When you have finished Sections A, B, and C, continue listening to the audio program to get the correct responses. This way you can evaluate how well you have learned the content of Unit Two.

Answer the following questions about the Chinese you have studied in this course.

Section A: Vocabulary

Identify the following questions by writing the correct letter in the space provided.

1. __C__
2. ___
3. ___
4. ___
5. ___
6. ___
7. ___
8. ___
9. ___
10. ___
11. ___
12. ___

A. Asks who or whom.
B. Asks how many books.
C. Asks how many pencils.
D. Asks which country.
E. Asks how things are going or the condition of things.
F. Asks what.
G. Asks how many or how much.
H. Asks where.
I. Asks how to deal with a situation.
J. Asks about what people are like.

Wǒmen xué zhōngwén.

Select the best description of the following place names by writing the correct letter in the space provided.

13. **A**
14. ___
15. ___
16. ___
17. ___
18. ___
19. ___
20. ___
21. ___
22. ___
23. ___
24. ___
25. ___
26. ___
27. ___
28. ___
29. ___
30. ___
31. ___
32. ___
33. ___
34. ___
35. ___
36. ___
37. ___

A. guójiā

B. Zhōngguó de chéngshì

C. Měiguó de chéngshì

D. Zhōngguó de dàxué

E. Rìběn de chéngshì

F. Fǎguó de chéngshì

G. Měiguó de dàxué

H. Yīngguó de chéngshì

Wǒ de zhōngwén lǎoshī

Associate the following words by writing the correct letter in the space provided.

38. __A__

39. ___

40. ___

41. ___

42. ___

43. ___

44. ___

45. ___

46. ___

47. ___

48. ___

49. ___

50. ___

51. ___

52. ___

53. ___

54. ___

55. ___

56. ___

57. ___

58. ___

59. ___

A. dōngxi

B. dìfang

C. rén

D. shùzì

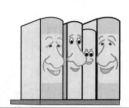

Wǒ de sìběn yīngwén shū

Counting things: when you hear a noun, choose the appropriate measure word and say the phrase that indicates two of those things.

Example: Instructor: **Rén.**
             Student: **Liǎngge rén.**

60. ___
61. ___
62. ___
63. ___
64. ___
65. ___
66. ___
67. ___
68. ___
69. ___
70. ___
71. ___
72. ___
73. ___
74. ___
75. ___
76. ___
77. ___
78. ___
79. ___
80. ___
81. ___
82. ___
83. ___
84. ___
85. ___

–wèi
–fēng
–tái
–jiàn
–běn
–dùn
–fèn
–guàn
–kuài
–píng
–zhāng
–zhī
–gè
–bù
–bēi

Numbers: Write the number you hear in Hindu-Arabic numerals.

86. ___
87. ___
88. ___
89. ___
90. ___
91. ___
92. ___
93. ___

Zhège shùzì duì ma?

94. ___
95. ___
96. ___
97. ___
98. ___
99. ___
100. ___

Section B: Structure

Ask an appropriate question for each of the following statements. The part to be focused on in your question will be repeated.

Example: Instructor: **Wǒ yào liǎngfèn(r).**   **(liǎngfèn(r))**
             Student: **Nǐ yào jǐfèn(r)?**

1. Tāmen wǔge rén zài gōngchǎng zuò shèjì gōngzuò.   (zài gōngchǎng)

_____

2. Tāmen wǔge rén zài gōngchǎng zuò shèjì gōngzuò.   (zuò shèjì gōngzuò)

_____

3. Tāmen wǔge rén zài gōngchǎng zuò shèjì gōngzuò.   (tāmen wǔge rén)

_____

4. Tāmen wǔge rén zài gōngchǎng zuò shèjì gōngzuò.   (shèjì)

_____

5. Tāmen wǔge rén zài gōngchǎng zuò shèjì gōngzuò.   (wǔge rén)

_____

6. Lǎo Chén, Xiǎo Lǐ hé Zhāng xiānsheng dōu shuō Bālí de jiē-shang hěn ānjìng.
                                         (Bālí de jiē-shang)

_____

7. Lǎo Chén, Xiǎo Lǐ hé Zhāng xiānsheng dōu shuō Bālí de jiē-shang hěn ānjìng.
(hěn ānjìng)

_____

8. Lǎo Chén, Xiǎo Lǐ hé Zhāng xiānsheng dōu shuō Bālí de jiē-shang hěn ānjìng.
(Bālí)

_____

9. Lǎo Chén, Xiǎo Lǐ hé Zhāng xiānsheng dōu shuō Bālí de jiē-shang hěn ānjìng.
(Lǎo Chén, Xiǎo Lǐ hé
Zhāng xiānsheng)

_____

10. Lǎo Chén, Xiǎo Lǐ hé Zhāng xiānsheng dōu shuō Bālí de jiē-shang hěn ānjìng.
(Bālí de jiē-shang hěn ānjìng)

_____

Ask an appropriate question for the situations given below.

11. You want to know a friend's telephone number.

_____

12. You want to know whether an acquaintance is married.

_____

13. You want to know whether I like this place.

_____

14. You want to know what her boyfriend looks like.

_____

15. You want to know my opinion.

_____

16. You want to know a stranger's name.

_____

17. You want to know where my company is located.

_____

18. You want to know how to handle the situation.

_____

19. You want to know Xiao Wang's given name.

_____

20. You want to know how your friend's wife is doing.

_____

Give a response to each of the following situations.

21. A friend is departing.

_____

22. The host has given you a cup of tea.

_____

23. You have failed to do something expected of you.

_____

24. An acquaintance comes into your home.

_____

25. A student has answered correctly.

_____

Complete the following sentences with one of the listed grammatical possibilities.

26.   (A) Zhōngguó Guójì Màoyì Zhōngxīn, nǐ zhīdao nàge dìfang ____?
        (B) Zhīdao. Nàr de shèbèi tǐng hǎo.

27.   (A) Dù Qiū bú-zài Běijīng ma?
        (B) ____, tā zài Běijīng.

28.   (A) Guójì Dà Fàndiàn zài Shànghǎi ba?
        (B) ____ zài Shànghǎi. Guójì Dà Fàndiàn zài Bālí.

29.   (A) Yǐqián nǐ bù-xǐhuan Zhōngguó chá ma?
        (B) Duì. Dànshì xiànzài xǐhuan ____.

30.   (A) Nǐ kàn Xiānggǎng zěnmeyàng?
        (B) Jiē-shang dōu tài chǎo ____.

31.   (A) Lín xiáojie zài chéng-li jiāoshū ba.
        (B) Tā bú-zài chéng-li jiāoshū. Tā ____ zài chéng-wài jiāoshū.

32.   (A) Nǐ shàng-guò kè le ma?
        (B) Wǒ hái ____ shàng-guò kè ne.

33.   (A) Huáshèngdùn shi nǎguó de chéngshì?
        (B) Shi Měiguó de ____.

34.   (A) Wǒ hái méi-you gàosu Wáng jīnglǐ. Nǐ ____?
        (B) Wǒ yě hái méi-gàosu tā.

35.   (A) Nǐ tàitai shi Rìběnrén ____?
        (B) Bù. Wǒ tàitai shi Zhōngguórén.

| méi- |
| bú/bù- |
| le |
| ma |
| ne |
| bei |
| ba |
| shì |

Chángchéng

After each sentence, explain in English what is generally being said. You can record your explanations either by writing them down, by recording them on a second tape recorder, or, if you have a language lab tape recorder, by recording your answer in the space provided after each sentence.

Example: Instructor: **Pān jīnglǐ, zhèfēng xìn zěnme bàn?**

                  <u>She's asking Pan, the manager, how to deal with this letter.</u>

36. Tā zài Liú tàitai nàr.

_____

37. Nǐ shi Měiguó nǎr de rén?

_____

38. Tā shi zài yóujú gōngzuò.

_____

39. Tā shuō zài Yǒuyì Shāngdiàn ménkǒu(r) děng wǒmen.

_____

40. Wǒ kàn tā tài wángù le.

_____

41. Wénjùdiàn zài shūdiàn de hòubiān(r).

_____

42. Yóupiào zěnme mǎi?

_____

43. Tā àiren zài Zhōngguó, bú-zài Měiguó.

_____

44. Wǒmen de bàngōngshì shi shísìhào.

_____

45. Shīfu, wǒ mǎi bàozhǐ.

---

46. Qián zhènghǎo.

---

47. Qǐng gěi wǒ ná yífèn(r) bàozhǐ.

---

48. Zhège shāngdiàn tǐng hǎo.

---

49. Tā zhǎngde tǐng piàoliang.

---

50. Tā shi Qīnghuá Dàxué de yánjiūshēng.

Section C: Listening Comprehension

Listen to the segments of conversational exchanges and answer the questions as they are asked. The questions will be either in English or Chinese.

Conversation One
(real life)

1a. Where does this encounter probably take place?
    a). Taiwan
    b). Mainland China
    c). Hong Kong
    d). United States

2a. How many people are buying the same book?
    a). One
    b). Two
    c). Three
    d). Four

3a. How many copies of the book is the man buying?
  a). Twelve
  b). Twenty
  c). Twenty-one
  d). Twenty-two

Conversation One (studio)

1b. Where does this encounter probably take place?
  a). Yóujú
  b). Shūdiàn
  c). Wénjùdiàn
  d). Cāntīng

2b. How many people are in this conversation?
  a). Two
  b). Three
  c). Four
  d). Five

3b. How many copies of the book is the man buying?
  a). Twelve
  b). Twenty
  c). Twenty-one
  d). Twenty-two

Conversation Two

4. Nǚde yào shénme?
  a). Zázhì
  b). Yīngwén bàozhǐ
  c). Zhèr de bàozhǐ
  d). Yīngwén xìnfēng

5. Nánde shuō:
  a). Yīngwén bàozhǐ zài zhèr
  b). Yīngwén bàozhǐ zài nàr
  c). Zhèr méi-you yīngwén bàozhǐ
  d). Zhèr yǒu yīngwén xìnfēng

Conversation Three

6. Nánrén yào gàn shénme?
  a). Mǎi bàozhǐ
  b). Mài bàozhǐ
  c). Kàn bàozhǐ
  d). Ná bàozhǐ

7. Nǚrén shi gàn shénme gōngzuò de?
   a). Gōngrén
   b). Lǎoshī
   c). Shòuhuòyuán
   d). Xuésheng

8. Shuí zhīdao nǎr yǒu bàozhǐ?
   a). Nǚrén zhīdao
   b). Nánrén zhīdao
   c). Tāmen dōu zhīdao
   d). Tāmen dōu bù-zhīdao

Conversation Four

9. Bái Wén shi shuí?
   a). Shi Lǎo Zhāng de lǎoshī
   b). Shi Lǎo Zhāng de qīzi
   c). Shi Lǎo Zhāng de mǔqin
   d). Shi yíge yánjiūshēng

10. Bái Wén zài nǎr?
    a). Tā zài Zhōngguó
    b). Tā zài Měiguó
    c). Tā zài Àodàlìyà
    d). Tā zài Zhījiāgē

11. Lǎo Zhāng zài nǎr?
    a). Tā zài Zhōngguó
    b). Tā zài Měiguó
    c). Tā zài Àodàlìyà
    d). Tā zài Zhījiāgē

12. Bái Wén zuò shénme gōngzuò?
    a). Zuò yánjiū gōngzuò
    b). Zuò yīwù gōngzuò
    c). Zuò mìshū gōngzuò
    d). Zuò guǎnlǐ gōngzuò

Conversation Five

13. What is the woman looking for?
    a). The dining car
    b). The International Hotel
    c). A bookstore
    d). A shop

14. Where is it?
    a). In front of the International Hotel
    b). Beyond the International Hotel
    c). Behind the International Hotel
    d). Next to the International Hotel

Conversation Six

15. "Restroom" zhōngwén zěnme shuō?
    a). Qǐngwèn
    b). Jiùshì
    c). Cèsuǒ
    d). Xiūxishì

16. Shuí zhīdao cèsuǒ zài nǎr?
    a). Yuēhàn zhīdao
    b). Lǎo Lǐ zhīdao
    c). Yuēhàn hé Lǎo Lǐ dōu zhīdao
    d). Yuēhàn hé Lǎo Lǐ dōu bù-zhīdao

17. Cèsuǒ zài nǎr?
    a). Zài wàibiān(r)
    b). Zài lǐbiān(r)
    c). Zài Zhījiāgē
    d). Zài hòubiān(r)

Conversation Seven

18. Nánrén xìng shénme?
    a). Xìng Lín
    b). Xìng Shǐmìsī
    c). Xìng Lǐ
    d). Xìng Shǐ

19. Shuí bú-zài zhèr?
    a). Nánrén de qīzi bú-zài zhèr
    b). Nǚrén de xiānsheng bú-zài zhèr
    c). Tāmen de àiren dōu bú-zài zhèr
    d). Nánrén, nǚrén dōu bú-zài zhèr

20. Shuí zài Běijīng?
    a). Nánrén de qīzi zài Běijīng
    b). Nǚrén de xiānsheng zài Běijīng
    c). Nánrén zài Běijīng
    d). Nǚrén zài Běijīng

Appendices

The vocabulary introduced in this program is presented in three glossaries.

Unit/Stage Glossary: The words and phrases in each stage are presented according to the part of speech (POS). This glossary will allow you to review vocabulary for a particular lesson.

Pinyin **Glossary**: Words and phrases are listed according to their conventional spellings. *Pinyin* follows the order of the English alphabet.

English Glossary: The English equivalents to the vocabulary are listed in the right column.

This list begins with functional descriptions which are indicated by parentheses. After these, the English equivalents are listed according to alphabetical order.

Unit/Stage Glossary

Pīnyīn	Hànzì	POS	Stage	English
lǎoshī	老师/老師	adr	0.1.	*teacher*
tóngxuémen	同学们/同學們	adr	0.1.	*fellow students*
lǎoshī	老师/老師	noun	0.1.	*teacher [m: -gè, -wèi]*
tóngxué	同学/同學	noun	0.1.	*schoolmate [m: -gè, -wèi]*
tóngxuémen	同学们/同學們	noun	0.1.	*students of a particular school*
hǎo	好	phr	0.1.	*(greeting, ex: Nǐ hǎo.)*
nǐ	你	pron	0.1.	*you*
nǐmen	你们/你們	pron	0.1.	*you (pl.)*
bú-duì	不对/不對	phr	0.2.	*not correct*
duì le	对了/對了	phr	0.2.	*correct*
qǐng	请/請	prvb	0.2.	*please (do something)*
le	了	sptc	0.2.	*(new situation)*
xiànzài	现在/現在	time	0.2.	*now*
qǐng	请/請	verb	0.2.	*request, invite*
zuò	坐	verb	0.2.	*sit*
shàng=kè	上课/上課	vobj	0.2.	*attend class, give a lesson*
gēnzhe	跟着/跟著	phr	0.3.	*follow*
lǎo péngyou	老朋友	phr	0.3.	*old friend*
dàjiā	大家	pron	0.3.	*all, everybody*
wǒ	我	pron	0.3.	*I, me*
shuō	说/說	verb	0.3.	*speak, say*
tīng	听/聽	verb	0.3.	*listen*
zài	再	adv	0.4.	*again*

---

adj=adjective; *adr*=term of address; *adv*=adverb; *co-v*=co-verb; *comp*=complement; *conj*=conjunction; *dem*=demonstrative; *fam*=family name; *intr*=interjection; *mark*=grammatical marker; *mdl*=modal; *meas*=measure; *mnde*=modifying noun; *mptc*=modification particle; *nphr*=noun phrase; *num*=number; *phr*=phrase; *plce*=place; *plwd*=place word; *pn*=place name; *pre*=prefix; *prep*=preposition; *prn*=proper noun; *pron*=pronoun; *prvb*=pre-verb; *ques*=question word/phrase; *sptc*=sentence particle; *sufx*=suffix; *sv*=state verb; *timd*=time-(duration) word; *time*=time word; *timp*=time phrase; *tsfx*=time suffix; *vdir*=verb of direction; *vobj*=verb with set object; *vpot*=verb with potential

biàn	遍	meas	0.4.	*(one complete activity/action)*
zhōngwén	中文	noun	0.4.	*Chinese language*
yī, yí, yì	一	num	0.4.	*one, 1*
zěnme	怎么/怎麼	ques	0.4.	*how (to do something)*
dàsuàn	大蒜	noun	0.5.	*garlic [m: -kē, -tóu]*
wèntí	问题/問題	noun	0.5.	*question, problem [m: -gè]*
yīngwén	英文	noun	0.5.	*English language*
huídá	回答	verb	0.5.	*answer*
wèn	问/問	verb	0.5.	*ask*
tàng	烫/燙	adj	0.6.	*scalding hot*
táng	糖	noun	0.6.	*sugar/candy [m: -kuài, -kē]*
tāng	汤/湯	noun	0.6.	*soup*
Tāng tài tàng le!	汤太烫了！/ 湯太燙了！	phr	0.6.	*The soup is scalding hot!*
tǎng	躺	verb	0.6.	*lie down*
bù-, bú-	不	mark	0.7.	*(negates verbs and adjectives)*
ma	吗/嗎	sptc	0.7.	*(question)*
dǒng	懂	sv	0.7.	*understand*
zhīdao	知道	sv	0.7.	*know, have the information*
méi-	没/沒	mark	0.8.	*(negates yǒu)*
bú-kèqi	不客气/不客氣	phr	0.8.	*Don't be so polite, You're welcome. (response to xièxie)*

adj=adjective; *adr*=term of address; *adv*=adverb; *co-v*=co-verb; *comp*=complement; *conj*=conjunction; *dem*=demonstrative; *fam*=family name; *intr*=interjection; *mark*=grammatical marker; *mdl*=modal; *meas*=measure; *mnde*=modifying noun; *mptc*=modification particle; *nphr*=noun phrase; *num*=number; *phr*=phrase; *plce*=place; *plwd*=place word; *pn*=place name; *pre*=prefix; *prep*=preposition; *prn*=proper noun; *pron*=pronoun; *prvb*=pre-verb; *ques*=question word/phrase; *sptc*=sentence particle; *sufx*=suffix; *sv*=state verb; *timd*=time-(duration) word; *time*=time word; *timp*=time phrase; *tsfx*=time suffix; *vdir*=verb of direction; *vobj*=verb with set object; *vpot*=verb with potential

xièxie	谢谢/謝謝	phr	0.8.	*thanks (accept with gratitude)*
zàijiàn	再见/再見	phr	0.8.	*goodbye*
méi	没/沒	sv	0.8.	*not have, lacks (= méi-yǒu)*
yǒu	有	sv	0.8.	*have, there (exists)*
xià=kè	下课/下課	vobj	0.8.	*end class, dismiss class*
tòu	透	adj	0.9.	*penetrate*
tū	凸	adj	0.9.	*protruding*
tái	台/臺	noun	0.9.	*platform*
tǎn	毯	noun	0.9.	*blanket*
tàn	炭	noun	0.9.	*charcoal*
táo	桃	noun	0.9.	*peach [m: -gè]*
tǔ	土	noun	0.9.	*soil*
tǎo	讨/討	verb	0.9.	*demand*
tōu	偷	verb	0.9.	*steal*
lǎo + <u>surname</u>	老	adr	1.1.	*older friend*
nǔshì	女士	adr	1.1.	*Ms. (formal)*
tàitai	太太	adr	1.1.	*Mrs.*
xiānsheng	先生	adr	1.1.	*Mr., Honorable*
xiǎo + <u>surname</u>	小	adr	1.1.	*younger friend*
xiáojie	小姐	adr	1.1.	*Miss*
Bái	白	fam	1.1.	*Chinese surname (white)*
Huáng	黄/黃	fam	1.1.	*Chinese surname (yellow)*
Lǐ	李	fam	1.1.	*Chinese surname (plum)*
Liú	刘/劉	fam	1.1.	*Chinese surname*
Wáng	王	fam	1.1.	*Chinese surname (king)*
Zhāng	张/張	fam	1.1.	*Chinese surname*

adj=adjective; *adr*=term of address; *adv*=adverb; *co-v*=co-verb; *comp*=complement; *conj*=conjunction; *dem*=demonstrative; *fam*=family name; *intr*=interjection; *mark*=grammatical marker; *mdl*=modal; *meas*=measure; *mnde*=modifying noun; *mptc*=modification particle; *nphr*=noun phrase; *num*=number; *phr*=phrase; *plce*=place; *plwd*=place word; *pn*=place name; *pre*=prefix; *prep*=preposition; *prn*=proper noun; *pron*=pronoun; *prvb*=pre-verb; *ques*=question word/phrase; *sptc*=sentence particle; *sufx*=suffix; *sv*=state verb; *timd*=time-(duration) word; *time*=time word; *timp*=time phrase; *tsfx*=time suffix; *vdir*=verb of direction; *vobj*=verb with set object; *vpot*=verb with potential

wèn X hǎo	问X好/問X好	phr	1.1.	*remember me to X, greet X*
tóngzhì	同志	adr	1.2.	*comrade*
Ōuyáng	欧阳/歐陽	fam	1.2.	*Chinese surname*
Chén	陈/陳	fam	1.2.	*Chinese surname*
Dù	杜	fam	1.2.	*Chinese surname*
Fāng	方	fam	1.2.	*Chinese surname (square)*
Lín	林	fam	1.2.	*Chinese surname (forest)*
Shī	施	fam	1.2.	*Chinese surname*
Wú	吴/吳	fam	1.2.	*Chinese surname*
Zhào	赵/趙	fam	1.2.	*Chinese surname*
ò	哦	intr	1.2.	*oh! (implies recognition "I see")*
guìxìng	贵姓/貴姓	phr	1.2.	*What is your family name?*
qǐngwèn	请问/請問	phr	1.2.	*May I ask a question?*
nín	您	pron	1.2.	*you (polite)*
tā	他	pron	1.2.	*he, him*
tā	她	pron	1.2.	*she, her*
xìng	姓	sv	1.2.	*have the family name X*
fùjīnglǐ	副经理/副經理	adr	1.3.	*assistant manager*
jīnglǐ	经理/經理	adr	1.3.	*manager, boss*
mìshū	秘书/秘書	adr	1.3.	*secretary*
Huà	华/華	fam	1.3.	*Chinese surname*
fùjīnglǐ	副经理/副經理	noun	1.3.	*assistant manager [m: -gè, -wèi]*
jīnglǐ	经理/經理	noun	1.3.	*manager [m: -gè, -wèi]*

adj=adjective; *adr*=term of address; *adv*=adverb; *co-v*=co-verb; *comp*=complement; *conj*=conjunction; *dem*=demonstrative; *fam*=family name; *intr*=interjection; *mark*=grammatical marker; *mdl*=modal; *meas*=measure; *mnde*=modifying noun; *mptc*=modification particle; *nphr*=noun phrase; *num*=number; *phr*=phrase; *plce*=place; *plwd*=place word; *pn*=place name; *pre*=prefix; *prep*=preposition; *prn*=proper noun; *pron*=pronoun; *prvb*=pre-verb; *ques*=question word/phrase; *sptc*=sentence particle; *sufx*=suffix; *sv*=state verb; *timd*=time-(duration) word; *time*=time word; *timp*=time phrase; *tsfx*=time suffix; *vdir*=verb of direction; *vobj*=verb with set object; *vpot*=verb with potential

míngzi	名字	noun	1.3.	*name [m: -gè]*
mìshū	秘书/秘書	noun	1.3.	*secretary [m: -gè, -wèi]*
rén	人	noun	1.3.	*person [m: -gè]*
xuésheng	学生/學生	noun	1.3.	*student [m: -gè, -wèi]*
shénme rén	什么人/甚麼人	phr	1.3.	*(asking about a person's profession or status)*
shéi/shuí	谁/誰	ques	1.3.	*who, whom*
shénme	什么/甚麼	ques	1.3.	*what*
jiào X	叫X	sv	1.3.	*named, be called X*
shì	是	sv	1.3.	*be, is, am, are, was, were*
bù-shūfu	不舒服	adj	1.4.	*unwell, indisposed, uncomfortable*
cōngming	聪明/聰明	adj	1.4.	*intelligent, clever*
hǎo	好	adj	1.4.	*fine, good, okay*
kāitong	开通/開通	adj	1.4.	*open-minded*
lǎn	懒/懶	adj	1.4.	*lazy*
lèi	累	adj	1.4.	*tired*
línghuó	灵活/靈活	adj	1.4.	*physically or mentally flexible, agile*
luōsuo	罗嗦/囉嗦	adj	1.4.	*talkative*
máng	忙	adj	1.4.	*busy*
nǔlì	努力	adj	1.4.	*hard working*
shūfu	舒服	adj	1.4.	*comfortable*
wángù	顽固/頑固	adj	1.4.	*stubborn, hard-headed*
dōu	都	adv	1.4.	*all (at head of predicate)*
hěn	很	adv	1.4.	*very (pre-adjective)*
yě	也	adv	1.4.	*also (before predicate)*
tóngshì	同事	noun	1.4.	*colleague*

adj=adjective; *adr*=term of address; *adv*=adverb; *co-v*=co-verb; *comp*=complement; *conj*=conjunction; *dem*=demonstrative; *fam*=family name; *intr*=interjection; *mark*=grammatical marker; *mdl*=modal; *meas*=measure; *mnde*=modifying noun; *mptc*=modification particle; *nphr*=noun phrase; *num*=number; *phr*=phrase; *plce*=place; *plwd*=place word; *pn*=place name; *pre*=prefix; *prep*=preposition; *prn*=proper noun; *pron*=pronoun; *prvb*=pre-verb; *ques*=question word/phrase; *sptc*=sentence particle; *sufx*=suffix; *sv*=state verb; *timd*=time-(duration) word; *time*=time word; *timp*=time phrase; *tsfx*=time suffix; *vdir*=verb of direction; *vobj*=verb with set object; *vpot*=verb with potential

tóngshìmen	同事们/同事們	noun	1.4.	colleagues
gǎnmào le	感冒了	phr	1.4	catch cold, have the flu
yǒu yìdiǎn(r)	有一点儿/ 有一點兒	phr	1.4.	somewhat (undesirable attribute)
tāmen	她们/她們	pron	1.4.	they, them (female)
tāmen	他们/他們	pron	1.4.	they, them (gender free)
X zěnmeyàng	X 怎么样/X 怎麼樣	ques	1.4.	how is X, what is X like
le	了	sptc	1.4.	(indicates changes)
ne	呢	sptc	1.4.	(question)
-men	们/們	sufx	1.4.	(pluralizes definite human nouns)
yǐqián	以前	time	1.4.	before, previously
zuìjìn	最近	time	1.4.	recently
āngzāng	肮脏/骯髒	adj	1.5.	dirty, foul
ānjìng	安静/安靜	adj	1.5.	peaceful, quiet
è	饿/餓	adj	1.5.	hungry
kě	渴	adj	1.5.	thirsty
chìzi	翅子	noun	1.5.	fin (usually from the shark)
jī	鸡/雞	noun	1.5.	chicken [m: -zhī]
jīn	金	noun	1.5.	gold, money
mǎ	马/馬	noun	1.5.	horse [m: -pǐ]
mántou	馒头/饅頭	noun	1.5.	steamed bun [m: -gè]
mèng	梦/夢	noun	1.5.	dream [m: -gè]
rénmín	人民	noun	1.5.	people, masses
rìzi	日子	noun	1.5.	days on the calendar
sè	色	noun	1.5.	lust, sensuality
shēngyīn	声音/聲音	noun	1.5.	sound [m: -zhǒng]
shìzi	式子	noun	1.5.	math equation [m: -gè]

adj=adjective; *adr*=term of address; *adv*=adverb; *co-v*=co-verb; *comp*=complement; *conj*=conjunction; *dem*=demonstrative; *fam*=family name; *intr*=interjection; *mark*=grammatical marker; *mdl*=modal; *meas*=measure; *mnde*=modifying noun; *mptc*=modification particle; *nphr*=noun phrase; *num*=number; *phr*=phrase; *plce*=place; *plwd*=place word; *pn*=place name; *pre*=prefix; *prep*=preposition; *prn*=proper noun; *pron*=pronoun; *prvb*=pre-verb; *ques*=question word/phrase; *sptc*=sentence particle; *sufx*=suffix; *sv*=state verb; *timd*=time-(duration) word; *time*=time word; *timp*=time phrase; *tsfx*=time suffix; *vdir*=verb of direction; *vobj*=verb with set object; *vpot*=verb with potential

sī	丝/絲	noun	1.5.	silk
yīngxióng	英雄	noun	1.5.	hero [m: -gè, -wèi]
zhìzi	稚子	noun	1.5.	young child
zī	资/資	noun	1.5.	capital
sà	卅	num	1.5.	thirty
sì	四	num	1.5.	four, 4
Chī ba.	吃吧。	phr	1.5.	Please eat.
Hē ba.	喝吧。	phr	1.5.	Please have a drink!
Wǒ è le.	我饿了。/我餓了。	phr	1.5.	I am hungry.
Wǒ kě le.	我渴了。	phr	1.5.	I am thirsty.
cī	呲	verb	1.5.	give a tongue-lashing to
mǎi	买/買	verb	1.5.	buy
mèn	焖/燜	verb	1.5.	braise, stew, cook in a covered pot over a low heat
ǎi	矮	adj	1.6.	short (height)
dà	大	adj	1.6.	large, great, old
gāo	高	adj	1.6.	tall
lǎo	老	adj	1.6.	old (anim), obsolete (inan)
miànshóu/ miànshú	面熟	adj	1.6.	familiar looking
nánkàn	难看/難看	adj	1.6.	unattractive, ugly
niánqīng	年轻/年輕	adj	1.6.	young (human)
pàng	胖	adj	1.6.	fat, plump
piàoliang	漂亮	adj	1.6.	attractive
shòu	瘦	adj	1.6.	slight (physical build), thin
xiǎo	小	adj	1.6.	small, young
zhuàng	壮/壯	adj	1.6.	stout, strong build

adj=adjective; adr=term of address; adv=adverb; co-v=co-verb; comp=complement; conj=conjunction; dem=demonstrative; fam=family name; intr=interjection; mark=grammatical marker; mdl=modal; meas=measure; mnde=modifying noun; mptc=modification particle; nphr=noun phrase; num=number; phr=phrase; plce=place; plwd=place word; pn=place name; pre=prefix; prep=preposition; prn=proper noun; pron=pronoun; prvb=pre-verb; ques=question word/phrase; sptc=sentence particle; sufx=suffix; sv=state verb; timd=time-(duration) word; time=time word; timp=time phrase; tsfx=time suffix; vdir=verb of direction; vobj=verb with set object; vpot=verb with potential

jiàoshòu	教授	adr	1.6.	*professor*
bǐjiào	比较/比較	adv	1.6.	*relatively, comparatively*
hé	和	conj	1.6.	*(joins nouns)*
nà/nèi	那	dem	1.6.	*that*
zhè/zhèi	这/這	dem	1.6.	*this*
gè	个/個	meas	1.6.	*(general measure for persons)*
wèi	位	meas	1.6.	*(persons-polite measure)*
nánde	男的	noun	1.6.	*man [m: -gè]*
nánrén	男人	noun	1.6.	*man [m: -gè]*
nǔde	女的	noun	1.6.	*woman [m: -gè]*
nǔrén	女人	noun	1.6.	*woman [m: -gè]*
rén	人	noun	1.6.	*person, people*
X zhǎngde zěnmeyàng	X长得怎么样/ X長得怎麼樣	phr	1.6.	*What does X look like?*
zhǎngde + adj.	长得/長得	phr	1.6.	*look(s) adj. (physical attribute)*
ba	吧	sptc	1.6.	*(assumes-state, suggests-event)*
bǐ	比	verb	1.6.	*compare to*
bǐjiào	比较/比較	verb	1.6.	*compare*
bèn	笨	adj	1.7.	*stupid, awkward*
dàfang	大方	adj	1.7.	*generous, liberal-minded*
jǐnzhāng	紧张/緊張	adj	1.7.	*anxious, nervous, tense*
nénggàn	能干/能幹	adj	1.7.	*competent, able*

adj=adjective; *adr*=term of address; *adv*=adverb; *co-v*=co-verb; *comp*=complement; *conj*=conjunction; *dem*=demonstrative; *fam*=family name; *intr*=interjection; *mark*=grammatical marker; *mdl*=modal; *meas*=measure; *mnde*=modifying noun; *mptc*=modification particle; *nphr*=noun phrase; *num*=number; *phr*=phrase; *plce*=place; *plwd*=place word; *pn*=place name; *pre*=prefix; *prep*=preposition; *prn*=proper noun; *pron*=pronoun; *prvb*=pre-verb; *ques*=question word/phrase; *sptc*=sentence particle; *sufx*=suffix; *sv*=state verb; *timd*=time-(duration) word; *time*=time word; *timp*=time phrase; *tsfx*=time suffix; *vdir*=verb of direction; *vobj*=verb with set object; *vpot*=verb with potential

píngjìng	平静/平靜	adj	1.7.	*calm, tranquil, composed*
qīngchu	清楚	adj	1.7.	*clear, clearheaded, aware*
wúnéng	无能/無能	adj	1.7.	*incompetent*
xiǎoqi	小气/小氣	adj	1.7.	*petty, stingy, narrow-minded*
nǎ/něi	哪	dem	1.7.	*which*
de	的	mptc	1.7.	*(after modifier of nominal)*
kèren	客人	noun	1.7.	*guest, visitor, customer*
bù-qīngchu	不清楚	phr	1.7.	*unclear, unaware*
méi-kòng	没空	phr	1.7.	*busy, do not have free time*
yòu <u>adj1</u> yòu <u>adj2</u>	又<u>adj1</u>又<u>adj2</u>	phr	1.7.	*both <u>adj1</u> and <u>adj2</u>*
yǒu kòng	有空	phr	1.7.	*have free time*
wǒmen	我们/我們	pron	1.7.	*we, us*
zánmen	咱们/咱們	pron	1.7.	*we, us (includes the addressee)*
nǎge/něige	哪个	ques	1.7.	*which one*
nǎwèi/něiwèi	哪位	ques	1.7.	*which person, who*
jiùshi	就是	sv	1.7.	*(emphatic) am, are, is, was, were*
huài	坏/壞	adj	1.8.	*broken*
kùn	困	adj	1.8.	*sleepy*
suān	酸	adj	1.8.	*sour*
wā	哇	intr	1.8.	*(expression of wonderment)*
duǒ	朵	meas	1.8.	*(measure for flowers)*
bózi	脖子	noun	1.8.	*neck*

adj=adjective; *adr*=term of address; *adv*=adverb; *co-v*=co-verb; *comp*=complement; *conj*=conjunction; *dem*=demonstrative; *fam*=family name; *intr*=interjection; *mark*=grammatical marker; *mdl*=modal; *meas*=measure; *mnde*=modifying noun; *mptc*=modification particle; *nphr*=noun phrase; *num*=number; *phr*=phrase; *plce*=place; *plwd*=place word; *pn*=place name; *pre*=prefix; *prep*=preposition; *prn*=proper noun; *pron*=pronoun; *prvb*=pre-verb; *ques*=question word/phrase; *sptc*=sentence particle; *sufx*=suffix; *sv*=state verb; *timd*=time-(duration) word; *time*=time word; *timp*=time phrase; *tsfx*=time suffix; *vdir*=verb of direction; *vobj*=verb with set object; *vpot*=verb with potential

bùzi	步子	noun	1.8.	*step*
dùzi	肚子	noun	1.8.	*belly*
fó	佛	noun	1.8.	*Buddha*
hóngshāo qiézi	红烧茄子/ 紅燒茄子	noun	1.8.	*Chinese entrée: eggplant braised in soy sauce*
huā	花	noun	1.8.	*flower [m: -duǒ, -zhī]*
huánzi	环子/環子	noun	1.8.	*ring [m: -gè]*
huǒ	火	noun	1.8.	*fire [m: -tuán, -bǎ]*
jiǎozi	饺子/餃子	noun	1.8.	*dumpling [m: -gè]*
jiǔ	酒	noun	1.8.	*alcohol beverage [m: -píng(r), -bēi]*
kùzi	裤子/褲子	noun	1.8.	*pants, trousers [m: -tiáo] (v: -chuān)*
lóng	龙/龍	noun	1.8.	*dragon [m: -tiáo]*
luàn	乱/亂	noun	1.8.	*chaos*
lúnzi	轮子/輪子	noun	1.8.	*wheel [m: -gè]*
lǜ	律	noun	1.8.	*law*
máo	毛	noun	1.8.	*fur, wool, bodyhair [m: -gēn]*
méi	眉	noun	1.8.	*eyebrow [m: -dào]*
mǐ	米	noun	1.8.	*rice [m: -kē, -lì]*
miàn	面	noun	1.8.	*noodle [m: -wǎn]*
mógu	蘑菇	noun	1.8.	*mushroom [m: -gè]*
pózi	婆子	noun	1.8.	*old woman [m: -gè]*
pùzi	铺子/鋪子	noun	1.8.	*shop [m: -gè]*
qiézi	茄子	noun	1.8.	*eggplant [m: -gè]*
ròuwán(r)	肉丸(儿)/ 肉丸(兒)	noun	1.8.	*meatball [m: -gè]*

adj=adjective; *adr*=term of address; *adv*=adverb; *co-v*=co-verb; *comp*=complement; *conj*=conjunction; *dem*=demonstrative; *fam*=family name; *intr*=interjection; *mark*=grammatical marker; *mdl*=modal; *meas*=measure; *mnde*=modifying noun; *mptc*=modification particle; *nphr*=noun phrase; *num*=number; *phr*=phrase; *plce*=place; *plwd*=place word; *pn*=place name; *pre*=prefix; *prep*=preposition; *prn*=proper noun; *pron*=pronoun; *prvb*=pre-verb; *ques*=question word/phrase; *sptc*=sentence particle; *sufx*=suffix; *sv*=state verb; *timd*=time-(duration) word; *time*=time word; *timp*=time phrase; *tsfx*=time suffix; *vdir*=verb of direction; *vobj*=verb with set object; *vpot*=verb with potential

suàn	蒜	noun	1.8.	*garlic [m: -bàn(r), -tóu]*
sùzi	粟子	noun	1.8.	*millet (also xiǎomǐ)*
tuǐ	腿	noun	1.8.	*leg [m: -tiáo]*
tùzi	兔子	noun	1.8.	*rabbit [m: -zhī]*
wánzi	丸子	noun	1.8.	*pill, ball [m: -gè]*
wěiba	尾巴	noun	1.8.	*tail [m: -tiáo, -gè]*
wénzi	蚊子	noun	1.8.	*mosquito [m: -zhī]*
xiā	虾/蝦	noun	1.8.	*shrimp [m: -zhī]*
xiǎomāo	小猫/小貓	noun	1.8.	*kitten [m: -zhī]*
xiézi	鞋子	noun	1.8.	*shoe(s) [m: -shuāng, -zhī]*
xióng	熊	noun	1.8.	*bear [m: -zhī, -tóu]*
xióngmāo	熊猫/熊貓	noun	1.8.	*panda [m: -zhī]*
yán	盐/鹽	noun	1.8.	*salt*
yàozi	鹞子/鷂子	noun	1.8.	*sparrow hawk*
yāzi	鸭子/鴨子	noun	1.8.	*duck [m: -zhī]*
yēzi	椰子	noun	1.8.	*coconut [m: -gè]*
yòuzi	柚子	noun	1.8.	*grapefruit, pomelo, shaddock [m: -gè]*
yú	鱼/魚	noun	1.8.	*fish [m: -tiáo]*
yuànzi	院子	noun	1.8.	*yard [m: -gè]*
yuè	月	noun	1.8.	*month [m: -gè]*
zhǐhuán	指环/指環	noun	1.8.	*finger ring [m: -gè]*
wǔ	五	num	1.8.	*five, 5*
wài	外	plwd	1.8.	*outside*
huáiyùn	怀孕/懷孕	verb	1.8.	*pregnant*
lüèduó	掠夺/掠奪	verb	1.8.	*plunder, rob*
mái	埋	verb	1.8.	*bury*
móuhuà	谋划/謀劃	verb	1.8.	*plan, scheme*

adj=adjective; *adr*=term of address; *adv*=adverb; *co-v*=co-verb; *comp*=complement; *conj*=conjunction; *dem*=demonstrative; *fam*=family name; *intr*=interjection; *mark*=grammatical marker; *mdl*=modal; *meas*=measure; *mnde*=modifying noun; *mptc*=modification particle; *nphr*=noun phrase; *num*=number; *phr*=phrase; *plce*=place; *plwd*=place word; *pn*=place name; *pre*=prefix; *prep*=preposition; *prn*=proper noun; *pron*=pronoun; *prvb*=pre-verb; *ques*=question word/phrase; *sptc*=sentence particle; *sufx*=suffix; *sv*=state verb; *timd*=time-(duration) word; *time*=time word; *timp*=time phrase; *tsfx*=time suffix; *vdir*=verb of direction; *vobj*=verb with set object; *vpot*=verb with potential

yòng	用	verb	1.8.	*use*
xiàozhǎng	校长/校長	adr	1.9.	*president (college), principal (school)*
yuànzhǎng	院长/院長	adr	1.9.	*dean (college), director (hospital)*
zhǔrèn	主任	adr	1.9.	*chairman, director (of an office)*
zhēn	真	adv	1.9.	*really, very, truly*
duìbuqǐ	对不起/對不起	phr	1.9.	*sorry (for not meeting expectations)*
huānyíng	欢迎/歡迎	phr	1.9.	*welcome (to outsiders)*
Wǒ gěi nǐmen jièshào yíxià.	我给你们介绍一下。/ 我給你們介紹一下。	phr	1.9.	*Let me introduce you.*
zìwǒ jièshào yíxià	自我介绍一下/ 自我介紹一下	phr	1.9.	*let me introduce myself*
dàxué	大学/大學	plce	1.9.	*university [m: -suǒ, -gè]*
gōngsī	公司	plce	1.9.	*company [m: -jiā, -gè]*
xuéxiào	学校/學校	plce	1.9.	*school [m: -suǒ, -gè]*
xuéyuàn	学院/學院	plce	1.9.	*college, institute [m: -gè]*
Běijīng Dàxué	北京大学/ 北京大學	pn	1.9.	*Beijing University (Beijing, China)*
Huáměi Màoyì Gōngsī	华美贸易公司/ 華美貿易公司	pn	1.9.	*Sino-American Trade Company*
Qīnghuá Dàxué	清华大学/ 清華大學	pn	1.9.	*Qinghua University (Beijing, China)*
Rénmín Dàxué	人民大学/ 人民大學	pn	1.9.	*People's University (Beijing, China)*

adj=adjective; *adr*=term of address; *adv*=adverb; *co-v*=co-verb; *comp*=complement; *conj*=conjunction; *dem*=demonstrative; *fam*=family name; *intr*=interjection; *mark*=grammatical marker; *mdl*=modal; *meas*=measure; *mnde*=modifying noun; *mptc*=modification particle; *nphr*=noun phrase; *num*=number; *phr*=phrase; *plce*=place; *plwd*=place word; *pn*=place name; *pre*=prefix; *prep*=preposition; *prn*=proper noun; *pron*=pronoun; *prvb*=pre-verb; *ques*=question word/phrase; *sptc*=sentence particle; *sufx*=suffix; *sv*=state verb; *timd*=time-(duration) word; *time*=time word; *timp*=time phrase; *tsfx*=time suffix; *vdir*=verb of direction; *vobj*=verb with set object; *vpot*=verb with potential

shīfàn dàxué	师范大学/ 師範大學	pn	1.9.	*normal (teachers) university*
zìwǒ	自我	pron	1.9.	*(reflexive) myself*
ā (yā, na)	啊 (呀，哪)	sptc	1.9.	*(emphasizes intentions)*
<u>V</u> yíxià	<u>V</u>一下	timd	1.9.	*try to <u>V</u> , <u>V</u> for a while*
chēnghu	称呼/稱呼	verb	1.9.	*call, address*
jièshào	介绍/介紹	verb	1.9.	*introduce*
tǐng	挺	adv	2.1.	*very, really*
zài	在	co-v	2.1.	*(at the place of action, event or state)*
dìfang	地方	noun	2.1.	*place, area*
shèbèi	设备/設備	noun	2.1.	*equipment*
shénme dìfang	什么地方/ 甚麼地方	phr	2.1.	*where, what place*
Bālí	巴黎	pn	2.1.	*Paris*
Běijīng	北京	pn	2.1.	*Beijing, Peking*
Dōngjīng	东京/東京	pn	2.1.	*Tokyo*
Guójì Dà Fàndiàn	国际大饭店/ 國際大飯店	pn	2.1.	*International Hotel*
Huáshèngdùn	华盛顿/華盛頓	pn	2.1.	*Washington D.C.*
Jiùjīnshān	旧金山/舊金山	pn	2.1.	*San Francisco*
Lúndūn	伦敦/倫敦	pn	2.1.	*London (Yīngguó)*
Niǔyuē	纽约/紐約	pn	2.1.	*New York*
Shànghǎi	上海	pn	2.1.	*Shanghai*
Shǒudū Jùchǎng	首都剧场/首都劇場	pn	2.1.	*Capital Theatre*
Xiānggǎng	香港	pn	2.1.	*Hong Kong*
Zhījiāgē	芝加哥	pn	2.1.	*Chicago*

adj=adjective; *adr*=term of address; *adv*=adverb; *co-v*=co-verb; *comp*=complement; *conj*=conjunction; *dem*=demonstrative; *fam*=family name; *intr*=interjection; *mark*=grammatical marker; *mdl*=modal; *meas*=measure; *mnde*=modifying noun; *mptc*=modification particle; *nphr*=noun phrase; *num*=number; *phr*=phrase; *plce*=place; *plwd*=place word; *pn*=place name; *pre*=prefix; *prep*=preposition; *prn*=proper noun; *pron*=pronoun; *prvb*=pre-verb; *ques*=question word/phrase; *sptc*=sentence particle; *sufx*=suffix; *sv*=state verb; *timd*=time-(duration) word; *time*=time word; *timp*=time phrase; *tsfx*=time suffix; *vdir*=verb of direction; *vobj*=verb with set object; *vpot*=verb with potential

Zhōngguó Guójì Màoyì Zhōngxīn	中国国际贸易中心/中國國際貿易中心	pn	2.1.	*China International Trade Center*
nǎli	哪里/哪裏	ques	2.1.	*where*
nǎr	哪儿/哪兒	ques	2.1.	*where*
rènshi	认识/認識	sv	2.1.	*know, recognize*
xǐhuan	喜欢/喜歡	sv	2.1.	*like, appreciate*
zài	在	sv	2.1.	*be at/in/on, exist*
shì	是	mark	2.2.	*(emphasizes following element in a phrase)*
gōngzuò	工作	noun	2.2.	*work, job*
guǎnlǐ	管理	noun	2.2.	*management*
guójiā	国家/國家	noun	2.2.	*nation, country [m: -gè]*
jiàoxué	教学/教學	noun	2.2.	*teaching*
kuàijì	会计/會計	noun	2.2.	*accountant, accounting [m: -gè, -wèi]*
línshígōng	临时工/臨時工	noun	2.2.	*part-time work (worker), temporary work (worker) [m: -gè, -wèi]*
shèjì	设计/設計	noun	2.2.	*design, plan, scheme [m: -gè, -zhǒng]*
yánjiū	研究	noun	2.2.	*research*
yīwù	医务/醫務	noun	2.2.	*medical duties, medical profession*
zuò X gōngzuò	做X工作	phr	2.2.	*work at/as X*
gōngchǎng	工厂/工廠	plce	2.2.	*factory [m: -gè, - jiā]*
jiā	家	plce	2.2.	*family, home, house [m: -gè]*

adj=adjective; *adr*=term of address; *adv*=adverb; *co-v*=co-verb; *comp*=complement; *conj*=conjunction; *dem*=demonstrative; *fam*=family name; *intr*=interjection; *mark*=grammatical marker; *mdl*=modal; *meas*=measure; *mnde*=modifying noun; *mptc*=modification particle; *nphr*=noun phrase; *num*=number; *phr*=phrase; *plce*=place; *plwd*=place word; *pn*=place name; *pre*=prefix; *prep*=preposition; *prn*=proper noun; *pron*=pronoun; *prvb*=pre-verb; *ques*=question word/phrase; *sptc*=sentence particle; *sufx*=suffix; *sv*=state verb; *timd*=time-(duration) word; *time*=time word; *timp*=time phrase; *tsfx*=time suffix; *vdir*=verb of direction; *vobj*=verb with set object; *vpot*=verb with potential

shāngdiàn	商店	plce	2.2.	store, shop [m: -gè, -jiā]
yīyuàn	医院/醫院	plce	2.2.	hospital [m: -gè, - jiā]
Àodàlìyà	澳大利亚/澳大利亞	pn	2.2.	Australia
Fùdàn Dàxué	复旦大学/復旦大學	pn	2.2.	Fudan University (Shanghai, China)
Gēlúnbù	哥伦布/哥倫布	pn	2.2.	Columbus
Guǎngzhōu	广州/廣州	pn	2.2.	city in Guangdong; Canton
Jiānádà	加拿大	pn	2.2.	Canada
Jìnán Dàxué	暨南大学/暨南大學	pn	2.2.	Jinan University (Guangzhou, China)
Luòshānjī	洛杉矶/洛杉磯	pn	2.2.	Los Angeles (Jiāzhōu)
Měiguó	美国/美國	pn	2.2.	United States, America
Qīngdǎo	青岛/青島	pn	2.2.	Tsingtao (city in Shandong)
Rìběn	日本	pn	2.2.	Japan
Wǔhàn	武汉/武漢	pn	2.2.	city in Hubei
Yīngguó	英国/英國	pn	2.2.	England
Zhōngguó	中国/中國	pn	2.2.	China
nǎguó/něiguó	哪国/哪國	ques	2.2.	which country
gōngzuò	工作	verb	2.2.	work
shèjì	设计/設計	verb	2.2.	design
yánjiū	研究	verb	2.2.	research
zuò	做	verb	2.2.	do
jiāo=shū	教书/教書	vobj	2.2.	teach (in a school setting)
ānjìng	安静/安靜	adj	2.3.	quiet, peaceful
bú-cuò	不错/不錯	adj	2.3.	good, not bad

adj=adjective; adr=term of address; adv=adverb; co-v=co-verb; comp=complement; conj=conjunction; dem=demonstrative; fam=family name; intr=interjection; mark=grammatical marker; mdl=modal; meas=measure; mnde=modifying noun; mptc=modification particle; nphr=noun phrase; num=number; phr=phrase; plce=place; plwd=place word; pn=place name; pre=prefix; prep=preposition; prn=proper noun; pron=pronoun; prvb=pre-verb; ques=question word/phrase; sptc=sentence particle; sufx=suffix; sv=state verb; timd=time-(duration) word; time=time word; timp=time phrase; tsfx=time suffix; vdir=verb of direction; vobj=verb with set object; vpot=verb with potential

chǎo	吵	adj	2.3.	noisy, raucous
gānjìng	干净/乾淨	adj	2.3.	clean
hǎowán(r)	好玩(儿)/好玩(兒)	adj	2.3.	fun, amusing
měi	美	adj	2.3.	beautiful
méi(yǒu)yìsi	没(有)意思/沒(有)意思	adj	2.3.	boring, uninteresting
pǔtōng	普通	adj	2.3.	common, wide-spread
rènao	热闹/熱鬧	adj	2.3.	lively, active, bustling
yōngjǐ	拥挤/擁擠	adj	2.3.	crowded, packed in
yǒu yìsi	有意思	adj	2.3.	interesting, amusing
zāng	脏/髒	adj	2.3.	dirty
chǎngzhǎng	厂长/廠長	adr	2.3.	factory chief or general manager
dàochù	到处/到處	adv	2.3.	everywhere
tài	太	adv	2.3.	too, excessive
chǎngzhǎng	厂长/廠長	noun	2.3.	factory chief
chéng	城	noun	2.3.	city
Nǐ kàn zěnmeyàng?	你看怎么样?/你看怎麽樣?	phr	2.3.	What do you think?
yǒu yìsi	有意思	phr	2.3.	interesting
chéng-lǐ	城里/城裏	plwd	2.3.	in town, in the city
chéng-wài	城外	plwd	2.3.	outside of town
chuāngkǒu	窗口	plwd	2.3.	ticket window [m: -gè]
chūkǒu	出口	plwd	2.3.	exit [m: -gè]
hǎi-biān(r)	海边(儿)/海邊(兒)	plwd	2.3.	seashore, by the sea
jiǎnpiàokǒu	剪票口	plwd	2.3.	ticket gate [m: -gè]

adj=adjective; adr=term of address; adv=adverb; co-v=co-verb; comp=complement; conj=conjunction; dem=demonstrative; fam=family name; intr=interjection; mark=grammatical marker; mdl=modal; meas=measure; mnde=modifying noun; mptc=modification particle; nphr=noun phrase; num=number; phr=phrase; plce=place; plwd=place word; pn=place name; pre=prefix; prep=preposition; prn=proper noun; pron=pronoun; prvb=pre-verb; ques=question word/phrase; sptc=sentence particle; sv=state verb; timd=time-(duration) word; time=time word; timp=time phrase; tsfx=time suffix; vdir=verb of direction; vobj=verb with set object; vpot=verb with potential

jiē-shang	街上	plwd	2.3.	on the street(s), in the street(s)
lùkǒu	路口	plwd	2.3.	intersection of streets or roadways [m: -gè]
ménkǒu	门口/門口	plwd	2.3.	doorway, gateway
rùkǒu	入口	plwd	2.3.	entrance [m: -gè]
shān-xià	山下	plwd	2.3.	at the foot of the mountain(s)
děng	等	verb	2.3.	wait
jiàn	见/見	verb	2.3.	meet, perceive, see
jiǎn=piào	剪票	vobj	2.3.	punch a ticket
bà(ba)	爸(爸)	adr	2.4.	dad, daddy, papa
diē	爹	adr	2.4.	dad, paw (non-urban)
mā(ma)	妈(妈)/媽(媽)	adr	2.4.	mom, mum, mama, ma
niáng	娘	adr	2.4	maw, ma (non-urban)
hái	还/還	adv	2.4.	in addition to, also (continuing state or event)
yǐjing	已经/已經	adv	2.4.	(achieved state or completed event)
méi(yǒu)	没(有)/沒(有)	mark	2.4.	(negates past events)
V guò X le	V 过X了/V 過X了	mark	2.4.	(completion of an expected event)
àiren	爱人/愛人	noun	2.4.	spouse (PRC)
bà(ba)	爸(爸)	noun	2.4.	dad
diē	爹	noun	2.4.	dad (non-urban)
duìxiàng	对象/對象	noun	2.4.	potential mate, sweetheart, counterpart
fùmǔ	父母	noun	2.4.	parents
fùqin	父亲/父親	noun	2.4.	father

adj=adjective; *adr*=term of address; *adv*=adverb; *co-v*=co-verb; *comp*=complement; *conj*=conjunction; *dem*=demonstrative; *fam*=family name; *intr*=interjection; *mark*=grammatical marker; *mdl*=modal; *meas*=measure; *mnde*=modifying noun; *mptc*=modification particle; *nphr*=noun phrase; *num*=number; *phr*=phrase; *plce*=place; *plwd*=place word; *pn*=place name; *pre*=prefix; *prep*=preposition; *prn*=proper noun; *pron*=pronoun; *prvb*=pre-verb; *ques*=question word/phrase; *sptc*=sentence particle; *sufx*=suffix; *sv*=state verb; *timd*=time-(duration) word; *time*=time word; *timp*=time phrase; *tsfx*=time suffix; *vdir*=verb of direction; *vobj*=verb with set object; *vpot*=verb with potential

fūren	夫人	noun	2.4.	*wife (formal)*
hēirén	黑人	noun	2.4.	*person of African descent*
huáqiáo	华侨/華僑	noun	2.4.	*overseas Chinese*
huárén	华人/華人	noun	2.4.	*Chinese person*
huáyì	华裔/華裔	noun	2.4.	*person of Chinese descent*
huáyǔ	华语/華語	noun	2.4.	*Chinese language*
mā(ma)	妈(妈)/媽(媽)	noun	2.4.	*mom*
mǔqin	母亲/母親	noun	2.4.	*mother*
nàkǒuzi/ nèikǒuzi	那口子	noun	2.4.	*spouse (informal), wife (informal)*
niáng	娘	noun	2.4	*mom (non-urban)*
qīzi	妻子	noun	2.4.	*wife (formal)*
Rìběnrén	日本人	noun	2.4.	*Japanese person*
xiānsheng	先生	noun	2.4.	*husband (formal)*
yóutàirén	犹太人/猶太人	noun	2.4.	*Jew*
zhàngfu	丈夫	noun	2.4.	*husband (formal)*
gàn shénme?	干什么?/ 幹什麼?	phr	2.4.	*What is (somebody) doing?*
hái méi(yǒu) jié=hūn	还没(有)结婚/ 還沒(有)結婚	phr	2.4.	*still not married*
jié=hūn le	结婚了/結婚了	phr	2.4.	*married*
jié=hūn le méi-you?	结婚了没有?/ 結婚了沒有?	phr	2.4.	*Are you married?*
hòu-biān(r)	后边(儿)/ 後邊(兒)	plwd	2.4.	*in the rear, back*
lǐ-biān(r)	里边(儿)/ 裏邊(兒)	plwd	2.4.	*inside*

adj=adjective; *adr*=term of address; *adv*=adverb; *co-v*=co-verb; *comp*=complement; *conj*=conjunction; *dem*=demonstrative; *fam*=family name; *intr*=interjection; *mark*=grammatical marker; *mdl*=modal; *meas*=measure; *mnde*=modifying noun; *mptc*=modification particle; *nphr*=noun phrase; *num*=number; *phr*=phrase; *plce*=place; *plwd*=place word; *pn*=place name; *pre*=prefix; *prep*=preposition; *prn*=proper noun; *pron*=pronoun; *prvb*=pre-verb; *ques*=question word/phrase; *sptc*=sentence particle; *sufx*=suffix; *sv*=state verb; *timd*=time-(duration) word; *time*=time word; *timp*=time phrase; *tsfx*=time suffix; *vdir*=verb of direction; *vobj*=verb with set object; *vpot*=verb with potential

páng-biān(r)	旁边（儿）/ 旁邊（兒）	plwd	2.4.	*on the side, beside*
qián-biān (r)	前边（儿）/ 前邊（兒）	plwd	2.4.	*in the front, front*
shàng-biān(r)	上边（儿）/ 上邊（兒）	plwd	2.4.	*on, on top*
shēn-biān(r)	身边（儿）/ 身邊（兒）	plwd	2.4.	*beside a person*
wài-biān(r)	外边（儿）/ 外邊（兒）	plwd	2.4.	*outside*
xià-biān(r)	下边（儿）/ 下邊（兒）	plwd	2.4.	*on the bottom, beneath*
Huáběi	华北/華北	pn	2.4.	*North China*
měijí-	美籍	pre	2.4.	*American (citizen)*
rìjí-	日籍	pre	2.4.	*Japanese (citizen)*
<u>V</u> le méiyǒu?	<u>V</u>了没有?/ <u>V</u>了沒有?	ques	2.4.	*<u>V</u> done yet?*
le	了	sptc	2.4.	*(completed event, achieved state)*
jié=hūn	结婚/結婚	vobj	2.4.	*get married*
bāozi	包子	noun	2.5.	*steamed stuffed bun [m: -gè]*
chóuzi	绸子/綢子	noun	2.5.	*silk fabric [m: -kuài]*
cuózi	矬子	noun	2.5.	*short person, dwarf [m: -gè]*
dízi	笛子	noun	2.5.	*bamboo flute [m: -zhī]*
fēizi	妃子	noun	2.5.	*imperial concubine [m: -gè]*
gēzi	鸽子/鴿子	noun	2.5.	*pigeon [m: -zhī]*

adj=adjective; *adr*=term of address; *adv*=adverb; *co-v*=co-verb; *comp*=complement; *conj*=conjunction; *dem*=demonstrative; *fam*=family name; *intr*=interjection; *mark*=grammatical marker; *mdl*=modal; *meas*=measure; *mnde*=modifying noun; *mptc*=modification particle; *nphr*=noun phrase; *num*=number; *phr*=phrase; *plce*=place; *plwd*=place word; *pn*=place name; *pre*=prefix; *prep*=preposition; *prn*=proper noun; *pron*=pronoun; *prvb*=pre-verb; *ques*=question word/phrase; *sptc*=sentence particle; *sufx*=suffix; *sv*=state verb; *timd*=time-(duration) word; *time*=time word; *timp*=time phrase; *tsfx*=time suffix; *vdir*=verb of direction; *vobj*=verb with set object; *vpot*=verb with potential

hézi	盒子	noun	2.5.	*box [m: -gè]*
jīzi	机子/機子	noun	2.5.	*small machine [m: -tái, -bù, -gè]*
kézi	壳子/殼子	noun	2.5.	*shell, packaging case [m: -gè]*
lǎozi	老子	noun	2.5.	*father, I (used jocularly or in anger)*
mèizi	妹子	noun	2.5.	*younger sister [m: -gè]*
nǎozi	脑子/腦子	noun	2.5.	*brain [m: -gè]*
páozi	袍子	noun	2.5.	*gown, robe [m: -jiàn]*
shìzi	柿子	noun	2.5.	*persimmon [m: -gè]*
suǒzi	锁子/鎖子	noun	2.5.	*lock [m: -bǎ]*
tízi	蹄子	noun	2.5.	*hoof [m: -gè]*
xízi	席子	noun	2.5.	*mat [m: -zhāng]*
zhóuzi	轴子/軸子	noun	2.5.	*roller [m: -gè]*
zuòzi	座子	noun	2.5.	*base, pedestal (for a machine) [m: -gè]*
dāngrán	当然/當然	adv	2.6.	*of course, naturally*
yòng	用	co-v	2.6.	*(indicates instrument: with, by)*
fēng	封	meas	2.6.	*(letters)*
tái	台/臺	meas	2.6.	*(machines/ chuánzhēnjī...)*
bǐ	笔/筆	noun	2.6.	*writing instrument [m: -zhī]*
chuánzhēn	传真/傳真	noun	2.6.	*fax [m: -fèn(r)]*
chuánzhēnjī	传真机/傳真機	noun	2.6.	*fax machine [m: -tái]*
diànhuà	电话/電話	noun	2.6.	*telephone [m: -bù]*
diànnǎo	电脑/電腦	noun	2.6.	*computer [m: -tái]*

adj=adjective; *adr*=term of address; *adv*=adverb; *co-v*=co-verb; *comp*=complement; *conj*=conjunction; *dem*=demonstrative; *fam*=family name; *intr*=interjection; *mark*=grammatical marker; *mdl*=modal; *meas*=measure; *mnde*=modifying noun; *mptc*=modification particle; *nphr*=noun phrase; *num*=number; *phr*=phrase; *plce*=place; *plwd*=place word; *pn*=place name; *pre*=prefix; *prep*=preposition; *prn*=proper noun; *pron*=pronoun; *prvb*=pre-verb; *ques*=question word/phrase; *sptc*=sentence particle; *sufx*=suffix; *sv*=state verb; *timd*=time-(duration) word; *time*=time word; *timp*=time phrase; *tsfx*=time suffix; *vdir*=verb of direction; *vobj*=verb with set object; *vpot*=verb with potential

hàomǎ(r)	号码(儿) / 號碼(兒)	noun	2.6.	number (telephone) [m: -gè]
shùzì	数字/數字	noun	2.6.	number [m: -gè]
xìn	信	noun	2.6.	letter, piece of correspondence [m: -fēng]
bā	八	num	2.6.	eight, 8
èr	二	num	2.6.	two, 2
jiǔ	九	num	2.6.	nine, 9
líng	零	num	2.6.	zero, 0
liù	六	num	2.6.	six, 6
qī	七	num	2.6.	seven, 7
sān	三	num	2.6.	three, 3
shí	十	num	2.6.	ten, 10
yāo	幺/么	num	2.6.	one (as a serial or code number) , 1
diànhuà hàomǎ(r) (shì) duōshǎo?	电话号码(儿) (是)多少？/ 電話號碼(兒) (是)多少？	phr	2.6.	asking for a telephone number
zěnme bàn?	怎么办？/ 怎麼辦？	phr	2.6.	How shall (we) handle this?
nàli	那里/那裏	plwd	2.6.	there, that place
nàr	那儿/那兒	plwd	2.6.	there, that place
zhèlǐ	这里/這裡	plwd	2.6.	here, this place
zhèr	这儿/這兒	plwd	2.6.	here, this place
bei	呗/唄	sptc	2.6.	(indicates obviousness)
-hào	号/號	sufx	2.6.	(room number, size, days of month)
dǎ	打	verb	2.6.	send (by electrical transmission)

adj=adjective; adr=term of address; adv=adverb; co-v=co-verb; comp=complement; conj=conjunction; dem=demonstrative; fam=family name; intr=interjection; mark=grammatical marker; mdl=modal; meas=measure; mnde=modifying noun; mptc=modification particle; nphr=noun phrase; num=number; phr=phrase; plce=place; plwd=place word; pn=place name; pre=prefix; prep=preposition; prn=proper noun; pron=pronoun; prvb=pre-verb; ques=question word/phrase; sptc=sentence particle; sufx=suffix; sv=state verb; timd=time-(duration) word; time=time word; timp=time phrase; tsfx=time suffix; vdir=verb of direction; vobj=verb with set object; vpot=verb with potential

fā	发/發	verb	2.6.	*dispatch, send, distribute, issue*
gàosu	告诉/告訴	verb	2.6.	*tell, relate, inform*
jì	寄	verb	2.6.	*send by mail*
tōngzhī	通知	verb	2.6.	*notify, inform*
xiě	写/寫	verb	2.6.	*write, compose*
yòng	用	verb	2.6.	*use*
chà	差	adj	2.7.	*poor quality, not up to standard*
duō	多	adj	2.7.	*many, much*
shǎo	少	adj	2.7.	*few, little (of something)*
chàbuduō	差不多	adv	2.7.	*almost, approximately*
zhǐ	只/祇	adv	2.7.	*only, merely*
jiān	间/間	meas	2.7.	*(rooms)*
gōngrén	工人	noun	2.7.	*worker [m: -gè, -wèi]*
yánjiūshēng	研究生	noun	2.7.	*graduate student [m: -gè, -wèi]*
bǎi	百	num	2.7.	*hundred, 100*
liǎng + <u>measure</u>	俩+<u>量词</u>/ 俩+<u>量詞</u>	num	2.7.	*two of, a couple of*
qiān	千	num	2.7.	*thousand, 1,000*
wàn	万	num	2.7.	*ten thousand, 10,000*
yī + <u>measure</u>	一+<u>量词</u>/ 一+<u>量詞</u>	num	2.7.	*one (of something)*
chàbuduō	差不多	phr	2.7.	*almost, That's about it.*
<u>X</u> de shì zěnmeyàng le?	<u>X</u>的事怎么样了？	phr	2.7.	*What about the matter of <u>X</u>?*
bàngōngshì	办公室/辦公室	plce	2.7.	*office [m: -jiān, -gè]*

adj=adjective; *adr*=term of address; *adv*=adverb; *co-v*=co-verb; *comp*=complement; *conj*=conjunction; *dem*=demonstrative; *fam*=family name; *intr*=interjection; *mark*=grammatical marker; *mdl*=modal; *meas*=measure; *mnde*=modifying noun; *mptc*=modification particle; *nphr*=noun phrase; *num*=number; *phr*=phrase; *plce*=place; *plwd*=place word; *pn*=place name; *pre*=prefix; *prep*=preposition; *prn*=proper noun; *pron*=pronoun; *prvb*=pre-verb; *ques*=question word/phrase; *sptc*=sentence particle; *sufx*=suffix; *sv*=state verb; *timd*=time-(duration) word; *time*=time word; *timp*=time phrase; *tsfx*=time suffix; *vdir*=verb of direction; *vobj*=verb with set object; *vpot*=verb with potential

yánjiūshēng yuàn	研究生院	plce	2.7.	graduate school [m: -gè]
duōshao	多少	ques	2.7.	how many/much
jǐ + <u>measure</u>	几+量词/ 幾+量詞	ques	2.7.	how many (small amount)
chà	差	verb	2.7.	lack, be short of
xūyào	需要	verb	2.7.	need, require
shīfu	师傅/師傅	adr	2.8.	master (for service workers) [m: -gè]
gěi	给/給	co-v	2.8.	(marks beneficiary of an action)
bēi	杯	meas	2.8.	(cups, glasses/chá, qìshuǐ)
běn(r)	本(儿)/本(兒)	meas	2.8.	(bound volumes/shū, zázhì)
dùn	顿/頓	meas	2.8.	(meals/fàn)
fèn(r)	份(儿)/份(兒)	meas	2.8.	(portions/fàn; issues/ bàozhǐ)
gè	个/個	meas	2.8.	(general measure for objects, people…)
guàn(r)	罐(儿)/罐(兒)	meas	2.8.	(cans/qìshuǐ)
kuài(r)	块(儿)/塊(兒)	meas	2.8.	(basic monetary unit/ qián), =yuán
píng(r)	瓶(儿)/瓶(兒)	meas	2.8.	(bottle/qìshuǐ)
xiē	些	meas	2.8.	(general plural measure)
zhāng	张/張	meas	2.8.	(flat things or flat surfaces/zhǐ)
zhī	支	meas	2.8.	(sticklike things/bǐ, qiānbǐ)

adj=adjective; *adr*=term of address; *adv*=adverb; *co-v*=co-verb; *comp*=complement; *conj*=conjunction; *dem*=demonstrative; *fam*=family name; *intr*=interjection; *mark*=grammatical marker; *mdl*=modal; *meas*=measure; *mnde*=modifying noun; *mptc*=modification particle; *nphr*=noun phrase; *num*=number; *phr*=phrase; *plce*=place; *plwd*=place word; *pn*=place name; *pre*=prefix; *prep*=preposition; *prn*=proper noun; *pron*=pronoun; *prvb*=pre-verb; *ques*=question word/phrase; *sptc*=sentence particle; *sufx*=suffix; *sv*=state verb; *timd*=time-(duration) word; *time*=time word; *timp*=time phrase; *tsfx*=time suffix; *vdir*=verb of direction; *vobj*=verb with set object; *vpot*=verb with potential

bāoguǒ	包裹	noun	2.8.	*parcel, package [m: -gè]*
bàozhǐ	报纸/報紙	noun	2.8.	*newspaper [m: -fèn(r), -zhāng]*
běnzi	本子	noun	2.8.	*notebook [m: -gè]*
cānquàn(r)	餐券(儿)/餐券(兒)	noun	2.8	*meal coupon [m: -zhāng]*
chá	茶	noun	2.8.	*tea [m: -bēi]*
dōngxi	东西/東西	noun	2.8.	*thing [m: -gè]*
fàn	饭/飯	noun	2.8.	*food, meal [m: -fèn(r), -dùn]*
fúwùyuán(r)	服务员(儿)/服務員(兒)	noun	2.8.	*service person, attendant [m: -gè, -wèi]*
héfàn	盒饭/盒飯	noun	2.8.	*box lunch [m: -fèn(r), -gè]*
jìniàn yóupiào	纪念邮票/紀念郵票	noun	2.8.	*commemorative stamp [m: -zhāng]*
lǚkè	旅客	noun	2.8.	*passenger [m: -gè, -wèi]*
míngxìnpiàn(r)	明信片(儿)/明信片(兒)	noun	2.8.	*post card [m: -zhāng]*
piào	票	noun	2.8.	*ticket [m: -zhāng]*
qián	钱/錢	noun	2.8.	*money [kuài/yuán=basic monetary unit]*
qiānbǐ	铅笔/鉛筆	noun	2.8.	*pencil [m: -zhī]*
qìshuǐ(r)	汽水(儿)/汽水(兒)	noun	2.8.	*soda, pop [m: -píng(r), -guàn(r)]*
shū	书/書	noun	2.8.	*book [m: -běn(r)]*
xìnfēng(r)	信封(儿)/信封(兒)	noun	2.8.	*envelope [m: -gè]*

adj=adjective; *adr*=term of address; *adv*=adverb; *co-v*=co-verb; *comp*=complement; *conj*=conjunction; *dem*=demonstrative; *fam*=family name; *intr*=interjection; *mark*=grammatical marker; *mdl*=modal; *meas*=measure; *mnde*=modifying noun; *mptc*=modification particle; *nphr*=noun phrase; *num*=number; *phr*=phrase; *plce*=place; *plwd*=place word; *pn*=place name; *pre*=prefix; *prep*=preposition; *prn*=proper noun; *pron*=pronoun; *prvb*=pre-verb; *ques*=question word/phrase; *sptc*=sentence particle; *sufx*=suffix; *sv*=state verb; *timd*=time-(duration) word; *time*=time word; *timp*=time phrase; *tsfx*=time suffix; *vdir*=verb of direction; *vobj*=verb with set object; *vpot*=verb with potential

xìnzhǐ	信纸/信紙	noun	2.8.	letter paper [m: -zhāng]
yóupiào	邮票/郵票	noun	2.8.	postage stamp [m: -zhāng]
yuánzhūbǐ	圆珠笔/圓珠筆	noun	2.8.	ball point pen [m: -zhī]
zázhì	杂志/雜誌	noun	2.8.	magazine [m: -běn(r), -fèn(r)]
qián zhènghǎo	钱正好/錢正好	phr	2.8.	correct change
cānchē	餐车/餐車	plce	2.8.	dining car (on a train) [m: -jié]
shūdiàn	书店/書店	plce	2.8.	book store [m: -gè, -jiā]
wénjùdiàn	文具店	plce	2.8.	stationery shop [m: -gè, -jiā]
yóujú (yóudiànjú)	邮局(邮电局)/ 郵局(郵電局)	plce	2.8.	post office [m: -gè, -jiā]
chī	吃	verb	2.8.	eat
gěi	给/給	verb	2.8.	give
hē	喝	verb	2.8.	drink
kàn	看	verb	2.8.	read, look, see, watch
mài	卖/賣	verb	2.8.	sell
mǎi	买/買	verb	2.8.	buy
ná	拿	verb	2.8.	take, hold
yào	要	verb	2.8.	want, require, demand, order (food), = xūyào
báicài	白菜	noun	2.9.	napa cabbage [m: -kē]
bǐnggān	饼干/餅乾	noun	2.9.	cracker, cookie [m: -kuài(r)]
cǎoméi	草莓	noun	2.9.	strawberry [m: -kē]
chūnjuǎn(r)	春卷(儿)/ 春卷(兒)	noun	2.9.	spring roll [m: -gè]
dàmǐ	大米	noun	2.9.	rice [m: -lì]

adj=adjective; adr=term of address; adv=adverb; co-v=co-verb; comp=complement; conj=conjunction; dem=demonstrative; fam=family name; intr=interjection; mark=grammatical marker; mdl=modal; meas=measure; mnde=modifying noun; mptc=modification particle; nphr=noun phrase; num=number; phr=phrase; plce=place; plwd=place word; pn=place name; pre=prefix; prep=preposition; prn=proper noun; pron=pronoun; prvb=pre-verb; ques=question word/phrase; sptc=sentence particle; sufx=suffix; sv=state verb; timd=time-(duration) word; time=time word; timp=time phrase; tsfx=time suffix; vdir=verb of direction; vobj=verb with set object; vpot=verb with potential

guōtiē	锅贴/鍋貼	noun	2.9.	potsticker, fried dumpling [m: -gè, -fèn(r)]
hóngchá	红茶/紅茶	noun	2.9.	black tea [m: -bēi]
huángguā	黄瓜/黃瓜	noun	2.9.	cucumber [m: -gēn]
jiàngyóu	酱油/醬油	noun	2.9.	soy sauce [m: -píng]
kǎoyā	烤鸭/烤鴨	noun	2.9.	roast duck [m: -zhī]
kuàizi	筷子	noun	2.9.	chopsticks [m: -shuāng]
lízi	梨子	noun	2.9.	pear [m: -gè]
lǐzi	李子	noun	2.9.	plum [m: -gè]
lìzi	栗子	noun	2.9.	chestnut [m: -gè]
lǜchá	绿茶/綠茶	noun	2.9.	green tea [m: -bēi]
lǜdòu	绿豆/綠豆	noun	2.9.	mung bean [m: -kē]
miànbāo	面包/麵包	noun	2.9.	bread [m: -kuài]
mǐfàn	米饭/米飯	noun	2.9.	cooked rice [m: -wǎn]
mùguā	木瓜	noun	2.9.	papaya [m: -gè]
nǎilào	奶酪	noun	2.9.	cheese [m: -kuài(r)]
nǎiyóu	奶油	noun	2.9.	cream [m: -kuài(r)]
niúnǎi	牛奶	noun	2.9.	milk [m: -píng, -hé, -tǒng, -guàn(r)]
niúpái	牛排	noun	2.9.	beefsteak [m: -kuài(r)]
píngguǒ	苹果/蘋果	noun	2.9.	apple [m: - gè]
Pǔ'ěrchá	普洱茶	noun	2.9.	Pu'er tea [m: -hú, -bēi, -kuài(r)]
qíncài	芹菜	noun	2.9.	celery [m: -bǎ, -gēn]
Qīngdǎo píjiǔ	青岛啤酒/青島啤酒	noun	2.9.	Tsingtao beer [m: -píng, -bēi, -tǒng, -guàn(r)]
shāobǐng	烧饼/燒餅	noun	2.9.	sesame griddle cake [m: -gè] (also shāobing)

adj=adjective; adr=term of address; adv=adverb; co-v=co-verb; comp=complement; conj=conjunction; dem=demonstrative; fam=family name; intr=interjection; mark=grammatical marker; mdl=modal; meas=measure; mnde=modifying noun; mptc=modification particle; nphr=noun phrase; num=number; phr=phrase; plce=place; plwd=place word; pn=place name; pre=prefix; prep=preposition; prn=proper noun; pron=pronoun; prvb=pre-verb; ques=question word/phrase; sptc=sentence particle; sufx=suffix; sv=state verb; timd=time-(duration) word; time=time word; timp=time phrase; tsfx=time suffix; vdir=verb of direction; vobj=verb with set object; vpot=verb with potential

shāyú	鲨鱼/鯊魚	noun	2.9.	shark [m: -tiáo]
shīzitóu	狮子头/ 獅子頭	noun	2.9.	Chinese entrée: meatball [m: -gè]
shūcài	蔬菜	noun	2.9.	vegetable [m: -zhǒng]
shuǐjiǎo	水饺/水餃	noun	2.9.	dumpling (boiled) [m: -gè]
tǔdòu	土豆	noun	2.9.	potato [m: -kē]
tùròu	兔肉	noun	2.9.	rabbit meat [m: -kuài(r)]
xiāngjiāo	香蕉	noun	2.9.	banana [m: -zhī (single), -bǎ (bunch)]
xiāngyóu	香油	noun	2.9.	sesame oil [m: -dī, -píng]
xiǎomǐ	小米	noun	2.9.	millet, also sùzi [m: -kē, -lì]
xiǎomǐ xīfàn	小米稀饭/ 小米稀飯	noun	2.9.	millet porridge [m: -wǎn]
xiēzi	蝎子	noun	2.9.	scorpion [m: -gè]
xīfàn	稀饭/稀飯	noun	2.9.	porridge [m: -wǎn]
yángcōng	洋葱/洋蔥	noun	2.9.	onion [m: -kē]
yùmǐ	玉米	noun	2.9.	corn [m: -gè]
zhīmayóu	芝麻油	noun	2.9.	sesame oil [m: -dī, -píng]
Zhōngguócài	中国菜/ 中國菜	noun	2.9.	Chinese food [m: -fèn(r)]
Dùzi è le.	肚子饿了。/ 肚子餓了。	phr	2.9	(I am) hungry.
Qǐng gěi wǒ yìshuāng kuàizi.	请给我一双筷子。/ 請給我一雙筷子。	phr	2.9	Please give me a pair of chopsticks.

adj=adjective; adr=term of address; adv=adverb; co-v=co-verb; comp=complement; conj=conjunction; dem=demonstrative; fam=family name; intr=interjection; mark=grammatical marker; mdl=modal; meas=measure; mnde=modifying noun; mptc=modification particle; nphr=noun phrase; num=number; phr=phrase; plce=place; plwd=place word; pn=place name; pre=prefix; prep=preposition; prn=proper noun; pron=pronoun; prvb=pre-verb; ques=question word/phrase; sptc=sentence particle; sufx=suffix; sv=state verb; timd=time-(duration) word; time=time word; timp=time phrase; tsfx=time suffix; vdir=verb of direction; vobj=verb with set object; vpot=verb with potential

Qǐng lái yìbēi lùchá.	请来一杯绿茶。 / 請來一杯綠茶。	phr	2.9	*Please give me a cup of green tea.*
Bǎodìng	保定	pn	2.9.	*Baoding (city in Hebei)*
Běihǎi	北海	pn	2.9.	*Beihai (city in Guangxi)*
Běihǎi Gōngyuán	北海公园	pn	2.9.	*Beihai Park (park in Beijing)*
Bèngbù	蚌埠	pn	2.9.	*Bengbu (city in Anhui)*
Chóngqìng	重庆/重慶	pn	2.9.	*Chongqing (city in China)*
Dàlǐ	大理	pn	2.9.	*Dali (city in Yunnan)*
Fènghuà	奉化	pn	2.9.	*Fenghua (city in Zhejiang)*
Fújiàn	福建	pn	2.9.	*Fujian (province in China)*
Gānsù	甘肃/甘蕭	pn	2.9.	*Gansu (province in China)*
Hànchéng	汉城/漢城	pn	2.9.	*Seoul (city in Korea)*
Jīnhuá	金华/金華	pn	2.9.	*Jinhua (city in Zhejiang)*
Jiǔlóng	九龙/九龍	pn	2.9.	*Jiulong (district in Hong Kong)*
Kūnmíng	昆明	pn	2.9.	*Kunming (city in Yunnan)*
Liáoníng	辽宁/遼寧	pn	2.9.	*Liaoning (province in China)*
Nánchāng	南昌	pn	2.9.	*Nanchang (city in Jiangxi)*
Nánhǎi	南海	pn	2.9.	*South China Sea*
Pǔ'ěr	普洱	pn	2.9.	*Pu'er (county in Yunnan)*

adj=adjective; *adr*=term of address; *adv*=adverb; *co-v*=co-verb; *comp*=complement; *conj*=conjunction; *dem*=demonstrative; *fam*=family name; *intr*=interjection; *mark*=grammatical marker; *mdl*=modal; *meas*=measure; *mnde*=modifying noun; *mptc*=modification particle; *nphr*=noun phrase; *num*=number; *phr*=phrase; *plce*=place; *plwd*=place word; *pn*=place name; *pre*=prefix; *prep*=preposition; *prn*=proper noun; *pron*=pronoun; *prvb*=pre-verb; *ques*=question word/phrase; *sptc*=sentence particle; *sufx*=suffix; *sv*=state verb; *timd*=time-(duration) word; *time*=time word; *timp*=time phrase; *tsfx*=time suffix; *vdir*=verb of direction; *vobj*=verb with set object; *vpot*=verb with potential

Shāndōng	山东/山東	pn	2.9.	Shandong (province in China)
Shěnyáng	沈阳/瀋陽	pn	2.9.	Shenyang (city in Liaoning)
Sìchuān	四川	pn	2.9.	Sichuan (province in China)
Táiběi	台北/臺北	pn	2.9.	Taipei (city in Taiwan)
Táiwān	台湾/臺灣	pn	2.9.	Taiwan
Tàiyuán	太原	pn	2.9.	Taiyuan (city in Shanxi)
Tiānjīn	天津	pn	2.9.	Tianjin (city in China)
Xīzàng	西藏	pn	2.9.	Tibet (region in China)
Yúnnán	云南/雲南	pn	2.9.	Yunnan (province in China)
Zhèjiāng	浙江	pn	2.9.	Zhejiang (province in China)

adj=adjective; *adr*=term of address; *adv*=adverb; *co-v*=co-verb; *comp*=complement; *conj*=conjunction; *dem*=demonstrative; *fam*=family name; *intr*=interjection; *mark*=grammatical marker; *mdl*=modal; *meas*=measure; *mnde*=modifying noun; *mptc*=modification particle; *nphr*=noun phrase; *num*=number; *phr*=phrase; *plce*=place; *plwd*=place word; *pn*=place name; *pre*=prefix; *prep*=preposition; *prn*=proper noun; *pron*=pronoun; *prvb*=pre-verb; *ques*=question word/phrase; *sptc*=sentence particle; *sufx*=suffix; *sv*=state verb; *timd*=time-(duration) word; *time*=time word; *timp*=time phrase; *tsfx*=time suffix; *vdir*=verb of direction; *vobj*=verb with set object; *vpot*=verb with potential

Pinyin Glossary

Pīnyīn	**Hànzì**	**POS**	**Stage**	**English**
ā (yā, na)	啊（呀，哪）	sptc	1.9.	*(emphasizes intentions)*
ǎi	矮	adj	1.6.	*short (height)*
àiren	爱人/愛人	noun	2.4.	*spouse (PRC)*
āngzāng	肮脏/骯髒	adj	1.5.	*dirty, foul*
ānjìng	安静/安靜	adj	1.5.	*peaceful, quiet*
Àodàlìyà	澳大利亚/ 澳大利亞	pn	2.2.	*Australia*
ba	吧	sptc	1.6.	*(assumes-state, suggests-event)*
bā	八	num	2.6.	*eight, 8*
bà(ba)	爸（爸）	noun	2.4.	*dad*
Bái	白	fam	1.1.	*Chinese surname (white)*
bǎi	百	num	2.7.	*hundred, 100*
báicài	白菜	noun	2.9.	*napa cabbage [m: -kē]*
Bālí	巴黎	pn	2.1.	*Paris*
bàngōngshì	办公室/辦公室	plce	2.7.	*office [m: -jiān, -gè]*
Bǎodìng	保定	pn	2.9.	*Baoding (city in Hebei)*
bāoguǒ	包裹	noun	2.8.	*parcel, package [m: -gè]*
bàozhǐ	报纸/報紙	noun	2.8.	*newspaper [m: -fèn(r), -zhāng]*
bāozi	包子	noun	2.5.	*steamed stuffed bun [m: -gè]*
bei	呗/唄	sptc	2.6.	*(indicates obviousness)*

adj=adjective; *adr*=term of address; *adv*=adverb; *co-v*=co-verb; *comp*=complement; *conj*=conjunction; *dem*=demonstrative; *fam*=family name; *intr*=interjection; *mark*=grammatical marker; *mdl*=modal; *meas*=measure; *mnde*=modifying noun; *mptc*=modification particle; *nphr*=noun phrase; *num*=number; *phr*=phrase; *plce*=place; *plwd*=place word; *pn*=place name; *pre*=prefix; *prep*=preposition; *prn*=proper noun; *pron*=pronoun; *prvb*=pre-verb; *ques*=question word/phrase; *sptc*=sentence particle; *sufx*=suffix; *sv*=state verb; *timd*=time-(duration) word; *time*=time word; *timp*=time phrase; *tsfx*=time suffix; *vdir*=verb of direction; *vobj*=verb with set object; *vpot*=verb with potential

bēi	杯	meas	2.8.	*(cups, glasses/chá, qìshuǐ)*
Běihǎi	北海	pn	2.9.	*Beihai (city in Guangxi)*
Běihǎi Gōngyuán	北海公园	pn	2.9.	*Beihai Park (park in Beijing)*
Běijīng	北京	pn	2.1.	*Beijing, Peking*
Běijīng Dàxué	北京大学/北京大學	pn	1.9.	*Beijing University (Beijing, China)*
běn(r)	本（儿）/本（兒）	meas	2.8.	*(bound volumes/shū, zázhì)*
bèn	笨	adj	1.7.	*stupid, awkward*
Bèngbù	蚌埠	pn	2.9.	*Bengbu (city in Anhui)*
běnzi	本子	noun	2.8.	*notebook [m: -gè]*
bǐ	比	verb	1.6.	*compare to*
bǐ	笔/筆	noun	2.6.	*writing instrument [m: -zhī]*
biàn	遍	meas	0.4.	*(one complete activity/action)*
bǐjiào	比较/比較	adv	1.6.	*relatively, comparatively*
bǐjiào	比较/比較	verb	1.6.	*compare*
bǐnggān	饼干/餅乾	noun	2.9.	*cracker, cookie [m: -kuài(r)]*
bózi	脖子	noun	1.8.	*neck*
bù-, bú-	不	mark	0.7.	*(negates verbs and adjectives)*
bú-cuò	不错/不錯	adj	2.3.	*good, not bad*
bú-duì	不对/不對	phr	0.2.	*not correct*

adj=adjective; *adr*=term of address; *adv*=adverb; *co-v*=co-verb; *comp*=complement; *conj*=conjunction; *dem*=demonstrative; *fam*=family name; *intr*=interjection; *mark*=grammatical marker; *mdl*=modal; *meas*=measure; *mnde*=modifying noun; *mptc*=modification particle; *nphr*=noun phrase; *num*=number; *phr*=phrase; *plce*=place; *plwd*=place word; *pn*=place name; *pre*=prefix; *prep*=preposition; *prn*=proper noun; *pron*=pronoun; *prvb*=pre-verb; *ques*=question word/phrase; *sptc*=sentence particle; *sufx*=suffix; *sv*=state verb; *timd*=time-(duration) word; *time*=time word; *timp*=time phrase; *tsfx*=time suffix; *vdir*=verb of direction; *vobj*=verb with set object; *vpot*=verb with potential

bú-kèqi	不客气／不客氣	phr	0.8.	*Don't be so polite, You're welcome. (response to xièxie)*
bù-qīngchu	不清楚	phr	1.7.	*unclear, unaware*
bù-shūfu	不舒服	adj	1.4.	*unwell, indisposed, uncomfortable*
bùzi	步子	noun	1.8.	*step*
cānchē	餐车／餐車	plce	2.8.	*dining car (on a train) [m: -jié]*
cānquàn(r)	餐券(儿)／餐券(兒)	noun	2.8	*meal coupon [m: -zhāng]*
cǎoméi	草莓	noun	2.9.	*strawberry [m: -kē]*
chá	茶	noun	2.8.	*tea [m: -bēi]*
chà	差	adj	2.7.	*poor quality, not up to standard*
chà	差	verb	2.7.	*lack, be short of*
chàbuduō	差不多	adv	2.7.	*almost, approximately*
chàbuduō	差不多	phr	2.7.	*almost, That's about it.*
chǎngzhǎng	厂长／廠長	adr	2.3.	*factory chief or general manager*
chǎngzhǎng	厂长／廠長	noun	2.3.	*factory chief*
chǎo	吵	adj	2.3.	*noisy, raucous*
Chén	陈／陳	fam	1.2.	*Chinese surname*
chéng	城	noun	2.3.	*city*
chēnghu	称呼／稱呼	verb	1.9.	*call, address*
chéng-lǐ	城里／城裏	plwd	2.3.	*in town, in the city*
chéng-wài	城外	plwd	2.3.	*outside of town*
chī	吃	verb	2.8.	*eat*
Chī ba.	吃吧。	phr	1.5.	*Please eat.*

adj=adjective; *adr*=term of address; *adv*=adverb; *co-v*=co-verb; *comp*=complement; *conj*=conjunction; *dem*=demonstrative; *fam*=family name; *intr*=interjection; *mark*=grammatical marker; *mdl*=modal; *meas*=measure; *mnde*=modifying noun; *mptc*=modification particle; *nphr*=noun phrase; *num*=number; *phr*=phrase; *plce*=place; *plwd*=place word; *pn*=place name; *pre*=prefix; *prep*=preposition; *prn*=proper noun; *pron*=pronoun; *prvb*=pre-verb; *ques*=question word/phrase; *sptc*=sentence particle; *sufx*=suffix; *sv*=state verb; *timd*=time-(duration) word; *time*=time word; *timp*=time phrase; *tsfx*=time suffix; *vdir*=verb of direction; *vobj*=verb with set object; *vpot*=verb with potential

chìzi	翅子	noun	1.5.	*fin (usually from the shark)*
Chóngqìng	重庆/重慶	pn	2.9.	*Chongqing (city in China)*
chóuzi	绸子/綢子	noun	2.5.	*silk fabric [m: -kuài]*
chuāngkǒu	窗口	plwd	2.3.	*ticket window [m: -gè]*
chuánzhēn	传真/傳真	noun	2.6.	*fax [m: -fèn(r)]*
chuánzhēnjī	传真机/傳真機	noun	2.6.	*fax machine [m: -tái]*
chūkǒu	出口	plwd	2.3.	*exit [m: -gè]*
chūnjuǎn(r)	春卷(儿)/春卷(兒)	noun	2.9.	*spring roll [m: -gè]*
cī	呲	verb	1.5.	*give a tongue-lashing to*
cōngming	聪明/聰明	adj	1.4.	*intelligent, clever*
cuózi	矬子	noun	2.5.	*short person, dwarf [m: -gè]*
dǎ	打	verb	2.6.	*send (by electrical transmission)*
dà	大	adj	1.6.	*large, great, old*
dàfang	大方	adj	1.7.	*generous, liberal-minded*
dàjiā	大家	pron	0.3.	*all, everybody*
Dàlǐ	大理	pn	2.9.	*Dali (city in Yunnan)*
dàmǐ	大米	noun	2.9.	*rice [m: -lì]*
dāngrán	当然/當然	adv	2.6.	*of course, naturally*
dàochù	到处/到處	adv	2.3.	*everywhere*
dàsuàn	大蒜	noun	0.5.	*garlic [m: -kē, -tóu]*
dàxué	大学/大學	plce	1.9.	*university [m: -suǒ, -gè]*
de	的	mptc	1.7.	*(after modifier of nominal)*

adj=adjective; *adr*=term of address; *adv*=adverb; *co-v*=co-verb; *comp*=complement; *conj*=conjunction; *dem*=demonstrative; *fam*=family name; *intr*=interjection; *mark*=grammatical marker; *mdl*=modal; *meas*=measure; *mnde*=modifying noun; *mptc*=modification particle; *nphr*=noun phrase; *num*=number; *phr*=phrase; *plce*=place; *plwd*=place word; *pn*=place name; *pre*=prefix; *prep*=preposition; *prn*=proper noun; *pron*=pronoun; *prvb*=pre-verb; *ques*=question word/phrase; *sptc*=sentence particle; *sufx*=suffix; *sv*=state verb; *timd*=time-(duration) word; *time*=time word; *timp*=time phrase; *tsfx*=time suffix; *vdir*=verb of direction; *vobj*=verb with set object; *vpot*=verb with potential

děng	等	verb	2.3.	*wait*
diànhuà	电话/電話	noun	2.6.	*telephone [m: -bù]*
diànhuà hàomǎ(r) (shì) duōshǎo?	电话号码(儿) (是)多少？/ 電話號碼(兒) (是)多少？	phr	2.6.	*asking for a telephone number*
diànnǎo	电脑/電腦	noun	2.6.	*computer [m: -tái]*
diē	爹	noun	2.4.	*dad (non-urban)*
dìfang	地方	noun	2.1.	*place, area*
dízi	笛子	noun	2.5.	*bamboo flute [m: -zhī]*
dǒng	懂	sv	0.7.	*understand*
Dōngjīng	东京/東京	pn	2.1.	*Tokyo*
dōngxi	东西/東西	noun	2.8.	*thing [m: -gè]*
dōu	都	adv	1.4.	*all (at head of predicate)*
Dù	杜	fam	1.2.	*Chinese surname*
duì le	对了/對了	phr	0.2.	*correct*
duìbuqǐ	对不起/對不起	phr	1.9.	*sorry (for not meeting expectations)*
duìxiàng	对象/對象	noun	2.4.	*potential mate, sweetheart, counterpart*
dùn	顿/頓	meas	2.8.	*(meals/fàn)*
duō	多	adj	2.7.	*many, much*
duǒ	朵	meas	1.8.	*(measure for flowers)*
duōshao	多少	ques	2.7.	*how many/much*
dùzi	肚子	noun	1.8.	*belly*
Dùzi è le.	肚子饿了。/ 肚子餓了。	phr	2.9	*(I am) hungry.*
è	饿/餓	adj	1.5.	*hungry*

adj=adjective; *adr*=term of address; *adv*=adverb; *co-v*=co-verb; *comp*=complement; *conj*=conjunction; *dem*=demonstrative; *fam*=family name; *intr*=interjection; *mark*=grammatical marker; *mdl*=modal; *meas*=measure; *mnde*=modifying noun; *mptc*=modification particle; *nphr*=noun phrase; *num*=number; *phr*=phrase; *plce*=place; *plwd*=place word; *pn*=place name; *pre*=prefix; *prep*=preposition; *prn*=proper noun; *pron*=pronoun; *prvb*=pre-verb; *ques*=question word/phrase; *sptc*=sentence particle; *sufx*=suffix; *sv*=state verb; *timd*=time-(duration) word; *time*=time word; *timp*=time phrase; *tsfx*=time suffix; *vdir*=verb of direction; *vobj*=verb with set object; *vpot*=verb with potential

èr	二	num	2.6.	two, 2
fā	发/發	verb	2.6.	dispatch, send, distribute, issue
fàn	饭/飯	noun	2.8.	food, meal [m: -fèn(r), -dùn]
Fāng	方	fam	1.2.	Chinese surname (square)
fēizi	妃子	noun	2.5.	imperial concubine [m: -gè]
fèn(r)	份(儿)/份(兒)	meas	2.8.	(portions/fàn; issues/ bàozhǐ)
fēng	封	meas	2.6.	(letters)
Fènghuà	奉化	pn	2.9.	Fenghua (city in Zhejiang)
fó	佛	noun	1.8.	Buddha
Fùdàn Dàxué	复旦大学/ 復旦大學	pn	2.2.	Fudan University (Shanghai, China)
Fújiàn	福建	pn	2.9.	Fujian (province in China)
fùjīnglǐ	副经理/副經理	adr	1.3.	assistant manager
fùjīnglǐ	副经理/副經理	noun	1.3.	assistant manager [m: -gè, -wèi]
fùmǔ	父母	noun	2.4.	parents
fùqin	父亲/父親	noun	2.4.	father
fūren	夫人	noun	2.4.	wife (formal)
fúwùyuán(r)	服务员(儿)/ 服務員(兒)	noun	2.8.	service person, attendant [m: -gè, -wèi]
gàn shénme?	干什么?/ 幹什麼?	phr	2.4.	What is (somebody) doing?
gānjìng	干净/乾淨	adj	2.3.	clean

adj=adjective; *adr*=term of address; *adv*=adverb; *co-v*=co-verb; *comp*=complement; *conj*=conjunction; *dem*=demonstrative; *fam*=family name; *intr*=interjection; *mark*=grammatical marker; *mdl*=modal; *meas*=measure; *mnde*=modifying noun; *mptc*=modification particle; *nphr*=noun phrase; *num*=number; *phr*=phrase; *plce*=place; *plwd*=place word; *pn*=place name; *pre*=prefix; *prep*=preposition; *prn*=proper noun; *pron*=pronoun; *prvb*=pre-verb; *ques*=question word/phrase; *sptc*=sentence particle; *sufx*=suffix; *sv*=state verb; *timd*=time-(duration) word; *time*=time word; *timp*=time phrase; *tsfx*=time suffix; *vdir*=verb of direction; *vobj*=verb with set object; *vpot*=verb with potential

gǎnmào le	感冒了	phr	1.4	*catch cold, have the flu*
Gānsù	甘肃/甘肅	pn	2.9.	*Gansu (province in China)*
gāo	高	adj	1.6.	*tall*
gàosu	告诉/告訴	verb	2.6.	*tell, relate, inform*
gè	个/個	meas	1.6.	*(general measure for persons)*
gè	个/個	meas	2.8.	*(general measure for objects, people…)*
gěi	给/給	co-v	2.8.	*(marks beneficiary of an action)*
gěi	给/給	verb	2.8.	*give*
Gēlúnbù	哥伦布/哥倫布	pn	2.2.	*Columbus*
gēnzhe	跟着/跟著	phr	0.3.	*follow*
gēzi	鸽子/鴿子	noun	2.5.	*pigeon [m: -zhī]*
gōngchǎng	工厂/工廠	plce	2.2.	*factory [m: -gè, - jiā]*
gōngrén	工人	noun	2.7.	*worker [m: -gè, -wèi]*
gōngsī	公司	plce	1.9.	*company [m: -jiā, -gè]*
gōngzuò	工作	noun	2.2.	*work, job*
gōngzuò	工作	verb	2.2.	*work*
guàn(r)	罐(儿)/罐(兒)	meas	2.8.	*(cans/qìshuǐ)*
Guǎngzhōu	广州/廣州	pn	2.2.	*city in Guangdong; Canton*
guǎnlǐ	管理	noun	2.2.	*management*
guìxìng	贵姓/貴姓	phr	1.2.	*What is your family name?*
Guójì Dà Fàndiàn	国际大饭店/國際大飯店	pn	2.1.	*International Hotel*
guójiā	国家/國家	noun	2.2.	*nation, country [m: -gè]*

adj=adjective; *adr*=term of address; *adv*=adverb; *co-v*=co-verb; *comp*=complement; *conj*=conjunction; *dem*=demonstrative; *fam*=family name; *intr*=interjection; *mark*=grammatical marker; *mdl*=modal; *meas*=measure; *mnde*=modifying noun; *mptc*=modification particle; *nphr*=noun phrase; *num*=number; *phr*=phrase; *plce*=place; *plwd*=place word; *pn*=place name; *pre*=prefix; *prep*=preposition; *prn*=proper noun; *pron*=pronoun; *prvb*=pre-verb; *ques*=question word/phrase; *sptc*=sentence particle; *sufx*=suffix; *sv*=state verb; *timd*=time-(duration) word; *time*=time word; *timp*=time phrase; *tsfx*=time suffix; *vdir*=verb of direction; *vobj*=verb with set object; *vpot*=verb with potential

guōtiē	锅贴/鍋貼	noun	2.9.	*potsticker, fried dumpling [m: -gè, -fèn(r)]*
hái	还/還	adv	2.4.	*in addition to, also (continuing state or event)*
hái méi(yǒu) jié=hūn	还没(有)结婚/ 還沒(有)結婚	phr	2.4.	*still not married*
hǎi-biān(r)	海边(儿)/ 海邊(兒)	plwd	2.3.	*seashore, by the sea*
Hànchéng	汉城/漢城	pn	2.9.	*Seoul (city in Korea)*
-hào	号/號	sufx	2.6.	*(room number, size, days of month)*
hǎo	好	adj	1.4.	*fine, good, okay*
hǎo	好	phr	0.1.	*(greeting, ex: Nǐ hǎo.)*
hàomǎ(r)	号码(儿)/ 號碼(兒)	noun	2.6.	*number (telephone) [m: -gè]*
hǎowán(r)	好玩(儿)/ 好玩(兒)	adj	2.3.	*fun, amusing*
hē	喝	verb	2.8.	*drink*
hé	和	conj	1.6.	*(joins nouns)*
Hē ba.	喝吧。	phr	1.5.	*Please have a drink!*
héfàn	盒饭/盒飯	noun	2.8.	*box lunch [m: -fèn(r), -gè]*
hēirén	黑人	noun	2.4.	*person of African descent*
hěn	很	adv	1.4.	*very (pre-adjective)*
hézi	盒子	noun	2.5.	*box [m: -gè]*
hóngchá	红茶/紅茶	noun	2.9.	*black tea [m: -bēi]*

adj=adjective; *adr*=term of address; *adv*=adverb; *co-v*=co-verb; *comp*=complement; *conj*=conjunction; *dem*=demonstrative; *fam*=family name; *intr*=interjection; *mark*=grammatical marker; *mdl*=modal; *meas*=measure; *mnde*=modifying noun; *mptc*=modification particle; *nphr*=noun phrase; *num*=number; *phr*=phrase; *plce*=place; *plwd*=place word; *pn*=place name; *pre*=prefix; *prep*=preposition; *prn*=proper noun; *pron*=pronoun; *prvb*=pre-verb; *ques*=question word/phrase; *sptc*=sentence particle; *sufx*=suffix; *sv*=state verb; *timd*=time-(duration) word; *time*=time word; *timp*=time phrase; *tsfx*=time suffix; *vdir*=verb of direction; *vobj*=verb with set object; *vpot*=verb with potential

hóngshāo qiézi	红烧茄子/ 紅燒茄子	noun	1.8.	*Chinese entrée:* *eggplant braised in soy* *sauce*
hòu-biān(r)	后边(儿)/ 後邊(兒)	plwd	2.4.	*in the rear, back*
huā	花	noun	1.8.	*flower [m: -duǒ, -zhī]*
Huà	华/華	fam	1.3.	*Chinese surname*
Huáběi	华北/華北	pn	2.4.	*North China*
huài	坏/壞	adj	1.8.	*broken*
huáiyùn	怀孕/懷孕	verb	1.8.	*pregnant*
Huáměi Màoyì Gōngsī	华美贸易公司/ 華美貿易公司	pn	1.9.	*Sino-American Trade* *Company*
Huáng	黄/黃	fam	1.1.	*Chinese surname* *(yellow)*
huángguā	黄瓜/黃瓜	noun	2.9.	*cucumber [m: -gēn]*
huānyíng	欢迎/歡迎	phr	1.9.	*welcome (to outsiders)*
huánzi	环子/環子	noun	1.8.	*ring [m: -gè]*
huáqiáo	华侨/華僑	noun	2.4.	*overseas Chinese*
huárén	华人/華人	noun	2.4.	*Chinese person*
Huáshèngdùn	华盛顿/華盛頓	pn	2.1.	*Washington D.C.*
huáyì	华裔/華裔	noun	2.4.	*person of Chinese* *descent*
huáyǔ	华语/華語	noun	2.4.	*Chinese language*
huídá	回答	verb	0.5.	*answer*
huǒ	火	noun	1.8.	*fire [m: -tuán, -bǎ]*
jì	寄	verb	2.6.	*send by mail*
jī	鸡/雞	noun	1.5.	*chicken [m: -zhī]*
jǐ + <u>measure</u>	几+<u>量词</u>/ 幾+<u>量詞</u>	ques	2.7.	*how many (small* *amount)*

adj=adjective; *adr*=term of address; *adv*=adverb; *co-v*=co-verb; *comp*=complement; *conj*=conjunction; *dem*=demonstrative; *fam*=family name; *intr*=interjection; *mark*=grammatical marker; *mdl*=modal; *meas*=measure; *mnde*=modifying noun; *mptc*=modification particle; *nphr*=noun phrase; *num*=number; *phr*=phrase; *plce*=place; *plwd*=place word; *pn*=place name; *pre*=prefix; *prep*=preposition; *prn*=proper noun; *pron*=pronoun; *prvb*=pre-verb; *ques*=question word/phrase; *sptc*=sentence particle; *sufx*=suffix; *sv*=state verb; *timd*=time-(duration) word; *time*=time word; *timp*=time phrase; *tsfx*=time suffix; *vdir*=verb of direction; *vobj*=verb with set object; *vpot*=verb with potential

jiā	家	plce	2.2.	*family, home, house [m: -gè]*
jiān	间/間	meas	2.7.	*(rooms)*
jiàn	见/見	verb	2.3.	*meet, perceive, see*
jiǎn=piào	剪票	vobj	2.3.	*punch a ticket*
Jiānádà	加拿大	pn	2.2.	*Canada*
jiàngyóu	酱油/醬油	noun	2.9.	*soy sauce [m: -píng]*
jiǎnpiàokǒu	剪票口	plwd	2.3.	*ticket gate [m: -gè]*
jiào X	叫 X	sv	1.3.	*named, be called X*
jiāo=shū	教书/教書	vobj	2.2.	*teach (in a school setting)*
jiàoshòu	教授	adr	1.6.	*professor*
jiàoxué	教学/教學	noun	2.2.	*teaching*
jiǎozi	饺子/餃子	noun	1.8.	*dumpling [m: -gè]*
jié=hūn	结婚/結婚	vobj	2.4.	*get married*
jié=hūn le	结婚了/結婚了	phr	2.4.	*married*
jié=hūn le méi-you?	结婚了没有?/結婚了沒有?	phr	2.4.	*Are you married?*
jiē-shang	街上	plwd	2.3.	*on the street(s), in the street(s)*
jièshào	介绍/介紹	verb	1.9.	*introduce*
jīn	金	noun	1.5.	*gold, money*
Jìnán Dàxué	暨南大学/暨南大學	pn	2.2.	*Jinan University (Guangzhou, China)*
jīnglǐ	经理/經理	adr	1.3.	*manager, boss*
jīnglǐ	经理/經理	noun	1.3.	*manager [m: -gè, -wèi]*
Jīnhuá	金华/金華	pn	2.9.	*Jinhua (city in Zhejiang)*
jìniàn yóupiào	纪念邮票/紀念郵票	noun	2.8.	*commemorative stamp [m: -zhāng]*
jǐnzhāng	紧张/緊張	adj	1.7.	*anxious, nervous, tense*

adj=adjective; *adr*=term of address; *adv*=adverb; *co-v*=co-verb; *comp*=complement; *conj*=conjunction; *dem*=demonstrative; *fam*=family name; *intr*=interjection; *mark*=grammatical marker; *mdl*=modal; *meas*=measure; *mnde*=modifying noun; *mptc*=modification particle; *nphr*=noun phrase; *num*=number; *phr*=phrase; *plce*=place; *plwd*=place word; *pn*=place name; *pre*=prefix; *prep*=preposition; *prn*=proper noun; *pron*=pronoun; *prvb*=pre-verb; *ques*=question word/phrase; *sptc*=sentence particle; *sufx*=suffix; *sv*=state verb; *timd*=time-(duration) word; *time*=time word; *timp*=time phrase; *tsfx*=time suffix; *vdir*=verb of direction; *vobj*=verb with set object; *vpot*=verb with potential

jiǔ	酒	noun	1.8.	*alcohol beverage [m: -píng(r), -bēi]*
jiǔ	九	num	2.6.	*nine, 9*
Jiùjīnshān	旧金山/舊金山	pn	2.1.	*San Francisco*
Jiǔlóng	九龙/九龍	pn	2.9.	*Jiulong (district in Hong Kong)*
jiùshi	就是	sv	1.7.	*(emphatic) am, are, is, was, were*
jīzi	机子/機子	noun	2.5.	*small machine [m: -tái, -bù, -gè]*
kāitong	开通/開通	adj	1.4.	*open-minded*
kàn	看	verb	2.8.	*read, look, see, watch*
kǎoyā	烤鸭/烤鴨	noun	2.9.	*roast duck [m: -zhī]*
kèren	客人	noun	1.7.	*guest, visitor, customer*
kézi	壳子/殼子	noun	2.5.	*shell, packaging case [m: -gè]*
kuài(r)	块(儿)/塊(兒)	meas	2.8.	*(basic monetary unit/ qián), =yuán*
kuàijì	会计/會計	noun	2.2.	*accountant, accounting [m: -gè, -wèi]*
kuàizi	筷子	noun	2.9.	*chopsticks [m: -shuāng]*
kùn	困	adj	1.8.	*sleepy*
Kūnmíng	昆明	pn	2.9.	*Kunming (city in Yunnan)*
kùzi	裤子/褲子	noun	1.8.	*pants, trousers [m: -tiáo] (v: -chuān)*
lǎn	懒/懶	adj	1.4.	*lazy*
lǎo	老	adj	1.6.	*old (anim), obsolete (inan)*
lǎo + <u>surname</u>	老	adr	1.1.	*older friend*

adj=adjective; *adr*=term of address; *adv*=adverb; *co-v*=co-verb; *comp*=complement; *conj*=conjunction; *dem*=demonstrative; *fam*=family name; *intr*=interjection; *mark*=grammatical marker; *mdl*=modal; *meas*=measure; *mnde*=modifying noun; *mptc*=modification particle; *nphr*=noun phrase; *num*=number; *phr*=phrase; *plce*=place; *plwd*=place word; *pn*=place name; *pre*=prefix; *prep*=preposition; *prn*=proper noun; *pron*=pronoun; *prvb*=pre-verb; *ques*=question word/phrase; *sptc*=sentence particle; *sufx*=suffix; *sv*=state verb; *timd*=time-(duration) word; *time*=time word; *timp*=time phrase; *tsfx*=time suffix; *vdir*=verb of direction; *vobj*=verb with set object; *vpot*=verb with potential

lǎo péngyou	老朋友	phr	0.3.	*old friend*
lǎoshī	老师/老師	adr	0.1.	*teacher*
lǎoshī	老师/老師	noun	0.1.	*teacher [m: -gè, -wèi]*
lǎozi	老子	noun	2.5.	*father, I (used jocularly or in anger)*
le	了	sptc	0.2.	*(new situation)*
le	了	sptc	1.4.	*(indicates changes)*
le	了	sptc	2.4.	*(completed event, achieved state)*
lèi	累	adj	1.4.	*tired*
Lǐ	李	fam	1.1.	*Chinese surname (plum)*
liǎng + <u>measure</u>	俩+量词/ 俩+量詞	num	2.7.	*two of, a couple of*
Liáoníng	辽宁/遼寧	pn	2.9.	*Liaoning (province in China)*
lǐ-biān(r)	里边(儿)/ 裏邊(兒)	plwd	2.4.	*inside*
Lín	林	fam	1.2.	*Chinese surname (forest)*
líng	零	num	2.6.	*zero, 0*
línghuó	灵活/靈活	adj	1.4.	*physically or mentally flexible, agile*
línshígōng	临时工/臨時工	noun	2.2.	*part-time work (worker), temporary work (worker) [m: -gè, -wèi]*
Liú	刘/劉	fam	1.1.	*Chinese surname*
liù	六	num	2.6.	*six, 6*
lízi	梨子	noun	2.9.	*pear [m: -gè]*
lǐzi	李子	noun	2.9.	*plum [m: -gè]*
lìzi	栗子	noun	2.9.	*chestnut [m: -gè]*

adj=adjective; *adr*=term of address; *adv*=adverb; *co-v*=co-verb; *comp*=complement; *conj*=conjunction; *dem*=demonstrative; *fam*=family name; *intr*=interjection; *mark*=grammatical marker; *mdl*=modal; *meas*=measure; *mnde*=modifying noun; *mptc*=modification particle; *nphr*=noun phrase; *num*=number; *phr*=phrase; *plce*=place; *plwd*=place word; *pn*=place name; *pre*=prefix; *prep*=preposition; *prn*=proper noun; *pron*=pronoun; *prvb*=pre-verb; *ques*=question word/phrase; *sptc*=sentence particle; *sufx*=suffix; *sv*=state verb; *timd*=time-(duration) word; *time*=time word; *timp*=time phrase; *tsfx*=time suffix; *vdir*=verb of direction; *vobj*=verb with set object; *vpot*=verb with potential

lóng	龙/龍	noun	1.8.	dragon [m: -tiáo]
lǜ	律	noun	1.8.	law
luàn	乱/亂	noun	1.8.	chaos
lǜchá	绿茶/綠茶	noun	2.9.	green tea [m: -bēi]
lǜdòu	绿豆/綠豆	noun	2.9.	mung bean [m: -kē]
lüèduó	掠夺/掠奪	verb	1.8.	plunder, rob
lǚkè	旅客	noun	2.8.	passenger [m: -gè, -wèi]
lùkǒu	路口	plwd	2.3.	intersection of streets or roadways [m: -gè]
Lúndūn	伦敦/倫敦	pn	2.1.	London (Yīngguó)
lúnzi	轮子/輪子	noun	1.8.	wheel [m: -gè]
Luòshānjī	洛杉矶/洛杉磯	pn	2.2.	Los Angeles (Jiāzhōu)
luōsuo	罗嗦/囉嗦	adj	1.4.	talkative
ma	吗/嗎	sptc	0.7.	(question)
mā(ma)	妈(妈)/媽(媽)	noun	2.4.	mom
mǎ	马/馬	noun	1.5.	horse [m: -pǐ]
mái	埋	verb	1.8.	bury
mǎi	买/買	verb	1.5.	buy
mǎi	买/買	verb	2.8.	buy
mài	卖/賣	verb	2.8.	sell
máng	忙	adj	1.4.	busy
mántou	馒头/饅頭	noun	1.5.	steamed bun [m: -gè]
máo	毛	noun	1.8.	fur, wool, bodyhair [m: -gēn]
méi	没/沒	sv	0.8.	not have, lacks (= méi-yǒu)
méi	眉	noun	1.8.	eyebrow [m: -dào]
měi	美	adj	2.3.	beautiful
méi-	没/沒	mark	0.8.	(negates yǒu)

adj=adjective; *adr*=term of address; *adv*=adverb; *co-v*=co-verb; *comp*=complement; *conj*=conjunction; *dem*=demonstrative; *fam*=family name; *intr*=interjection; *mark*=grammatical marker; *mdl*=modal; *meas*=measure; *mnde*=modifying noun; *mptc*=modification particle; *nphr*=noun phrase; *num*=number; *phr*=phrase; *plce*=place; *plwd*=place word; *pn*=place name; *pre*=prefix; *prep*=preposition; *prn*=proper noun; *pron*=pronoun; *prvb*=pre-verb; *ques*=question word/phrase; *sptc*=sentence particle; *sufx*=suffix; *sv*=state verb; *timd*=time-(duration) word; *time*=time word; *timp*=time phrase; *tsfx*=time suffix; *vdir*=verb of direction; *vobj*=verb with set object; *vpot*=verb with potential

méi(yǒu)	没(有)/沒(有)	mark	2.4.	*(negates past events)*
méi(yǒu)yìsi	没(有)意思/ 沒(有)意思	adj	2.3.	*boring, uninteresting*
Měiguó	美国/美國	pn	2.2.	*United States, America*
méi-kòng	没空	phr	1.7.	*busy, do not have free time*
měijí-	美籍	pre	2.4.	*American (citizen)*
mèizi	妹子	noun	2.5.	*younger sister [m: -gè]*
-men	们/們	sufx	1.4.	*(pluralizes definite human nouns)*
mèn	焖/燜	verb	1.5.	*braise, stew, cook in a covered pot over a low heat*
mèng	梦/夢	noun	1.5.	*dream [m: -gè]*
ménkǒu	门口/門口	plwd	2.3.	*doorway, gateway*
mǐ	米	noun	1.8.	*rice [m: -kē, -lì]*
miàn	面	noun	1.8.	*noodle [m: -wǎn]*
miànbāo	面包/麵包	noun	2.9.	*bread [m: -kuài]*
miànshóu/ miànshú	面熟	adj	1.6.	*familiar looking*
mǐfàn	米饭/米飯	noun	2.9.	*cooked rice [m: -wǎn]*
míngxìnpiàn(r)	明信片(儿)/ 明信片(兒)	noun	2.8.	*post card [m: -zhāng]*
míngzi	名字	noun	1.3.	*name [m: -gè]*
mìshū	秘书/秘書	adr	1.3.	*secretary*
mìshū	秘书/秘書	noun	1.3.	*secretary [m: -gè, -wèi]*
mógu	蘑菇	noun	1.8.	*mushroom [m: -gè]*
móuhuà	谋划/謀劃	verb	1.8.	*plan, scheme*
mùguā	木瓜	noun	2.9.	*papaya [m: -gè]*
mǔqin	母亲/母親	noun	2.4.	*mother*

adj=adjective; *adr*=term of address; *adv*=adverb; *co-v*=co-verb; *comp*=complement; *conj*=conjunction; *dem*=demonstrative; *fam*=family name; *intr*=interjection; *mark*=grammatical marker; *mdl*=modal; *meas*=measure; *mnde*=modifying noun; *mptc*=modification particle; *nphr*=noun phrase; *num*=number; *phr*=phrase; *plce*=place; *plwd*=place word; *pn*=place name; *pre*=prefix; *prep*=preposition; *prn*=proper noun; *pron*=pronoun; *prvb*=pre-verb; *ques*=question word/phrase; *sptc*=sentence particle; *sufx*=suffix; *sv*=state verb; *timd*=time-(duration) word; *time*=time word; *timp*=time phrase; *tsfx*=time suffix; *vdir*=verb of direction; *vobj*=verb with set object; *vpot*=verb with potential

ná	拿	verb	2.8.	take, hold
nǎ/něi	哪	dem	1.7.	which
nà/nèi	那	dem	1.6.	that
nǎge/něige	哪个	ques	1.7.	which one
nǎguó/něiguó	哪国/哪國	ques	2.2.	which country
nǎilào	奶酪	noun	2.9.	cheese [m: -kuài(r)]
nǎiyóu	奶油	noun	2.9.	cream [m: -kuài(r)]
nǎli	哪里/哪裏	ques	2.1.	where
nàli	那里/那裏	plwd	2.6.	there, that place
Nánchāng	南昌	pn	2.9.	Nanchang (city in Jiangxi)
nánde	男的	noun	1.6.	man [m: -gè]
Nánhǎi	南海	pn	2.9.	South China Sea
nánkàn	难看/難看	adj	1.6.	unattractive, ugly
nánrén	男人	noun	1.6.	man [m: -gè]
nǎozi	脑子/腦子	noun	2.5.	brain [m: -gè]
nǎr	哪儿/哪兒	ques	2.1.	where
nàr	那儿/那兒	plwd	2.6.	there, that place
nǎwèi/něiwèi	哪位	ques	1.7.	which person, who
ne	呢	sptc	1.4.	(question)
nàkǒuzi/nèikǒuzi	那口子	noun	2.4.	spouse (informal), wife (informal)
nénggàn	能干/能幹	adj	1.7.	competent, able
nǐ	你	pron	0.1.	you
Nǐ kàn zěnmeyàng?	你看怎么样?/你看怎麽樣?	phr	2.3.	What do you think?
niáng	娘	noun	2.4	mom (non-urban)
niánqīng	年轻/年輕	adj	1.6.	young (human)

adj=adjective; *adr*=term of address; *adv*=adverb; *co-v*=co-verb; *comp*=complement; *conj*=conjunction; *dem*=demonstrative; *fam*=family name; *intr*=interjection; *mark*=grammatical marker; *mdl*=modal; *meas*=measure; *mnde*=modifying noun; *mptc*=modification particle; *nphr*=noun phrase; *num*=number; *phr*=phrase; *plce*=place; *plwd*=place word; *pn*=place name; *pre*=prefix; *prep*=preposition; *prn*=proper noun; *pron*=pronoun; *prvb*=pre-verb; *ques*=question word/phrase; *sptc*=sentence particle; *sufx*=suffix; *sv*=state verb; *timd*=time-(duration) word; *time*=time word; *timp*=time phrase; *tsfx*=time suffix; *vdir*=verb of direction; *vobj*=verb with set object; *vpot*=verb with potential

nǐmen	你们/你們	pron	0.1.	*you (pl.)*
nín	您	pron	1.2.	*you (polite)*
niúnǎi	牛奶	noun	2.9.	*milk [m: -píng, -hé,* *-tǒng, -guàn(r)]*
niúpái	牛排	noun	2.9.	*beefsteak [m: -kuài(r)]*
Niǔyuē	纽约/紐約	pn	2.1.	*New York*
nǔlì	努力	adj	1.4.	*hard working*
nǚde	女的	noun	1.6.	*woman [m: -gè]*
nǚrén	女人	noun	1.6.	*woman [m: -gè]*
nǚshì	女士	adr	1.1.	*Ms. (formal)*
ò	哦	intr	1.2.	*oh! (implies recognition "I see")*
Ōuyáng	欧阳/歐陽	fam	1.2.	*Chinese surname*
pàng	胖	adj	1.6.	*fat, plump*
páng-biān(r)	旁边(儿)/ 旁邊(兒)	plwd	2.4.	*on the side, beside*
páozi	袍子	noun	2.5.	*gown, robe [m: -jiàn]*
piào	票	noun	2.8.	*ticket [m: -zhāng]*
piàoliang	漂亮	adj	1.6.	*attractive*
píng(r)	瓶(儿)/瓶(兒)	meas	2.8.	*(bottle/qìshuǐ)*
píngguǒ	苹果/蘋果	noun	2.9.	*apple [m: - gè]*
píngjìng	平静/平静	adj	1.7.	*calm, tranquil, composed*
pózi	婆子	noun	1.8.	*old woman [m: -gè]*
Pǔ'ěr	普洱	pn	2.9.	*Pu'er (county in Yunnan)*
Pǔ'ěrchá	普洱茶	noun	2.9.	*Pu'er tea [m: -hú, -bēi, -kuài(r)]*
pǔtōng	普通	adj	2.3.	*common, wide-spread*
pùzi	铺子/鋪子	noun	1.8.	*shop [m: -gè]*

adj=adjective; *adr*=term of address; *adv*=adverb; *co-v*=co-verb; *comp*=complement; *conj*=conjunction; *dem*=demonstrative; *fam*=family name; *intr*=interjection; *mark*=grammatical marker; *mdl*=modal; *meas*=measure; *mnde*=modifying noun; *mptc*=modification particle; *nphr*=noun phrase; *num*=number; *phr*=phrase; *plce*=place; *plwd*=place word; *pn*=place name; *pre*=prefix; *prep*=preposition; *prn*=proper noun; *pron*=pronoun; *prvb*=pre-verb; *ques*=question word/phrase; *sptc*=sentence particle; *sufx*=suffix; *sv*=state verb; *timd*=time-(duration) word; *time*=time word; *timp*=time phrase; *tsfx*=time suffix; *vdir*=verb of direction; *vobj*=verb with set object; *vpot*=verb with potential

qī	七	num	2.6.	seven, 7
qiān	千	num	2.7.	thousand, 1,000
qián	钱/錢	noun	2.8.	money [kuài/yuán=basic monetary unit]
qián zhènghǎo	钱正好/錢正好	phr	2.8.	correct change
qiānbǐ	铅笔/鉛筆	noun	2.8.	pencil [m: -zhī]
qián-biān (r)	前边(儿)/前邊(兒)	plwd	2.4.	in the front, front
qiézi	茄子	noun	1.8.	eggplant [m: -gè]
qíncài	芹菜	noun	2.9.	celery [m: -bǎ, -gēn]
qǐng	请/請	prvb	0.2.	please (do something)
qǐng	请/請	verb	0.2.	request, invite
Qǐng gěi wǒ yìshuāng kuàizi.	请给我一双筷子。/請給我一雙筷子。	phr	2.9	Please give me a pair of chopsticks.
Qǐng lái yìbēi lǜchá.	请来一杯绿茶。/請來一杯綠茶。	phr	2.9	Please give me a cup of green tea.
qīngchu	清楚	adj	1.7.	clear, clearheaded, aware
Qīngdǎo	青岛/青島	pn	2.2.	Tsingtao (city in Shandong)
Qīngdǎo píjiǔ	青岛啤酒/青島啤酒	noun	2.9.	Tsingtao beer [m: -píng, -bēi, -tǒng, -guàn(r)]
Qīnghuá Dàxué	清华大学/清華大學	pn	1.9.	Qinghua University (Beijing, China)
qǐngwèn	请问/請問	phr	1.2.	May I ask a question?
qìshuǐ(r)	汽水(儿)/汽水(兒)	noun	2.8.	soda, pop [m: -píng(r), -guàn(r)]
qīzi	妻子	noun	2.4.	wife (formal)

adj=adjective; adr=term of address; adv=adverb; co-v=co-verb; comp=complement; conj=conjunction; dem=demonstrative; fam=family name; intr=interjection; mark=grammatical marker; mdl=modal; meas=measure; mnde=modifying noun; mptc=modification particle; nphr=noun phrase; num=number; phr=phrase; plce=place; plwd=place word; pn=place name; pre=prefix; prep=preposition; prn=proper noun; pron=pronoun; prvb=pre-verb; ques=question word/phrase; sptc=sentence particle; sufx=suffix; sv=state verb; timd=time-(duration) word; time=time word; timp=time phrase; tsfx=time suffix; vdir=verb of direction; vobj=verb with set object; vpot=verb with potential

rén	人	noun	1.3.	*person [m: -gè]*
rén	人	noun	1.6.	*person, people*
rènao	热闹/熱鬧	adj	2.3.	*lively, active, bustling*
rénmín	人民	noun	1.5.	*people, masses*
Rénmín Dàxué	人民大学/ 人民大學	pn	1.9.	*People's University (Beijing, China)*
rènshi	认识/認識	sv	2.1.	*know, recognize*
Rìběn	日本	pn	2.2.	*Japan*
Rìběnrén	日本人	noun	2.4.	*Japanese person*
rìjí-	日籍	pre	2.4.	*Japanese (citizen)*
rìzi	日子	noun	1.5.	*days on the calendar*
ròuwán(r)	肉丸(儿)/ 肉丸(兒)	noun	1.8.	*meatball [m: -gè]*
rùkǒu	入口	plwd	2.3.	*entrance [m: -gè]*
sà	卅	num	1.5.	*thirty*
sān	三	num	2.6.	*three,3*
sè	色	noun	1.5.	*lust, sensuality*
Shāndōng	山东/山東	pn	2.9.	*Shandong (province in China)*
shàng=kè	上课/上課	vobj	0.2.	*attend class, give a lesson*
shàng-biān(r)	上边(儿)/ 上邊(兒)	plwd	2.4.	*on, on top*
shāngdiàn	商店	plce	2.2.	*store, shop [m: -gè, -jiā]*
Shànghǎi	上海	pn	2.1.	*Shanghai*
shān-xià	山下	plwd	2.3.	*at the foot of the mountain(s)*
shǎo	少	adj	2.7.	*few, little (of something)*

adj=adjective; *adr*=term of address; *adv*=adverb; *co-v*=co-verb; *comp*=complement; *conj*=conjunction; *dem*=demonstrative; *fam*=family name; *intr*=interjection; *mark*=grammatical marker; *mdl*=modal; *meas*=measure; *mnde*=modifying noun; *mptc*=modification particle; *nphr*=noun phrase; *num*=number; *phr*=phrase; *plce*=place; *plwd*=place word; *pn*=place name; *pre*=prefix; *prep*=preposition; *prn*=proper noun; *pron*=pronoun; *prvb*=pre-verb; *ques*=question word/phrase; *sptc*=sentence particle; *sufx*=suffix; *sv*=state verb; *timd*=time-(duration) word; *time*=time word; *timp*=time phrase; *tsfx*=time suffix; *vdir*=verb of direction; *vobj*=verb with set object; *vpot*=verb with potential

shāobǐng	烧饼/燒餅	noun	2.9.	sesame griddle cake [m: -gè] (also shāobing)
shāyú	鲨鱼/鯊魚	noun	2.9.	shark [m: -tiáo]
shèbèi	设备/設備	noun	2.1.	equipment
shéi/shuí	谁/誰	ques	1.3.	who, whom
shèjì	设计/設計	noun	2.2.	design, plan, scheme [m: -gè, -zhǒng]
shèjì	设计/設計	verb	2.2.	design
shēn-biān(r)	身边(儿)/身邊(兒)	plwd	2.4.	beside a person
shēngyīn	声音/聲音	noun	1.5.	sound [m: -zhǒng]
shénme	什么/甚麼	ques	1.3.	what
shénme dìfang	什么地方/甚麼地方	phr	2.1.	where, what place
shénme rén	什么人/甚麼人	phr	1.3.	(asking about a person's profession or status)
Shěnyáng	沈阳/瀋陽	pn	2.9.	Shenyang (city in Liaoning)
sī	丝/絲	noun	1.5.	silk
Shī	施	fam	1.2.	Chinese surname
shí	十	num	2.6.	ten, 10
shì	是	sv	1.3.	be, is, am, are, was, were
shì	是	mark	2.2.	(emphasizes following element in a phrase)
shīfàn dàxué	师范大学/師範大學	pn	1.9.	normal (teachers) university
shīfu	师傅/師傅	adr	2.8.	master (for service workers) [m: -gè]

adj=adjective; adr=term of address; adv=adverb; co-v=co-verb; comp=complement; conj=conjunction; dem=demonstrative; fam=family name; intr=interjection; mark=grammatical marker; mdl=modal; meas=measure; mnde=modifying noun; mptc=modification particle; nphr=noun phrase; num=number; phr=phrase; plce=place; plwd=place word; pn=place name; pre=prefix; prep=preposition; prn=proper noun; pron=pronoun; prvb=pre-verb; ques=question word/phrase; sptc=sentence particle; sufx=suffix; sv=state verb; timd=time-(duration) word; time=time word; timp=time phrase; tsfx=time suffix; vdir=verb of direction; vobj=verb with set object; vpot=verb with potential

shìzi	式子	noun	1.5.	*math equation [m: -gè]*
shìzi	柿子	noun	2.5.	*persimmon [m: -gè]*
shīzitóu	狮子头/ 獅子頭	noun	2.9.	*Chinese entrée: meatball [m: -gè]*
shòu	瘦	adj	1.6.	*slight (physical build), thin*
Shǒudū Jùchǎng	首都剧场/首都劇場	pn	2.1.	*Capital Theatre*
shū	书/書	noun	2.8.	*book [m: -běn(r)]*
shūcài	蔬菜	noun	2.9.	*vegetable [m: -zhǒng]*
shūdiàn	书店/書店	plce	2.8.	*book store [m: -gè, -jiā]*
shūfu	舒服	adj	1.4.	*comfortable*
shuǐjiǎo	水饺/水餃	noun	2.9.	*dumpling (boiled) [m: -gè]*
shuō	说/說	verb	0.3.	*speak, say*
shùzì	数字/數字	noun	2.6.	*number [m: -gè]*
sì	四	num	1.5.	*four, 4*
Sìchuān	四川	pn	2.9.	*Sichuan (province in China)*
suān	酸	adj	1.8.	*sour*
suàn	蒜	noun	1.8.	*garlic [m: -bàn(r), -tóu]*
suǒzi	锁子/鎖子	noun	2.5.	*lock [m: -bǎ]*
sùzi	粟子	noun	1.8.	*millet (also xiǎomǐ)*
tā	他	pron	1.2.	*he, him*
tā	她	pron	1.2.	*she, her*
tái	台/臺	noun	0.9.	*platform*
tái	台/臺	meas	2.6.	*(machines/ chuánzhēnjī...)*
tài	太	adv	2.3.	*too, excessive*
Táiběi	台北/臺北	pn	2.9.	*Taipei (city in Taiwan)*
tàitai	太太	adr	1.1.	*Mrs.*

adj=adjective; *adr*=term of address; *adv*=adverb; *co-v*=co-verb; *comp*=complement; *conj*=conjunction; *dem*=demonstrative; *fam*=family name; *intr*=interjection; *mark*=grammatical marker; *mdl*=modal; *meas*=measure; *mnde*=modifying noun; *mptc*=modification particle; *nphr*=noun phrase; *num*=number; *phr*=phrase; *plce*=place; *plwd*=place word; *pn*=place name; *pre*=prefix; *prep*=preposition; *prn*=proper noun; *pron*=pronoun; *prvb*=pre-verb; *ques*=question word/phrase; *sptc*=sentence particle; *sufx*=suffix; *sv*=state verb; *timd*=time-(duration) word; *time*=time word; *timp*=time phrase; *tsfx*=time suffix; *vdir*=verb of direction; *vobj*=verb with set object; *vpot*=verb with potential

Táiwān	台湾/臺灣	pn	2.9.	*Taiwan*
Tàiyuán	太原	pn	2.9.	*Taiyuan (city in Shanxi)*
tāmen	她们/她們	pron	1.4.	*they, them (female)*
tāmen	他们/他們	pron	1.4.	*they, them (gender free)*
tǎn	毯	noun	0.9.	*blanket*
tàn	炭	noun	0.9.	*charcoal*
tāng	汤/湯	noun	0.6.	*soup*
táng	糖	noun	0.6.	*sugar/candy [m: -kuài, -kē]*
tǎng	躺	verb	0.6.	*lie down*
tàng	烫/燙	adj	0.6.	*scalding hot*
Tāng tài tàng le!	汤太烫了！/ 湯太燙了！	phr	0.6.	*The soup is scalding hot!*
táo	桃	noun	0.9.	*peach [m: -gè]*
tǎo	讨/討	verb	0.9.	*demand*
Tiānjīn	天津	pn	2.9.	*Tianjin (city in China)*
tīng	听/聽	verb	0.3.	*listen*
tǐng	挺	adv	2.1.	*very, really*
tízi	蹄子	noun	2.5.	*hoof [m: -gè]*
tóngshì	同事	noun	1.4.	*colleague*
tóngshìmen	同事们/同事們	noun	1.4.	*colleagues*
tóngxué	同学/同學	noun	0.1.	*schoolmate [m: -gè, -wèi]*
tóngxuémen	同学们/同學們	adr	0.1.	*fellow students*
tóngxuémen	同学们/同學們	noun	0.1.	*students of a particular school*
tōngzhī	通知	verb	2.6.	*notify, inform*
tóngzhì	同志	adr	1.2.	*comrade*
tōu	偷	verb	0.9.	*steal*

adj=adjective; *adr*=term of address; *adv*=adverb; *co-v*=co-verb; *comp*=complement; *conj*=conjunction; *dem*=demonstrative; *fam*=family name; *intr*=interjection; *mark*=grammatical marker; *mdl*=modal; *meas*=measure; *mnde*=modifying noun; *mptc*=modification particle; *nphr*=noun phrase; *num*=number; *phr*=phrase; *plce*=place; *plwd*=place word; *pn*=place name; *pre*=prefix; *prep*=preposition; *prn*=proper noun; *pron*=pronoun; *prvb*=pre-verb; *ques*=question word/phrase; *sptc*=sentence particle; *sufx*=suffix; *sv*=state verb; *timd*=time-(duration) word; *time*=time word; *timp*=time phrase; *tsfx*=time suffix; *vdir*=verb of direction; *vobj*=verb with set object; *vpot*=verb with potential

tòu	透	adj	0.9.	*penetrate*
tū	凸	adj	0.9.	*protruding*
tǔ	土	noun	0.9.	*soil*
tǔdòu	土豆	noun	2.9.	*potato [m: -kē]*
tuǐ	腿	noun	1.8.	*leg [m: -tiáo]*
tùròu	兔肉	noun	2.9.	*rabbit meat [m: -kuài(r)]*
tùzi	兔子	noun	1.8.	*rabbit [m: -zhī]*
V̱ guò X̱ le	V̱ 过 X̱ 了/V̱ 過 X̱ 了	mark	2.4.	*(completion of an expected event)*
V̱ le méiyǒu?	V̱ 了没有?/ V̱ 了没有?	ques	2.4.	*V̱ done yet?*
V̱ yíxià	V̱ 一下	timd	1.9.	*try to V̱ , V̱ for a while*
wā	哇	intr	1.8.	*(expression of wonderment)*
wài	外	plwd	1.8.	*outside*
wài-biān(r)	外边(儿)/ 外邊(兒)	plwd	2.4.	*outside*
wàn	万	num	2.7.	*ten thousand, 10,000*
Wáng	王	fam	1.1.	*Chinese surname (king)*
wángù	顽固/頑固	adj	1.4.	*stubborn, hard-headed*
wánzi	丸子	noun	1.8.	*pill, ball [m: -gè]*
wèi	位	meas	1.6.	*(persons-polite measure)*
wěiba	尾巴	noun	1.8.	*tail [m: -tiáo, -gè]*
wèn	问/問	verb	0.5.	*ask*
wèn X̱ hǎo	问 X̱ 好/問 X̱ 好	phr	1.1.	*remember me to X̱ , greet X̱*
wénjùdiàn	文具店	plce	2.8.	*stationery shop [m: -gè, jiā]*

adj=adjective; *adr*=term of address; *adv*=adverb; *co-v*=co-verb; *comp*=complement; *conj*=conjunction; *dem*=demonstrative; *fam*=family name; *intr*=interjection; *mark*=grammatical marker; *mdl*=modal; *meas*=measure; *mnde*=modifying noun; *mptc*=modification particle; *nphr*=noun phrase; *num*=number; *phr*=phrase; *plce*=place; *plwd*=place word; *pn*=place name; *pre*=prefix; *prep*=preposition; *prn*=proper noun; *pron*=pronoun; *prvb*=pre-verb; *ques*=question word/phrase; *sptc*=sentence particle; *sufx*=suffix; *sv*=state verb; *timd*=time-(duration) word; *time*=time word; *timp*=time phrase; *tsfx*=time suffix; *vdir*=verb of direction; *vobj*=verb with set object; *vpot*=verb with potential

wèntí	问题/問題	noun	0.5.	*question, problem [m: -gè]*
wénzi	蚊子	noun	1.8.	*mosquito [m: -zhī]*
wǒ	我	pron	0.3.	*I, me*
Wǒ è le.	我饿了。/我餓了。	phr	1.5.	*I am hungry.*
Wǒ gěi nǐmen jièshào yíxià.	我给你们介绍一下。/ 我給你們介绍一下。	phr	1.9.	*Let me introduce you.*
Wǒ kě le.	我渴了。	phr	1.5.	*I am thirsty.*
wǒmen	我们/我們	pron	1.7.	*we, us*
Wú	吴/吳	fam	1.2.	*Chinese surname*
wǔ	五	num	1.8.	*five, 5*
Wǔhàn	武汉/武漢	pn	2.2.	*city in Hubei*
wúnéng	无能/無能	adj	1.7.	*incompetent*
X de shì zěnmeyàng le?	X的事怎么样了？	phr	2.7.	*What about the matter of X?*
X zěnmeyàng	X怎么样/X怎麼樣	ques	1.4.	*how is X, what is X like*
X zhǎngde zěnmeyàng	X长得怎么样/ X長得怎麼樣	phr	1.6.	*What does X look like?*
xiā	虾/蝦	noun	1.8.	*shrimp [m: -zhī]*
xià=kè	下课/下課	vobj	0.8.	*end class, dismiss class*
xià-biān(r)	下边（儿）/ 下邊（兒）	plwd	2.4.	*on the bottom, beneath*
Xiānggǎng	香港	pn	2.1.	*Hong Kong*
xiāngjiāo	香蕉	noun	2.9.	*banana [m: -zhī (single), -bǎ (bunch)]*
xiāngyóu	香油	noun	2.9.	*sesame oil [m: -dī, -píng]*

adj=adjective; *adr*=term of address; *adv*=adverb; *co-v*=co-verb; *comp*=complement; *conj*=conjunction; *dem*=demonstrative; *fam*=family name; *intr*=interjection; *mark*=grammatical marker; *mdl*=modal; *meas*=measure; *mnde*=modifying noun; *mptc*=modification particle; *nphr*=noun phrase; *num*=number; *phr*=phrase; *plce*=place; *plwd*=place word; *pn*=place name; *pre*=prefix; *prep*=preposition; *prn*=proper noun; *pron*=pronoun; *prvb*=pre-verb; *ques*=question word/phrase; *sptc*=sentence particle; *sufx*=suffix; *sv*=state verb; *timd*=time-(duration) word; *time*=time word; *timp*=time phrase; *tsfx*=time suffix; *vdir*=verb of direction; *vobj*=verb with set object; *vpot*=verb with potential

xiānsheng	先生	adr	1.1.	*Mr., Honorable*
xiānsheng	先生	noun	2.4.	*husband (formal)*
xiànzài	现在/現在	time	0.2.	*now*
xiǎo	小	adj	1.6.	*small, young*
xiǎo + <u>surname</u>	小	adr	1.1.	*younger friend*
xiáojie	小姐	adr	1.1.	*Miss*
xiǎomāo	小猫/小貓	noun	1.8.	*kitten [m: -zhī]*
xiǎomǐ	小米	noun	2.9.	*millet, also sùzi [m: -kē, -lì]*
xiǎomǐ xīfàn	小米稀饭/小米稀飯	noun	2.9.	*millet porridge [m: -wǎn]*
xiǎoqi	小气/小氣	adj	1.7.	*petty, stingy, narrow-minded*
xiàozhǎng	校长/校長	adr	1.9.	*president (college), principal (school)*
xiē	些	meas	2.8.	*(general plural measure)*
xiě	写/寫	verb	2.6.	*write, compose*
xièxie	谢谢/謝謝	phr	0.8.	*thanks (accept with gratitude)*
xiēzi	蝎子	noun	2.9.	*scorpion [m: -gè]*
xiézi	鞋子	noun	1.8.	*shoe(s) [m: -shuāng, -zhī]*
xīfàn	稀饭/稀飯	noun	2.9.	*porridge [m: -wǎn]*
xǐhuan	喜欢/喜歡	sv	2.1.	*like, appreciate*
xìn	信	noun	2.6.	*letter, piece of correspondence [m: -fēng]*
xìnfēng(r)	信封（儿）/信封（兒）	noun	2.8.	*envelope [m: -gè]*
xìng	姓	sv	1.2.	*have the family name <u>X</u>*

adj=adjective; *adr*=term of address; *adv*=adverb; *co-v*=co-verb; *comp*=complement; *conj*=conjunction; *dem*=demonstrative; *fam*=family name; *intr*=interjection; *mark*=grammatical marker; *mdl*=modal; *meas*=measure; *mnde*=modifying noun; *mptc*=modification particle; *nphr*=noun phrase; *num*=number; *phr*=phrase; *plce*=place; *plwd*=place word; *pn*=place name; *pre*=prefix; *prep*=preposition; *prn*=proper noun; *pron*=pronoun; *prvb*=pre-verb; *ques*=question word/phrase; *sptc*=sentence particle; *sufx*=suffix; *sv*=state verb; *timd*=time-(duration) word; *time*=time word; *timp*=time phrase; *tsfx*=time suffix; *vdir*=verb of direction; *vobj*=verb with set object; *vpot*=verb with potential

xìnzhǐ	信纸/信紙	noun	2.8.	*letter paper [m: -zhāng]*
xióng	熊	noun	1.8.	*bear [m: -zhī, -tóu]*
xióngmāo	熊猫/熊貓	noun	1.8.	*panda [m: -zhī]*
Xīzàng	西藏	pn	2.9.	*Tibet (region in China)*
xízi	席子	noun	2.5.	*mat [m: -zhāng]*
xuésheng	学生/學生	noun	1.3.	*student [m: -gè, -wèi]*
xuéxiào	学校/學校	plce	1.9.	*school [m: -suǒ, -gè]*
xuéyuàn	学院/學院	plce	1.9.	*college, institute [m: -gè]*
xūyào	需要	verb	2.7.	*need, require*
yán	盐/鹽	noun	1.8.	*salt*
yángcōng	洋葱/洋蔥	noun	2.9.	*onion [m: -kē]*
yánjiū	研究	noun	2.2.	*research*
yánjiū	研究	verb	2.2.	*research*
yánjiūshēng	研究生	noun	2.7.	*graduate student [m: -gè, -wèi]*
yánjiūshēng yuàn	研究生院	plce	2.7.	*graduate school [m: -gè]*
yāo	幺/么	num	2.6.	*one (as a serial or code number) , 1*
yào	要	verb	2.8.	*want, require, demand, order (food), = xūyào*
yàozi	鹞子/鷂子	noun	1.8.	*sparrow hawk*
yāzi	鸭子/鴨子	noun	1.8.	*duck [m: -zhī]*
yě	也	adv	1.4.	*also (before predicate)*
yēzi	椰子	noun	1.8.	*coconut [m: -gè]*
yī + <u>measure</u>	一+量词/一+量詞	num	2.7.	*one (of something)*
yī, yí, yì	一	num	0.4.	*one, 1*

adj=adjective; *adr*=term of address; *adv*=adverb; *co-v*=co-verb; *comp*=complement; *conj*=conjunction; *dem*=demonstrative; *fam*=family name; *intr*=interjection; *mark*=grammatical marker; *mdl*=modal; *meas*=measure; *mnde*=modifying noun; *mptc*=modification particle; *nphr*=noun phrase; *num*=number; *phr*=phrase; *plce*=place; *plwd*=place word; *pn*=place name; *pre*=prefix; *prep*=preposition; *prn*=proper noun; *pron*=pronoun; *prvb*=pre-verb; *ques*=question word/phrase; *sptc*=sentence particle; *sufx*=suffix; *sv*=state verb; *timd*=time-(duration) word; *time*=time word; *timp*=time phrase; *tsfx*=time suffix; *vdir*=verb of direction; *vobj*=verb with set object; *vpot*=verb with potential

yǐjing	已经/已經	adv	2.4.	*(achieved state or completed event)*
Yīngguó	英国/英國	pn	2.2.	*England*
yīngwén	英文	noun	0.5.	*English language*
yīngxióng	英雄	noun	1.5.	*hero [m: -gè, -wèi]*
yǐqián	以前	time	1.4.	*before, previously*
yīwù	医务/醫務	noun	2.2.	*medical duties, medical profession*
yīyuàn	医院/醫院	plce	2.2.	*hospital [m: -gè, - jiā]*
yòng	用	verb	1.8.	*use*
yòng	用	co-v	2.6.	*(indicates instrument: with, by)*
yòng	用	verb	2.6.	*use*
yōngjǐ	拥挤/擁擠	adj	2.3.	*crowded, packed in*
yǒu	有	sv	0.8.	*have, there (exists)*
yòu adj1 yòu adj2	又 adj1 又 adj2	phr	1.7.	*both adj1 and adj2*
yǒu kòng	有空	phr	1.7.	*have free time*
yǒu yìdiǎn(r)	有一点儿/ 有一點兒	phr	1.4.	*somewhat (undesirable attribute)*
yǒu yìsi	有意思	adj	2.3.	*interesting, amusing*
yǒu yìsi	有意思	phr	2.3.	*interesting*
yóujú (yóudiànjú)	邮局（邮电局）/ 郵局（郵電局）	plce	2.8.	*post office [m: -gè, -jiā]*
yóupiào	邮票/郵票	noun	2.8.	*postage stamp [m: -zhāng]*
yóutàirén	犹太人/猶太人	noun	2.4.	*Jew*
yòuzi	柚子	noun	1.8.	*grapefruit, pomelo, shaddock [m: -gè]*
yú	鱼/魚	noun	1.8.	*fish [m: -tiáo]*

adj=adjective; *adr*=term of address; *adv*=adverb; *co-v*=co-verb; *comp*=complement; *conj*=conjunction; *dem*=demonstrative; *fam*=family name; *intr*=interjection; *mark*=grammatical marker; *mdl*=modal; *meas*=measure; *mnde*=modifying noun; *mptc*=modification particle; *nphr*=noun phrase; *num*=number; *phr*=phrase; *plce*=place; *plwd*=place word; *pn*=place name; *pre*=prefix; *prep*=preposition; *prn*=proper noun; *pron*=pronoun; *prvb*=pre-verb; *ques*=question word/phrase; *sptc*=sentence particle; *sufx*=suffix; *sv*=state verb; *timd*=time-(duration) word; *time*=time word; *timp*=time phrase; *tsfx*=time suffix; *vdir*=verb of direction; *vobj*=verb with set object; *vpot*=verb with potential

yuànzhǎng	院长/院長	adr	1.9.	*dean (college), director (hospital)*
yuánzhūbǐ	圆珠笔/圓珠筆	noun	2.8.	*ball point pen [m: -zhī]*
yuànzi	院子	noun	1.8.	*yard [m: -gè]*
yuè	月	noun	1.8.	*month [m: -gè]*
yùmǐ	玉米	noun	2.9.	*corn [m: -gè]*
Yúnnán	云南/雲南	pn	2.9.	*Yunnan (province in China)*
zài	再	adv	0.4.	*again*
zài	在	co-v	2.1.	*(at the place of action, event or state)*
zài	在	sv	2.1.	*be at/in/on, exist*
zàijiàn	再见/再見	phr	0.8.	*goodbye*
zāng	脏/髒	adj	2.3.	*dirty*
zánmen	咱们/咱們	pron	1.7.	*we, us (includes the addressee)*
zázhì	杂志/雜誌	noun	2.8.	*magazine [m: -běn(r), -fèn(r)]*
zěnme	怎么/怎麼	ques	0.4.	*how (to do something)*
zěnme bàn?	怎么办？/ 怎麼辦？	phr	2.6.	*How shall (we) handle this?*
Zhāng	张/張	fam	1.1.	*Chinese surname*
zhāng	张/張	meas	2.8.	*(flat things or flat surfaces/zhǐ)*
zhǎngde + <u>adj.</u>	长得/長得	phr	1.6.	*look(s) <u>adj.</u> (physical attribute)*
zhàngfu	丈夫	noun	2.4.	*husband (formal)*
Zhào	赵/趙	fam	1.2.	*Chinese surname*
zhè/zhèi	这/這	dem	1.6.	*this*

adj=adjective; *adr*=term of address; *adv*=adverb; *co-v*=co-verb; *comp*=complement; *conj*=conjunction; *dem*=demonstrative; *fam*=family name; *intr*=interjection; *mark*=grammatical marker; *mdl*=modal; *meas*=measure; *mnde*=modifying noun; *mptc*=modification particle; *nphr*=noun phrase; *num*=number; *phr*=phrase; *plce*=place; *plwd*=place word; *pn*=place name; *pre*=prefix; *prep*=preposition; *prn*=proper noun; *pron*=pronoun; *prvb*=pre-verb; *ques*=question word/phrase; *sptc*=sentence particle; *sufx*=suffix; *sv*=state verb; *timd*=time-(duration) word; *time*=time word; *timp*=time phrase; *tsfx*=time suffix; *vdir*=verb of direction; *vobj*=verb with set object; *vpot*=verb with potential

Zhèjiāng	浙江	pn	2.9.	*Zhejiang (province in China)*
zhèlǐ	这里/這裡	plwd	2.6.	*here, this place*
zhēn	真	adv	1.9.	*really, very, truly*
zhèr	这儿/這兒	plwd	2.6.	*here, this place*
zhī	支	meas	2.8.	*(sticklike things/bǐ, qiānbǐ)*
zhǐ	只/祇	adv	2.7.	*only, merely*
zhīdao	知道	sv	0.7.	*know, have the information*
zhǐhuán	指环/指環	noun	1.8.	*finger ring [m: -gè]*
Zhījiāgē	芝加哥	pn	2.1.	*Chicago*
zhīmayóu	芝麻油	noun	2.9.	*sesame oil [m: -dī, -píng]*
zhìzi	稚子	noun	1.5.	*young child*
Zhōngguó Guójì Màoyì Zhōngxīn	中国国际贸易中心/中國國際貿易中心	pn	2.1.	*China International Trade Center*
Zhōngguó	中国/中國	pn	2.2.	*China*
Zhōngguócài	中国菜/中國菜	noun	2.9.	*Chinese food [m: -fèn(r)]*
zhōngwén	中文	noun	0.4.	*Chinese language*
zhóuzi	轴子/軸子	noun	2.5.	*roller [m: -gè]*
zhuàng	壮/壯	adj	1.6.	*stout, strong build*
zhǔrèn	主任	adr	1.9.	*chairman, director (of an office)*
zī	资/資	noun	1.5.	*capital*
zìwǒ	自我	pron	1.9.	*(reflexive) myself*

adj=adjective; *adr*=term of address; *adv*=adverb; *co-v*=co-verb; *comp*=complement; *conj*=conjunction; *dem*=demonstrative; *fam*=family name; *intr*=interjection; *mark*=grammatical marker; *mdl*=modal; *meas*=measure; *mnde*=modifying noun; *mptc*=modification particle; *nphr*=noun phrase; *num*=number; *phr*=phrase; *plce*=place; *plwd*=place word; *pn*=place name; *pre*=prefix; *prep*=preposition; *prn*=proper noun; *pron*=pronoun; *prvb*=pre-verb; *ques*=question word/phrase; *sptc*=sentence particle; *sufx*=suffix; *sv*=state verb; *timd*=time-(duration) word; *time*=time word; *timp*=time phrase; *tsfx*=time suffix; *vdir*=verb of direction; *vobj*=verb with set object; *vpot*=verb with potential

zìwǒ jièshào yíxià	自我介绍一下 / 自我介紹一下	phr	1.9.	*let me introduce myself*
zuìjìn	最近	time	1.4.	*recently*
zuò	坐	verb	0.2.	*sit*
zuò	做	verb	2.2.	*do*
zuò X gōngzuò	做 X 工作	phr	2.2.	*work at/as X*
zuòzi	座子	noun	2.5.	*base, pedestal (for a machine) [m: -gè]*

English Glossary

Pīnyīn	Hànzì	POS	Stage	English
yǐjing	已经/已經	adv	2.4.	*(achieved state or completed event)*
de	的	mptc	1.7.	*(after modifier of nominal)*
shénme rén	什么人/甚麼人	phr	1.3.	*(asking about a person's profession or status)*
ba	吧	sptc	1.6.	*(assumes-state, suggests-event)*
zài	在	co-v	2.1.	*(at the place of action, event or state)*
kuài(r)	块(儿)/塊(兒)	meas	2.8.	*(basic monetary unit/ qián), =yuán*
píng(r)	瓶(儿)/瓶(兒)	meas	2.8.	*(bottle/qìshuǐ)*
běn(r)	本(儿)/本(兒)	meas	2.8.	*(bound volumes/shū, zázhì)*
guàn(r)	罐(儿)/罐(兒)	meas	2.8.	*(cans/qìshuǐ)*
le	了	sptc	2.4.	*(completed event, achieved state)*
yǐjing......le	已经……了/ 已經……了	mark	2.4.	*(completed state or event)*
<u>V</u> guò <u>X</u> le	<u>V</u> 过 <u>X</u> 了/<u>V</u> 過 <u>X</u> 了	mark	2.4.	*(completion of an expected event)*
bēi	杯	meas	2.8.	*(cups, glasses/chá, qìshuǐ)*
shì	是	mark	2.2.	*(emphasizes following element in a phrase)*
ā (yā, na)	啊(呀，哪)	sptc	1.9.	*(emphasizes intentions)*

adj=adjective; *adr*=term of address; *adv*=adverb; *co-v*=co-verb; *comp*=complement; *conj*=conjunction; *dem*=demonstrative; *fam*=family name; *intr*=interjection; *mark*=grammatical marker; *mdl*=modal; *meas*=measure; *mnde*=modifying noun; *mptc*=modification particle; *nphr*=noun phrase; *num*=number; *phr*=phrase; *plce*=place; *plwd*=place word; *pn*=place name; *pre*=prefix; *prep*=preposition; *prn*=proper noun; *pron*=pronoun; *prvb*=pre-verb; *ques*=question word/phrase; *sptc*=sentence particle; *sufx*=suffix; *sv*=state verb; *timd*=time-(duration) word; *time*=time word; *timp*=time phrase; *tsfx*=time suffix; *vdir*=verb of direction; *vobj*=verb with set object; *vpot*=verb with potential

jiùshi	就是	sv	1.7.	(emphatic) am, are, is, was, were
wā	哇	intr	1.8.	(expression of wonderment)
zhāng	张/張	meas	2.8.	(flat things or flat surfaces/zhǐ)
gè	个/個	meas	1.6.	(general measure for persons)
gè	个/個	meas	2.8.	(general measure for objects, people...)
xiē	些	meas	2.8.	(general plural measure)
hǎo	好	phr	0.1.	(greeting, ex: Nǐ hǎo.)
Dùzi è le.	肚子饿了。/ 肚子餓了。	phr	2.9	(I am) hungry.
le	了	sptc	1.4.	(indicates changes)
yòng	用	co-v	2.6.	(indicates instrument: with, by)
bei	呗/唄	sptc	2.6.	(indicates obviousness)
hé	和	conj	1.6.	(joins nouns)
fēng	封	meas	2.6.	(letters)
tái	台/臺	meas	2.6.	(machines/chuánzhēnjī...)
gěi	给/給	co-v	2.8.	(marks beneficiary of an action)
dùn	顿/頓	meas	2.8.	(meals/fàn)
duǒ	朵	meas	1.8.	(measure for flowers)
méi(yǒu)	没(有)/沒(有)	mark	2.4.	(negates past events)
bù-, bú-	不	mark	0.7.	(negates verbs and adjectives)

adj=adjective; *adr*=term of address; *adv*=adverb; *co-v*=co-verb; *comp*=complement; *conj*=conjunction; *dem*=demonstrative; *fam*=family name; *intr*=interjection; *mark*=grammatical marker; *mdl*=modal; *meas*=measure; *mnde*=modifying noun; *mptc*=modification particle; *nphr*=noun phrase; *num*=number; *phr*=phrase; *plce*=place; *plwd*=place word; *pn*=place name; *pre*=prefix; *prep*=preposition; *prn*=proper noun; *pron*=pronoun; *prvb*=pre-verb; *ques*=question word/phrase; *sptc*=sentence particle; *sufx*=suffix; *sv*=state verb; *timd*=time-(duration) word; *time*=time word; *timp*=time phrase; *tsfx*=time suffix; *vdir*=verb of direction; *vobj*=verb with set object; *vpot*=verb with potential

méi-	没/沒	mark	0.8.	*(negates yǒu)*
le	了	sptc	0.2.	*(new situation)*
biàn	遍	meas	0.4.	*(one complete activity/action)*
wèi	位	meas	1.6.	*(persons-polite measure)*
-men	们/們	sufx	1.4.	*(pluralizes definite human nouns)*
fèn(r)	份(儿)/份(兒)	meas	2.8.	*(portions/fàn; issues/ bàozhǐ)*
ma	吗/嗎	sptc	0.7.	*(question)*
ne	呢	sptc	1.4.	*(question)*
zìwǒ	自我	pron	1.9.	*(reflexive) myself*
-hào	号/號	sufx	2.6.	*(room number, size, days of month)*
jiān	间/間	meas	2.7.	*(rooms)*
zhī	支	meas	2.8.	*(sticklike things/bǐ, qiānbǐ)*
kuàijì	会计/會計	noun	2.2.	*accountant, accounting [m: -gè, -wèi]*
zài	再	adv	0.4.	*again*
jiǔ	酒	noun	1.8.	*alcohol beverage [m: -píng(r), -bēi]*
dōu	都	adv	1.4.	*all (at head of predicate)*
dàjiā	大家	pron	0.3.	*all, everybody*
chàbuduō	差不多	adv	2.7.	*almost, approximately*
chàbuduō	差不多	phr	2.7.	*almost, That's about it.*
yě	也	adv	1.4.	*also (before predicate)*
měijí-	美籍	pre	2.4.	*American (citizen)*
huídá	回答	verb	0.5.	*answer*

adj=adjective; *adr*=term of address; *adv*=adverb; *co-v*=co-verb; *comp*=complement; *conj*=conjunction; *dem*=demonstrative; *fam*=family name; *intr*=interjection; *mark*=grammatical marker; *mdl*=modal; *meas*=measure; *mnde*=modifying noun; *mptc*=modification particle; *nphr*=noun phrase; *num*=number; *phr*=phrase; *plce*=place; *plwd*=place word; *pn*=place name; *pre*=prefix; *prep*=preposition; *prn*=proper noun; *pron*=pronoun; *prvb*=pre-verb; *ques*=question word/phrase; *sptc*=sentence particle; *sufx*=suffix; *sv*=state verb; *timd*=time-(duration) word; *time*=time word; *timp*=time phrase; *tsfx*=time suffix; *vdir*=verb of direction; *vobj*=verb with set object; *vpot*=verb with potential

jǐnzhāng	紧张/緊張	adj	1.7.	anxious, nervous, tense
píngguǒ	苹果/蘋果	noun	2.9.	apple [m: - gè]
jié=hūn le méi-you?	结婚了没有?/結婚了沒有?	phr	2.4.	Are you married?
wèn	问/問	verb	0.5.	ask
diànhuà hàomǎ(r) (shì) duōshǎo?	电话号码(儿)(是)多少? /電話號碼(兒)(是)多少?	phr	2.6.	asking for a telephone number
fùjīnglǐ	副经理/副經理	adr	1.3.	assistant manager
fùjīnglǐ	副经理/副經理	noun	1.3.	assistant manager [m: -gè, -wèi]
shān-xià	山下	plwd	2.3.	at the foot of the mountain(s)
shàng=kè	上课/上課	vobj	0.2.	attend class, give a lesson
piàoliang	漂亮	adj	1.6.	attractive
Àodàlìyà	澳大利亚/澳大利亞	pn	2.2.	Australia
yuánzhūbǐ	圆珠笔/圓珠筆	noun	2.8.	ball point pen [m: -zhī]
dízi	笛子	noun	2.5.	bamboo flute [m: -zhī]
xiāngjiāo	香蕉	noun	2.9.	banana [m: -zhī (single), -bǎ (bunch)]
Bǎodìng	保定	pn	2.9.	Baoding (city in Hebei)
zuòzi	座子	noun	2.5.	base, pedestal (for a machine) [m: -gè]
zài	在	sv	2.1.	be at/in/on, exist
shì	是	sv	1.3.	be, is, am, are, was, were
xióng	熊	noun	1.8.	bear [m: -zhī, -tóu]

adj=adjective; adr=term of address; adv=adverb; co-v=co-verb; comp=complement; conj=conjunction; dem=demonstrative; fam=family name; intr=interjection; mark=grammatical marker; mdl=modal; meas=measure; mnde=modifying noun; mptc=modification particle; nphr=noun phrase; num=number; phr=phrase; plce=place; plwd=place word; pn=place name; pre=prefix; prep=preposition; prn=proper noun; pron=pronoun; prvb=pre-verb; ques=question word/phrase; sptc=sentence particle; sufx=suffix; sv=state verb; timd=time-(duration) word; time=time word; timp=time phrase; tsfx=time suffix; vdir=verb of direction; vobj=verb with set object; vpot=verb with potential

měi	美	adj	2.3.	*beautiful*
niúpái	牛排	noun	2.9.	*beefsteak [m: -kuài(r)]*
yǐqián	以前	time	1.4.	*before, previously*
Běihǎi	北海	pn	2.9.	*Beihai (city in Guangxi)*
Běihǎi Gōngyuán	北海公园	pn	2.9.	*Beihai Park (park in Beijing)*
Běijīng Dàxué	北京大学/ 北京大學	pn	1.9.	*Beijing University (Beijing, China)*
Běijīng	北京	pn	2.1.	*Beijing, Peking*
dùzi	肚子	noun	1.8.	*belly*
Bèngbù	蚌埠	pn	2.9.	*Bengbu (city in Anhui)*
shēn-biān(r)	身边(儿)/ 身邊(兒)	plwd	2.4.	*beside a person*
hóngchá	红茶/紅茶	noun	2.9.	*black tea [m: -bēi]*
tǎn	毯	noun	0.9.	*blanket*
shū	书/書	noun	2.8.	*book [m: -běn(r)]*
shūdiàn	书店/書店	plce	2.8.	*book store [m: -gè, -jiā]*
méi(yǒu)yìsi	没(有)意思/ 沒(有)意思	adj	2.3.	*boring, uninteresting*
yòu adj1 yòu adj2	又 adj1 又 adj2	phr	1.7.	*both adj1 and adj2*
hézi	盒子	noun	2.5.	*box [m: -gè]*
héfàn	盒饭/盒飯	noun	2.8.	*box lunch [m: -fèn(r), -gè]*
nǎozi	脑子/腦子	noun	2.5.	*brain [m: -gè]*
mèn	焖/燜	verb	1.5.	*braise, stew, cook in a covered pot over a low heat*
miànbāo	面包/麵包	noun	2.9.	*bread [m: -kuài]*
huài	坏/壞	adj	1.8.	*broken*
fó	佛	noun	1.8.	*Buddha*

adj=adjective; *adr*=term of address; *adv*=adverb; *co-v*=co-verb; *comp*=complement; *conj*=conjunction; *dem*=demonstrative; *fam*=family name; *intr*=interjection; *mark*=grammatical marker; *mdl*=modal; *meas*=measure; *mnde*=modifying noun; *mptc*=modification particle; *nphr*=noun phrase; *num*=number; *phr*=phrase; *plce*=place; *plwd*=place word; *pn*=place name; *pre*=prefix; *prep*=preposition; *prn*=proper noun; *pron*=pronoun; *prvb*=pre-verb; *ques*=question word/phrase; *sptc*=sentence particle; *sufx*=suffix; *sv*=state verb; *timd*=time-(duration) word; *time*=time word; *timp*=time phrase; *tsfx*=time suffix; *vdir*=verb of direction; *vobj*=verb with set object; *vpot*=verb with potential

mái	埋	verb	1.8.	*bury*
máng	忙	adj	1.4.	*busy*
méi-kòng	没空	phr	1.7.	*busy, do not have free time*
mǎi	买/買	verb	1.5.	*buy*
mǎi	买/買	verb	2.8.	*buy*
chēnghu	称呼/稱呼	verb	1.9.	*call, address*
píngjìng	平静/平靜	adj	1.7.	*calm, tranquil, composed*
Jiānádà	加拿大	pn	2.2.	*Canada*
zī	资/資	noun	1.5.	*capital*
Shǒudū Jùchǎng	首都剧场/首都劇場	pn	2.1.	*Capital Theatre*
gǎnmào le	感冒了	phr	1.4	*catch cold, have the flu*
qíncài	芹菜	noun	2.9.	*celery [m: -bǎ, -gēn]*
zhǔrèn	主任	adr	1.9.	*chairman, director (of an office)*
luàn	乱/亂	noun	1.8.	*chaos*
tàn	炭	noun	0.9.	*charcoal*
nǎilào	奶酪	noun	2.9.	*cheese [m: -kuài(r)]*
lìzi	栗子	noun	2.9.	*chestnut [m: -gè]*
Zhījiāgē	芝加哥	pn	2.1.	*Chicago*
jī	鸡/雞	noun	1.5.	*chicken [m: -zhī]*
Zhōngguó	中国/中國	pn	2.2.	*China*
Zhōngguó Guójì Màoyì Zhōngxīn	中国国际贸易中心/中國國際貿易中心	pn	2.1.	*China International Trade Center*
shīzitóu	狮子头/獅子頭	noun	2.9.	*Chinese entrée: meatball [m: -gè]*

adj=adjective; *adr*=term of address; *adv*=adverb; *co-v*=co-verb; *comp*=complement; *conj*=conjunction; *dem*=demonstrative; *fam*=family name; *intr*=interjection; *mark*=grammatical marker; *mdl*=modal; *meas*=measure; *mnde*=modifying noun; *mptc*=modification particle; *nphr*=noun phrase; *num*=number; *phr*=phrase; *plce*=place; *plwd*=place word; *pn*=place name; *pre*=prefix; *prep*=preposition; *prn*=proper noun; *pron*=pronoun; *prvb*=pre-verb; *ques*=question word/phrase; *sptc*=sentence particle; *sufx*=suffix; *sv*=state verb; *timd*=time-(duration) word; *time*=time word; *timp*=time phrase; *tsfx*=time suffix; *vdir*=verb of direction; *vobj*=verb with set object; *vpot*=verb with potential

hóngshāo qiézi	红烧茄子/ 紅燒茄子	noun	1.8.	*Chinese entrée: eggplant braised in soy sauce*
Zhōngguócài	中国菜/ 中國菜	noun	2.9.	*Chinese food [m: -fèn(r)]*
zhōngwén	中文	noun	0.4.	*Chinese language*
huáyǔ	华语/華語	noun	2.4.	*Chinese language*
huárén	华人/華人	noun	2.4.	*Chinese person*
Liú	刘/劉	fam	1.1.	*Chinese surname*
Zhāng	张/張	fam	1.1.	*Chinese surname*
Ōuyáng	欧阳/歐陽	fam	1.2.	*Chinese surname*
Chén	陈/陳	fam	1.2.	*Chinese surname*
Dù	杜	fam	1.2.	*Chinese surname*
Wú	吴/吳	fam	1.2.	*Chinese surname*
Zhào	赵/趙	fam	1.2.	*Chinese surname*
Huà	华/華	fam	1.3.	*Chinese surname*
Lín	林	fam	1.2.	*Chinese surname (forest)*
Shī	施	fam	1.2.	*Chinese surname*
Wáng	王	fam	1.1.	*Chinese surname (king)*
Lǐ	李	fam	1.1.	*Chinese surname (plum)*
Fāng	方	fam	1.2.	*Chinese surname (square)*
Bái	白	fam	1.1.	*Chinese surname (white)*
Huáng	黄/黃	fam	1.1.	*Chinese surname (yellow)*
Chóngqìng	重庆/重慶	pn	2.9.	*Chongqing (city in China)*
kuàizi	筷子	noun	2.9.	*chopsticks [m: -shuāng]*

adj=adjective; *adr*=term of address; *adv*=adverb; *co-v*=co-verb; *comp*=complement; *conj*=conjunction; *dem*=demonstrative; *fam*=family name; *intr*=interjection; *mark*=grammatical marker; *mdl*=modal; *meas*=measure; *mnde*=modifying noun; *mptc*=modification particle; *nphr*=noun phrase; *num*=number; *phr*=phrase; *plce*=place; *plwd*=place word; *pn*=place name; *pre*=prefix; *prep*=preposition; *prn*=proper noun; *pron*=pronoun; *prvb*=pre-verb; *ques*=question word/phrase; *sptc*=sentence particle; *sufx*=suffix; *sv*=state verb; *timd*=time-(duration) word; *time*=time word; *timp*=time phrase; *tsfx*=time suffix; *vdir*=verb of direction; *vobj*=verb with set object; *vpot*=verb with potential

chéng	城	noun	2.3.	*city*
Guǎngzhōu	广州/廣州	pn	2.2.	*city in Guangdong; Canton*
Wǔhàn	武汉/武漢	pn	2.2.	*city in Hubei*
gānjìng	干净/乾淨	adj	2.3.	*clean*
qīngchu	清楚	adj	1.7.	*clear, clearheaded, aware*
yēzi	椰子	noun	1.8.	*coconut [m: -gè]*
tóngshì	同事	noun	1.4.	*colleague*
tóngshìmen	同事们/同事們	noun	1.4.	*colleagues*
xuéyuàn	学院/學院	plce	1.9.	*college, institute [m: -gè]*
Gēlúnbù	哥伦布/哥倫布	pn	2.2.	*Columbus*
shūfu	舒服	adj	1.4.	*comfortable*
jìniàn yóupiào	纪念邮票/纪念郵票	noun	2.8.	*commemorative stamp [m: -zhāng]*
pǔtōng	普通	adj	2.3.	*common, wide-spread*
gōngsī	公司	plce	1.9.	*company [m: -jiā, -gè]*
bǐjiào	比较/比較	verb	1.6.	*compare*
bǐ	比	verb	1.6.	*compare to*
nénggàn	能干/能幹	adj	1.7.	*competent, able*
diànnǎo	电脑/電腦	noun	2.6.	*computer [m: -tái]*
tóngzhì	同志	adr	1.2.	*comrade*
mǐfàn	米饭/米飯	noun	2.9.	*cooked rice [m: -wǎn]*
yùmǐ	玉米	noun	2.9.	*corn [m: -gè]*
duì le	对了/對了	phr	0.2.	*correct*
qián zhènghǎo	钱正好/錢正好	phr	2.8.	*correct change*
bǐnggān	饼干/餅乾	noun	2.9.	*cracker, cookie [m: -kuài(r)]*

adj=adjective; *adr*=term of address; *adv*=adverb; *co-v*=co-verb; *comp*=complement; *conj*=conjunction; *dem*=demonstrative; *fam*=family name; *intr*=interjection; *mark*=grammatical marker; *mdl*=modal; *meas*=measure; *mnde*=modifying noun; *mptc*=modification particle; *nphr*=noun phrase; *num*=number; *phr*=phrase; *plce*=place; *plwd*=place word; *pn*=place name; *pre*=prefix; *prep*=preposition; *prn*=proper noun; *pron*=pronoun; *prvb*=pre-verb; *ques*=question word/phrase; *sptc*=sentence particle; *sufx*=suffix; *sv*=state verb; *timd*=time-(duration) word; *time*=time word; *timp*=time phrase; *tsfx*=time suffix; *vdir*=verb of direction; *vobj*=verb with set object; *vpot*=verb with potential

nǎiyóu	奶油	noun	2.9.	cream [m: -kuài(r)]
yōngjǐ	拥挤/擁擠	adj	2.3.	crowded, packed in
huángguā	黄瓜/黃瓜	noun	2.9.	cucumber [m: -gēn]
bà(ba)	爸(爸)	noun	2.4.	dad
diē	爹	noun	2.4.	dad (non-urban)
Dàlǐ	大理	pn	2.9.	Dali (city in Yunnan)
rìzi	日子	noun	1.5.	days on the calendar
yuànzhǎng	院长/院長	adr	1.9.	dean (college), director (hospital)
tǎo	讨/討	verb	0.9.	demand
shèjì	设计/設計	verb	2.2.	design
shèjì	设计/設計	noun	2.2.	design, plan, scheme [m: -gè, -zhǒng]
cānchē	餐车/餐車	plce	2.8.	dining car (on a train) [m: -jié]
zāng	脏/髒	adj	2.3.	dirty
āngzāng	肮脏/骯髒	adj	1.5.	dirty, foul
fā	发/發	verb	2.6.	dispatch, send, distribute, issue
zuò	做	verb	2.2.	do
bú-kèqi	不客气/不客氣	phr	0.8.	Don't be so polite, You're welcome. (response to xièxie)
ménkǒu	门口/門口	plwd	2.3.	doorway, gateway
lóng	龙/龍	noun	1.8.	dragon [m: -tiáo]
mèng	梦/夢	noun	1.5.	dream [m: -gè]
hē	喝	verb	2.8.	drink
yāzi	鸭子/鴨子	noun	1.8.	duck [m: -zhī]

adj=adjective; *adr*=term of address; *adv*=adverb; *co-v*=co-verb; *comp*=complement; *conj*=conjunction; *dem*=demonstrative; *fam*=family name; *intr*=interjection; *mark*=grammatical marker; *mdl*=modal; *meas*=measure; *mnde*=modifying noun; *mptc*=modification particle; *nphr*=noun phrase; *num*=number; *phr*=phrase; *plce*=place; *plwd*=place word; *pn*=place name; *pre*=prefix; *prep*=preposition; *prn*=proper noun; *pron*=pronoun; *prvb*=pre-verb; *ques*=question word/phrase; *sptc*=sentence particle; *sufx*=suffix; *sv*=state verb; *timd*=time-(duration) word; *time*=time word; *timp*=time phrase; *tsfx*=time suffix; *vdir*=verb of direction; *vobj*=verb with set object; *vpot*=verb with potential

shuǐjiǎo	水饺/水餃	noun	2.9.	*dumpling (boiled)* *[m: -gè]*
jiǎozi	饺子/餃子	noun	1.8.	*dumpling [m: -gè]*
chī	吃	verb	2.8.	*eat*
qiézi	茄子	noun	1.8.	*eggplant [m: -gè]*
bā	八	num	2.6.	*eight, 8*
xià=kè	下课/下課	vobj	0.8.	*end class, dismiss class*
Yīngguó	英国/英國	pn	2.2.	*England*
yīngwén	英文	noun	0.5.	*English language*
rùkǒu	入口	plwd	2.3.	*entrance [m: -gè]*
xìnfēng(r)	信封(儿)/信封(兒)	noun	2.8.	*envelope [m: -gè]*
shèbèi	设备/設備	noun	2.1.	*equipment*
dàochù	到处/到處	adv	2.3.	*everywhere*
chūkǒu	出口	plwd	2.3.	*exit [m: -gè]*
méi	眉	noun	1.8.	*eyebrow [m: -dào]*
gōngchǎng	工厂/工廠	plce	2.2.	*factory [m: -gè, -jiā]*
chǎngzhǎng	厂长/廠長	noun	2.3.	*factory chief*
chǎngzhǎng	厂长/廠長	adr	2.3.	*factory chief or general manager*
miànshóu/ miànshú	面熟	adj	1.6.	*familiar looking*
jiā	家	plce	2.2.	*family, home, house [m: -gè]*
pàng	胖	adj	1.6.	*fat, plump*
fùqin	父亲/父親	noun	2.4.	*father*
lǎozi	老子	noun	2.5.	*father, I (used jocularly or in anger)*
chuánzhēn	传真/傳真	noun	2.6.	*fax [m: -fèn(r)]*

adj=adjective; *adr*=term of address; *adv*=adverb; *co-v*=co-verb; *comp*=complement; *conj*=conjunction; *dem*=demonstrative; *fam*=family name; *intr*=interjection; *mark*=grammatical marker; *mdl*=modal; *meas*=measure; *mnde*=modifying noun; *mptc*=modification particle; *nphr*=noun phrase; *num*=number; *phr*=phrase; *plce*=place; *plwd*=place word; *pn*=place name; *pre*=prefix; *prep*=preposition; *prn*=proper noun; *pron*=pronoun; *prvb*=pre-verb; *ques*=question word/phrase; *sptc*=sentence particle; *sufx*=suffix; *sv*=state verb; *timd*=time-(duration) word; *time*=time word; *timp*=time phrase; *tsfx*=time suffix; *vdir*=verb of direction; *vobj*=verb with set object; *vpot*=verb with potential

chuánzhēnjī	传真机/傳真機	noun	2.6.	*fax machine [m: -tái]*
tóngxuémen	同学们/同學們	adr	0.1.	*fellow students*
Fènghuà	奉化	pn	2.9.	*Fenghua (city in Zhejiang)*
shǎo	少	adj	2.7.	*few, little (of something)*
chìzi	翅子	noun	1.5.	*fin (usually from the shark)*
hǎo	好	adj	1.4.	*fine, good, okay*
zhǐhuán	指环/指環	noun	1.8.	*finger ring [m: -gè]*
huǒ	火	noun	1.8.	*fire [m: -tuán, -bǎ]*
yú	鱼/魚	noun	1.8.	*fish [m: -tiáo]*
wǔ	五	num	1.8.	*five, 5*
huā	花	noun	1.8.	*flower [m: -duǒ, -zhī]*
gēnzhe	跟着/跟著	phr	0.3.	*follow*
fàn	饭/飯	noun	2.8.	*food, meal [m: -fèn(r), -dùn]*
sì	四	num	1.5.	*four, 4*
Fùdàn Dàxué	复旦大学/復旦大學	pn	2.2.	*Fudan University (Shanghai, China)*
Fújiàn	福建	pn	2.9.	*Fujian (province in China)*
hǎowán(r)	好玩(儿)/好玩(兒)	adj	2.3.	*fun, amusing*
máo	毛	noun	1.8.	*fur, wool, bodyhair [m: -gēn]*
Gānsù	甘肃/甘肅	pn	2.9.	*Gansu (province in China)*
suàn	蒜	noun	1.8.	*garlic [m: -bàn(r), -tóu]*
dàsuàn	大蒜	noun	0.5.	*garlic [m: -kē, -tóu]*

adj=adjective; *adr*=term of address; *adv*=adverb; *co-v*=co-verb; *comp*=complement; *conj*=conjunction; *dem*=demonstrative; *fam*=family name; *intr*=interjection; *mark*=grammatical marker; *mdl*=modal; *meas*=measure; *mnde*=modifying noun; *mptc*=modification particle; *nphr*=noun phrase; *num*=number; *phr*=phrase; *plce*=place; *plwd*=place word; *pn*=place name; *pre*=prefix; *prep*=preposition; *prn*=proper noun; *pron*=pronoun; *prvb*=pre-verb; *ques*=question word/phrase; *sptc*=sentence particle; *sufx*=suffix; *sv*=state verb; *timd*=time-(duration) word; *time*=time word; *timp*=time phrase; *tsfx*=time suffix; *vdir*=verb of direction; *vobj*=verb with set object; *vpot*=verb with potential

dàfang	大方	adj	1.7.	*generous, liberal-minded*
jié=hūn	结婚/結婚	vobj	2.4.	*get married*
gěi	给/給	verb	2.8.	*give*
cī	呲	verb	1.5.	*give a tongue-lashing to*
jīn	金	noun	1.5.	*gold, money*
bú-cuò	不错/不錯	adj	2.3.	*good, not bad*
zàijiàn	再见/再見	phr	0.8.	*goodbye*
páozi	袍子	noun	2.5.	*gown, robe [m: -jiàn]*
yánjiūshēng yuàn	研究生院	plce	2.7.	*graduate school [m: -gè]*
yánjiūshēng	研究生	noun	2.7.	*graduate student [m: -gè, -wèi]*
yòuzi	柚子	noun	1.8.	*grapefruit, pomelo, shaddock [m: -gè]*
lǜchá	绿茶/綠茶	noun	2.9.	*green tea [m: -bēi]*
kèren	客人	noun	1.7.	*guest, visitor, customer*
nǔlì	努力	adj	1.4.	*hard working*
yǒu kòng	有空	phr	1.7.	*have free time*
xìng	姓	sv	1.2.	*have the family name <u>X</u>*
yǒu	有	sv	0.8.	*have, there (exists)*
tā	他	pron	1.2.	*he, him*
zhèlǐ	这里/這裡	plwd	2.6.	*here, this place*
zhèr	这儿/這兒	plwd	2.6.	*here, this place*
yīngxióng	英雄	noun	1.5.	*hero [m: -gè, -wèi]*
Xiānggǎng	香港	pn	2.1.	*Hong Kong*
tízi	蹄子	noun	2.5.	*hoof [m: -gè]*
mǎ	马/馬	noun	1.5.	*horse [m: -pǐ]*
yīyuàn	医院/醫院	plce	2.2.	*hospital [m: -gè, - jiā]*

adj=adjective; *adr*=term of address; *adv*=adverb; *co-v*=co-verb; *comp*=complement; *conj*=conjunction; *dem*=demonstrative; *fam*=family name; *intr*=interjection; *mark*=grammatical marker; *mdl*=modal; *meas*=measure; *mnde*=modifying noun; *mptc*=modification particle; *nphr*=noun phrase; *num*=number; *phr*=phrase; *plce*=place; *plwd*=place word; *pn*=place name; *pre*=prefix; *prep*=preposition; *prn*=proper noun; *pron*=pronoun; *prvb*=pre-verb; *ques*=question word/phrase; *sptc*=sentence particle; *sufx*=suffix; *sv*=state verb; *timd*=time-(duration) word; *time*=time word; *timp*=time phrase; *tsfx*=time suffix; *vdir*=verb of direction; *vobj*=verb with set object; *vpot*=verb with potential

zěnme	怎么／怎麼	ques	0.4.	*how (to do something)*
X zěnmeyàng	X怎么样／X怎麼樣	ques	1.4.	*how is X, what is X like*
jǐ + measure	几+量词／ 幾+量詞	ques	2.7.	*how many (small amount)*
duōshao	多少	ques	2.7.	*how many/much*
zěnme bàn?	怎么办？／ 怎麼辦？	phr	2.6.	*How shall (we) handle this?*
bǎi	百	num	2.7.	*hundred, 100*
è	饿／餓	adj	1.5.	*hungry*
xiānsheng	先生	noun	2.4.	*husband (formal)*
zhàngfu	丈夫	noun	2.4.	*husband (formal)*
Wǒ è le.	我饿了。／我餓了。	phr	1.5.	*I am hungry.*
Wǒ kě le.	我渴了。	phr	1.5.	*I am thirsty.*
wǒ	我	pron	0.3.	*I, me*
fēizi	妃子	noun	2.5.	*imperial concubine [m: -gè]*
hái	还／還	adv	2.4.	*in addition to, also (continuing state or event)*
qián-biān (r)	前边（儿）／ 前邊（兒）	plwd	2.4.	*in the front, front*
hòu-biān(r)	后边（儿）／ 後邊（兒）	plwd	2.4.	*in the rear, back*
chéng-lǐ	城里／城裏	plwd	2.3.	*in town, in the city*
wúnéng	无能／無能	adj	1.7.	*incompetent*
lǐ-biān(r)	里边（儿）／ 裏邊（兒）	plwd	2.4.	*inside*
cōngming	聪明／聰明	adj	1.4.	*intelligent, clever*
yǒu yìsi	有意思	phr	2.3.	*interesting*
yǒu yìsi	有意思	adj	2.3.	*interesting, amusing*

adj=adjective; *adr*=term of address; *adv*=adverb; *co-v*=co-verb; *comp*=complement; *conj*=conjunction; *dem*=demonstrative; *fam*=family name; *intr*=interjection; *mark*=grammatical marker; *mdl*=modal; *meas*=measure; *mnde*=modifying noun; *mptc*=modification particle; *nphr*=noun phrase; *num*=number; *phr*=phrase; *plce*=place; *plwd*=place word; *pn*=place name; *pre*=prefix; *prep*=preposition; *prn*=proper noun; *pron*=pronoun; *prvb*=pre-verb; *ques*=question word/phrase; *sptc*=sentence particle; *sufx*=suffix; *sv*=state verb; *timd*=time-(duration) word; *time*=time word; *timp*=time phrase; *tsfx*=time suffix; *vdir*=verb of direction; *vobj*=verb with set object; *vpot*=verb with potential

Guójì Dà Fàndiàn	国际大饭店/國際大飯店	pn	2.1.	*International Hotel*
lùkǒu	路口	plwd	2.3.	*intersection of streets or roadways [m: -gè]*
jièshào	介绍/介紹	verb	1.9.	*introduce*
Rìběn	日本	pn	2.2.	*Japan*
rìjí-	日籍	pre	2.4.	*Japanese (citizen)*
Rìběnrén	日本人	noun	2.4.	*Japanese person*
yóutàirén	犹太人/猶太人	noun	2.4.	*Jew*
Jìnán Dàxué	暨南大学/暨南大學	pn	2.2.	*Jinan University (Guangzhou, China)*
Jīnhuá	金华/金華	pn	2.9.	*Jinhua (city in Zhejiang)*
Jiǔlóng	九龙/九龍	pn	2.9.	*Jiulong (district in Hong Kong)*
xiǎomāo	小猫/小貓	noun	1.8.	*kitten [m: -zhī]*
zhīdao	知道	sv	0.7.	*know, have the information*
rènshi	认识/認識	sv	2.1.	*know, recognize*
Kūnmíng	昆明	pn	2.9.	*Kunming (city in Yunnan)*
chà	差	verb	2.7.	*lack, be short of*
dà	大	adj	1.6.	*large, great, old*
lǜ	律	noun	1.8.	*law*
lǎn	懒/懶	adj	1.4.	*lazy*
tuǐ	腿	noun	1.8.	*leg [m: -tiáo]*
zìwǒ jièshào yíxià	自我介绍一下/自我介紹一下	phr	1.9.	*let me introduce myself*

adj=adjective; *adr*=term of address; *adv*=adverb; *co-v*=co-verb; *comp*=complement; *conj*=conjunction; *dem*=demonstrative; *fam*=family name; *intr*=interjection; *mark*=grammatical marker; *mdl*=modal; *meas*=measure; *mnde*=modifying noun; *mptc*=modification particle; *nphr*=noun phrase; *num*=number; *phr*=phrase; *plce*=place; *plwd*=place word; *pn*=place name; *pre*=prefix; *prep*=preposition; *prn*=proper noun; *pron*=pronoun; *prvb*=pre-verb; *ques*=question word/phrase; *sptc*=sentence particle; *sufx*=suffix; *sv*=state verb; *timd*=time-(duration) word; *time*=time word; *timp*=time phrase; *tsfx*=time suffix; *vdir*=verb of direction; *vobj*=verb with set object; *vpot*=verb with potential

Wǒ gěi nǐmen jièshào yíxià.	我给你们介绍一下。/ 我給你們介紹一下。	phr	1.9.	*Let me introduce you.*
xìnzhǐ	信纸/信紙	noun	2.8.	*letter paper [m: -zhāng]*
xìn	信	noun	2.6.	*letter, piece of correspondence [m: -fēng]*
Liáoníng	辽宁/遼寧	pn	2.9.	*Liaoning (province in China)*
tǎng	躺	verb	0.6.	*lie down*
xǐhuan	喜欢/喜歡	sv	2.1.	*like, appreciate*
tīng	听/聽	verb	0.3.	*listen*
rènao	热闹/熱鬧	adj	2.3.	*lively, active, bustling*
suǒzi	锁子/鎖子	noun	2.5.	*lock [m: -bǎ]*
Lúndūn	伦敦/倫敦	pn	2.1.	*London (Yīngguó)*
zhǎngde + adj.	长得/長得	phr	1.6.	*look(s) adj. (physical attribute)*
Luòshānjī	洛杉矶/洛杉磯	pn	2.2.	*Los Angeles (Jiāzhōu)*
sè	色	noun	1.5.	*lust, sensuality*
zázhì	杂志/雜誌	noun	2.8.	*magazine [m: -běn(r), -fèn(r)]*
nánde	男的	noun	1.6.	*man [m: -gè]*
nánrén	男人	noun	1.6.	*man [m: -gè]*
guǎnlǐ	管理	noun	2.2.	*management*
jīnglǐ	经理/經理	noun	1.3.	*manager [m: -gè, -wèi]*
jīnglǐ	经理/經理	adr	1.3.	*manager, boss*
duō	多	adj	2.7.	*many, much*
jié=hūn le	结婚了/結婚了	phr	2.4.	*married*

adj=adjective; *adr*=term of address; *adv*=adverb; *co-v*=co-verb; *comp*=complement; *conj*=conjunction; *dem*=demonstrative; *fam*=family name; *intr*=interjection; *mark*=grammatical marker; *mdl*=modal; *meas*=measure; *mnde*=modifying noun; *mptc*=modification particle; *nphr*=noun phrase; *num*=number; *phr*=phrase; *plce*=place; *plwd*=place word; *pn*=place name; *pre*=prefix; *prep*=preposition; *prn*=proper noun; *pron*=pronoun; *prvb*=pre-verb; *ques*=question word/phrase; *sptc*=sentence particle; *sufx*=suffix; *sv*=state verb; *timd*=time-(duration) word; *time*=time word; *timp*=time phrase; *tsfx*=time suffix; *vdir*=verb of direction; *vobj*=verb with set object; *vpot*=verb with potential

shīfu	师傅/師傅	adr	2.8.	*master (for service workers) [m: -gè]*
xízi	席子	noun	2.5.	*mat [m: -zhāng]*
shìzi	式子	noun	1.5.	*math equation [m: -gè]*
qǐngwèn	请问/請問	phr	1.2.	*May I ask a question?*
cānquàn(r)	餐券(儿)/餐券(兒)	noun	2.8	*meal coupon [m: -zhāng]*
ròuwán(r)	肉丸(儿)/肉丸(兒)	noun	1.8.	*meatball [m: -gè]*
yīwù	医务/醫務	noun	2.2.	*medical duties, medical profession*
jiàn	见/見	verb	2.3.	*meet, perceive, see*
niúnǎi	牛奶	noun	2.9.	*milk [m: -píng, -hé, -tǒng, -guàn(r)]*
sùzi	粟子	noun	1.8.	*millet (also xiǎomǐ)*
xiǎomǐ xīfàn	小米稀饭/小米稀飯	noun	2.9.	*millet porridge [m: -wǎn]*
xiǎomǐ	小米	noun	2.9.	*millet, also sùzi [m: -kē, -lì]*
xiáojie	小姐	adr	1.1.	*Miss*
mā(ma)	妈(妈)/媽(媽)	noun	2.4.	*mom*
niáng	娘	noun	2.4	*mom (non-urban)*
qián	钱/錢	noun	2.8.	*money [kuài/yuán=basic monetary unit]*
yuè	月	noun	1.8.	*month [m: -gè]*
wénzi	蚊子	noun	1.8.	*mosquito [m: -zhī]*
mǔqin	母亲/母親	noun	2.4.	*mother*
xiānsheng	先生	adr	1.1.	*Mr., Honorable*

adj=adjective; *adr*=term of address; *adv*=adverb; *co-v*=co-verb; *comp*=complement; *conj*=conjunction; *dem*=demonstrative; *fam*=family name; *intr*=interjection; *mark*=grammatical marker; *mdl*=modal; *meas*=measure; *mnde*=modifying noun; *mptc*=modification particle; *nphr*=noun phrase; *num*=number; *phr*=phrase; *plce*=place; *plwd*=place word; *pn*=place name; *pre*=prefix; *prep*=preposition; *prn*=proper noun; *pron*=pronoun; *prvb*=pre-verb; *ques*=question word/phrase; *sptc*=sentence particle; *sufx*=suffix; *sv*=state verb; *timd*=time-(duration) word; *time*=time word; *timp*=time phrase; *tsfx*=time suffix; *vdir*=verb of direction; *vobj*=verb with set object; *vpot*=verb with potential

tàitai	太太	adr	1.1.	*Mrs.*
nǔshì	女士	adr	1.1.	*Ms. (formal)*
lùdòu	绿豆/綠豆	noun	2.9.	*mung bean [m: -kē]*
mógu	蘑菇	noun	1.8.	*mushroom [m: -gè]*
míngzi	名字	noun	1.3.	*name [m: -gè]*
jiào X	叫 X	sv	1.3.	*named, be called X*
Nánchāng	南昌	pn	2.9.	*Nanchang (city in Jiangxi)*
báicài	白菜	noun	2.9.	*napa cabbage [m: -kē]*
guójiā	国家/國家	noun	2.2.	*nation, country [m: -gè]*
bózi	脖子	noun	1.8.	*neck*
xūyào	需要	verb	2.7.	*need, require*
bàozhǐ	报纸/報紙	noun	2.8.	*newspaper [m: -fèn(r), -zhāng]*
Niǔyuē	纽约/紐約	pn	2.1.	*New York*
jiǔ	九	num	2.6.	*nine, 9*
chǎo	吵	adj	2.3.	*noisy, raucous*
miàn	面	noun	1.8.	*noodle [m: -wǎn]*
shīfàn dàxué	师范大学/師範大學	pn	1.9.	*normal (teachers) university*
Huáběi	华北/華北	pn	2.4.	*North China*
bú-duì	不对/不對	phr	0.2.	*not correct*
méi	没/沒	sv	0.8.	*not have, lacks (= méi-yǒu)*
běnzi	本子	noun	2.8.	*notebook [m: -gè]*
tōngzhī	通知	verb	2.6.	*notify, inform*
xiànzài	现在/現在	time	0.2.	*now*
hàomǎ(r)	号码(儿)/號碼(兒)	noun	2.6.	*number (telephone) [m: -gè]*
shùzì	数字/數字	noun	2.6.	*number [m: -gè]*

adj=adjective; *adr*=term of address; *adv*=adverb; *co-v*=co-verb; *comp*=complement; *conj*=conjunction; *dem*=demonstrative; *fam*=family name; *intr*=interjection; *mark*=grammatical marker; *mdl*=modal; *meas*=measure; *mnde*=modifying noun; *mptc*=modification particle; *nphr*=noun phrase; *num*=number; *phr*=phrase; *plce*=place; *plwd*=place word; *pn*=place name; *pre*=prefix; *prep*=preposition; *prn*=proper noun; *pron*=pronoun; *prvb*=pre-verb; *ques*=question word/phrase; *sptc*=sentence particle; *sufx*=suffix; *sv*=state verb; *timd*=time-(duration) word; *time*=time word; *timp*=time phrase; *tsfx*=time suffix; *vdir*=verb of direction; *vobj*=verb with set object; *vpot*=verb with potential

dāngrán	当然/當然	adv	2.6.	*of course, naturally*
bàngōngshì	办公室/辦公室	plce	2.7.	*office [m: -jiān, -gè]*
ò	哦	intr	1.2.	*oh! (implies recognition "I see")*
lǎo	老	adj	1.6.	*old (anim), obsolete (inan)*
lǎo péngyou	老朋友	phr	0.3.	*old friend*
pózi	婆子	noun	1.8.	*old woman [m: -gè]*
lǎo + surname	老	adr	1.1.	*older friend*
xià-biān(r)	下边(儿)/下邊(兒)	plwd	2.4.	*on the bottom, beneath*
páng-biān(r)	旁边(儿)/旁邊(兒)	plwd	2.4.	*on the side, beside*
jiē-shang	街上	plwd	2.3.	*on the street(s), in the street(s)*
shàng-biān(r)	上边(儿)/上邊(兒)	plwd	2.4.	*on, on top*
yāo	幺/么	num	2.6.	*one (as a serial or code number) , 1*
yī + measure	一+量词/一+量詞	num	2.7.	*one (of something)*
yī, yí, yì	一	num	0.4.	*one, 1*
yángcōng	洋葱/洋蔥	noun	2.9.	*onion [m: -kē]*
zhǐ	只/衹	adv	2.7.	*only, merely*
kāitong	开通/開通	adj	1.4.	*open-minded*
wài	外	plwd	1.8.	*outside*
wài-biān(r)	外边(儿)/外邊(兒)	plwd	2.4.	*outside*
chéng-wài	城外	plwd	2.3.	*outside of town*

adj=adjective; *adr*=term of address; *adv*=adverb; *co-v*=co-verb; *comp*=complement; *conj*=conjunction; *dem*=demonstrative; *fam*=family name; *intr*=interjection; *mark*=grammatical marker; *mdl*=modal; *meas*=measure; *mnde*=modifying noun; *mptc*=modification particle; *nphr*=noun phrase; *num*=number; *phr*=phrase; *plce*=place; *plwd*=place word; *pn*=place name; *pre*=prefix; *prep*=preposition; *prn*=proper noun; *pron*=pronoun; *prvb*=pre-verb; *ques*=question word/phrase; *sptc*=sentence particle; *sufx*=suffix; *sv*=state verb; *timd*=time-(duration) word; *time*=time word; *timp*=time phrase; *tsfx*=time suffix; *vdir*=verb of direction; *vobj*=verb with set object; *vpot*=verb with potential

huáqiáo	华侨/華僑	noun	2.4.	overseas Chinese
xióngmāo	熊猫/熊貓	noun	1.8.	panda [m: -zhī]
kùzi	裤子/褲子	noun	1.8.	pants, trousers [m: -tiáo] (v: -chuān)
mùguā	木瓜	noun	2.9.	papaya [m: -gè]
bāoguǒ	包裹	noun	2.8.	parcel, package [m: -gè]
fùmǔ	父母	noun	2.4.	parents
Bālí	巴黎	pn	2.1.	Paris
línshígōng	临时工/臨時工	noun	2.2.	part-time work (worker), temporary work (worker) [m: -gè, -wèi]
lǚkè	旅客	noun	2.8.	passenger [m: -gè, -wèi]
ānjìng	安静/安靜	adj	1.5.	peaceful, quiet
táo	桃	noun	0.9.	peach [m: -gè]
lízi	梨子	noun	2.9.	pear [m: -gè]
qiānbǐ	铅笔/鉛筆	noun	2.8.	pencil [m: -zhī]
tòu	透	adj	0.9.	penetrate
rénmín	人民	noun	1.5.	people, masses
Rénmín Dàxué	人民大学/人民大學	pn	1.9.	People's University (Beijing, China)
shìzi	柿子	noun	2.5.	persimmon [m: -gè]
rén	人	noun	1.3.	person [m: -gè]
hēirén	黑人	noun	2.4.	person of African descent
huáyì	华裔/華裔	noun	2.4.	person of Chinese descent
rén	人	noun	1.6.	person, people
xiǎoqi	小气/小氣	adj	1.7.	petty, stingy, narrow-minded

adj=adjective; *adr*=term of address; *adv*=adverb; *co-v*=co-verb; *comp*=complement; *conj*=conjunction; *dem*=demonstrative; *fam*=family name; *intr*=interjection; *mark*=grammatical marker; *mdl*=modal; *meas*=measure; *mnde*=modifying noun; *mptc*=modification particle; *nphr*=noun phrase; *num*=number; *phr*=phrase; *plce*=place; *plwd*=place word; *pn*=place name; *pre*=prefix; *prep*=preposition; *prn*=proper noun; *pron*=pronoun; *prvb*=pre-verb; *ques*=question word/phrase; *sptc*=sentence particle; *sufx*=suffix; *sv*=state verb; *timd*=time-(duration) word; *time*=time word; *timp*=time phrase; *tsfx*=time suffix; *vdir*=verb of direction; *vobj*=verb with set object; *vpot*=verb with potential

línghuó	灵活/靈活	adj	1.4.	*physically or mentally flexible, agile*
gēzi	鸽子/鴿子	noun	2.5.	*pigeon [m: -zhī]*
wánzi	丸子	noun	1.8.	*pill, ball [m: -gè]*
dìfang	地方	noun	2.1.	*place, area*
móuhuà	谋划/謀劃	verb	1.8.	*plan, scheme*
tái	台/臺	noun	0.9.	*platform*
qǐng	请/請	prvb	0.2.	*please (do something)*
Chī ba.	吃吧。	phr	1.5.	*Please eat.*
Qǐng lái yìbēi lǜchá.	请来一杯绿茶。/ 請來一杯綠茶。	phr	2.9	*Please give me a cup of green tea.*
Qǐng gěi wǒ yìshuāng kuàizi.	请给我一双筷子。/ 請給我一雙筷子。	phr	2.9	*Please give me a pair of chopsticks.*
Hē ba.	喝吧。	phr	1.5.	*Please have a drink!*
lǐzi	李子	noun	2.9.	*plum [m: -gè]*
lüèduó	掠夺/掠奪	verb	1.8.	*plunder, rob*
chà	差	adj	2.7.	*poor quality, not up to standard*
xīfàn	稀饭/稀飯	noun	2.9.	*porridge [m: -wǎn]*
míngxìnpiàn(r)	明信片(儿)/ 明信片(兒)	noun	2.8.	*post card [m: -zhāng]*
yóujú (yóudiànjú)	邮局(邮电局)/ 郵局(郵電局)	plce	2.8.	*post office [m: -gè, -jiā]*
yóupiào	邮票/郵票	noun	2.8.	*postage stamp [m: -zhāng]*
tǔdòu	土豆	noun	2.9.	*potato [m: -kē]*
duìxiàng	对象/對象	noun	2.4.	*potential mate, sweetheart, counterpart*

adj=adjective; *adr*=term of address; *adv*=adverb; *co-v*=co-verb; *comp*=complement; *conj*=conjunction; *dem*=demonstrative; *fam*=family name; *intr*=interjection; *mark*=grammatical marker; *mdl*=modal; *meas*=measure; *mnde*=modifying noun; *mptc*=modification particle; *nphr*=noun phrase; *num*=number; *phr*=phrase; *plce*=place; *plwd*=place word; *pn*=place name; *pre*=prefix; *prep*=preposition; *prn*=proper noun; *pron*=pronoun; *prvb*=pre-verb; *ques*=question word/phrase; *sptc*=sentence particle; *sufx*=suffix; *sv*=state verb; *timd*=time-(duration) word; *time*=time word; *timp*=time phrase; *tsfx*=time suffix; *vdir*=verb of direction; *vobj*=verb with set object; *vpot*=verb with potential

guōtiē	锅贴/鍋貼	noun	2.9.	*potsticker, fried dumpling [m: -gè, -fèn(r)]*
huáiyùn	怀孕/懷孕	verb	1.8.	*pregnant*
xiàozhǎng	校长/校長	adr	1.9.	*president (college), principal (school)*
jiàoshòu	教授	adr	1.6.	*professor*
tū	凸	adj	0.9.	*protruding*
Pǔ'ěr	普洱	pn	2.9.	*Pu'er (county in Yunnan)*
Pǔ'ěrchá	普洱茶	noun	2.9.	*Pu'er tea [m: -hú, -bēi, -kuài(r)]*
jiǎn=piào	剪票	vobj	2.3.	*punch a ticket*
Qīnghuá Dàxué	清华大学/清華大學	pn	1.9.	*Qinghua University (Beijing, China)*
wèntí	问题/問題	noun	0.5.	*question, problem [m: -gè]*
tùzi	兔子	noun	1.8.	*rabbit [m: -zhī]*
tùròu	兔肉	noun	2.9.	*rabbit meat [m: -kuài(r)]*
kàn	看	verb	2.8.	*read, look, see, watch*
zhēn	真	adv	1.9.	*really, very, truly*
zuìjìn	最近	time	1.4.	*recently*
bǐjiào	比较/比較	adv	1.6.	*relatively, comparatively*
wèn X hǎo	问 X 好/問 X 好	phr	1.1.	*remember me to X, greet X*
qǐng	请/請	verb	0.2.	*request, invite*
yánjiū	研究	noun	2.2.	*research*
yánjiū	研究	verb	2.2.	*research*
mǐ	米	noun	1.8.	*rice [m: -kē, -lì]*

adj=adjective; *adr*=term of address; *adv*=adverb; *co-v*=co-verb; *comp*=complement; *conj*=conjunction; *dem*=demonstrative; *fam*=family name; *intr*=interjection; *mark*=grammatical marker; *mdl*=modal; *meas*=measure; *mnde*=modifying noun; *mptc*=modification particle; *nphr*=noun phrase; *num*=number; *phr*=phrase; *plce*=place; *plwd*=place word; *pn*=place name; *pre*=prefix; *prep*=preposition; *prn*=proper noun; *pron*=pronoun; *prvb*=pre-verb; *ques*=question word/phrase; *sptc*=sentence particle; *sufx*=suffix; *sv*=state verb; *timd*=time-(duration) word; *time*=time word; *timp*=time phrase; *tsfx*=time suffix; *vdir*=verb of direction; *vobj*=verb with set object; *vpot*=verb with potential

dàmǐ	大米	noun	2.9.	rice [m: -lì]
huánzi	环子/環子	noun	1.8.	ring [m: -gè]
kǎoyā	烤鸭/烤鴨	noun	2.9.	roast duck [m: -zhī]
zhóuzi	轴子/軸子	noun	2.5.	roller [m: -gè]
yán	盐/鹽	noun	1.8.	salt
Jiùjīnshān	旧金山/舊金山	pn	2.1.	San Francisco
tàng	烫/燙	adj	0.6.	scalding hot
xuéxiào	学校/學校	plce	1.9.	school [m: -suǒ, -gè]
tóngxué	同学/同學	noun	0.1.	schoolmate [m: -gè, -wèi]
xiēzi	蝎子	noun	2.9.	scorpion [m: -gè]
hǎi-biān(r)	海边(儿)/海邊(兒)	plwd	2.3.	seashore, by the sea
mìshū	秘书/秘書	adr	1.3.	secretary
mìshū	秘书/秘書	noun	1.3.	secretary [m: -gè, -wèi]
mài	卖/賣	verb	2.8.	sell
dǎ	打	verb	2.6.	send (by electrical transmission)
jì	寄	verb	2.6.	send by mail
Hànchéng	汉城/漢城	pn	2.9.	Seoul (city in Korea)
fúwùyuán(r)	服务员(儿)/服務員(兒)	noun	2.8.	service person, attendant [m: -gè, -wèi]
shāobǐng	烧饼/燒餅	noun	2.9.	sesame griddle cake [m: -gè] (also shāobing)
xiāngyóu	香油	noun	2.9.	sesame oil [m: -dī, -píng]
zhīmayóu	芝麻油	noun	2.9.	sesame oil [m: -dī, -píng]
qī	七	num	2.6.	seven, 7

adj=adjective; adr=term of address; adv=adverb; co-v=co-verb; comp=complement; conj=conjunction; dem=demonstrative; fam=family name; intr=interjection; mark=grammatical marker; mdl=modal; meas=measure; mnde=modifying noun; mptc=modification particle; nphr=noun phrase; num=number; phr=phrase; plce=place; plwd=place word; pn=place name; pre=prefix; prep=preposition; prn=proper noun; pron=pronoun; prvb=pre-verb; ques=question word/phrase; sptc=sentence particle; sufx=suffix; sv=state verb; timd=time-(duration) word; time=time word; timp=time phrase; tsfx=time suffix; vdir=verb of direction; vobj=verb with set object; vpot=verb with potential

Shāndōng	山东/山東	pn	2.9.	Shandong (province in China)
Shànghǎi	上海	pn	2.1.	Shanghai
shāyú	鲨鱼/鯊魚	noun	2.9.	shark [m: -tiáo]
tā	她	pron	1.2.	she, her
kézi	壳子/殼子	noun	2.5.	shell, packaging case [m: -gè]
Shěnyáng	沈阳/瀋陽	pn	2.9.	Shenyang (city in Liaoning)
xiézi	鞋子	noun	1.8.	shoe(s) [m: -shuāng, -zhī]
pùzi	铺子/鋪子	noun	1.8.	shop [m: -gè]
ǎi	矮	adj	1.6.	short (height)
cuózi	矬子	noun	2.5.	short person, dwarf [m: -gè]
xiā	虾/蝦	noun	1.8.	shrimp [m: -zhī]
Sìchuān	四川	pn	2.9.	Sichuan (province in China)
sī	丝/絲	noun	1.5.	silk
chóuzi	绸子/綢子	noun	2.5.	silk fabric [m: -kuài]
Huáměi Màoyì Gōngsī	华美贸易公司/華美貿易公司	pn	1.9.	Sino-American Trade Company
zuò	坐	verb	0.2.	sit
liù	六	num	2.6.	six, 6
kùn	困	adj	1.8.	sleepy
shòu	瘦	adj	1.6.	slight (physical build), thin
jīzi	机子/機子	noun	2.5.	small machine [m: -tái, -bù, -gè]
xiǎo	小	adj	1.6.	small, young

adj=adjective; adr=term of address; adv=adverb; co-v=co-verb; comp=complement; conj=conjunction; dem=demonstrative; fam=family name; intr=interjection; mark=grammatical marker; mdl=modal; meas=measure; mnde=modifying noun; mptc=modification particle; nphr=noun phrase; num=number; phr=phrase; plce=place; plwd=place word; pn=place name; pre=prefix; prep=preposition; prn=proper noun; pron=pronoun; prvb=pre-verb; ques=question word/phrase; sptc=sentence particle; sufx=suffix; sv=state verb; timd=time-(duration) word; time=time word; timp=time phrase; tsfx=time suffix; vdir=verb of direction; vobj=verb with set object; vpot=verb with potential

qìshuǐ(r)	汽水（儿）/ 汽水（兒）	noun	2.8.	*soda, pop [m: -píng(r), -guàn(r)]*
tǔ	土	noun	0.9.	*soil*
yǒu yìdiǎn(r)	有一点儿/ 有一點兒	phr	1.4.	*somewhat (undesirable attribute)*
duìbuqǐ	对不起/對不起	phr	1.9.	*sorry (for not meeting expectations)*
shēngyīn	声音/聲音	noun	1.5.	*sound [m: -zhǒng]*
tāng	汤/湯	noun	0.6.	*soup*
suān	酸	adj	1.8.	*sour*
Nánhǎi	南海	pn	2.9.	*South China Sea*
jiàngyóu	酱油/醬油	noun	2.9.	*soy sauce [m: -píng]*
yàozi	鹞子/鷂子	noun	1.8.	*sparrow hawk*
shuō	说/說	verb	0.3.	*speak, say*
nàkǒuzi/ nèikǒuzi	那口子	noun	2.4.	*spouse (informal), wife (informal)*
àiren	爱人/愛人	noun	2.4.	*spouse (PRC)*
chūnjuǎn(r)	春卷（儿）/ 春卷（兒）	noun	2.9.	*spring roll [m: -gè]*
wénjùdiàn	文具店	plce	2.8.	*stationery shop [m: -gè, -jiā]*
tōu	偷	verb	0.9.	*steal*
mántou	馒头/饅頭	noun	1.5.	*steamed bun [m: -gè]*
bāozi	包子	noun	2.5.	*steamed stuffed bun [m: -gè]*
bùzi	步子	noun	1.8.	*step*
hái méi(yǒu) jié=hūn	还没（有）结婚/ 還沒（有）結婚	phr	2.4.	*still not married*

adj=adjective; *adr*=term of address; *adv*=adverb; *co-v*=co-verb; *comp*=complement; *conj*=conjunction; *dem*=demonstrative; *fam*=family name; *intr*=interjection; *mark*=grammatical marker; *mdl*=modal; *meas*=measure; *mnde*=modifying noun; *mptc*=modification particle; *nphr*=noun phrase; *num*=number; *phr*=phrase; *plce*=place; *plwd*=place word; *pn*=place name; *pre*=prefix; *prep*=preposition; *prn*=proper noun; *pron*=pronoun; *prvb*=pre-verb; *ques*=question word/phrase; *sptc*=sentence particle; *sufx*=suffix; *sv*=state verb; *timd*=time-(duration) word; *time*=time word; *timp*=time phrase; *tsfx*=time suffix; *vdir*=verb of direction; *vobj*=verb with set object; *vpot*=verb with potential

shāngdiàn	商店	plce	2.2.	*store, shop [m: -gè, -jiā]*
zhuàng	壮/壯	adj	1.6.	*stout, strong build*
cǎoméi	草莓	noun	2.9.	*strawberry [m: -kē]*
wángù	顽固/頑固	adj	1.4.	*stubborn, hard-headed*
xuésheng	学生/學生	noun	1.3.	*student [m: -gè, -wèi]*
tóngxuémen	同学们/同學們	noun	0.1.	*students of a particular school*
bèn	笨	adj	1.7.	*stupid, awkward*
táng	糖	noun	0.6.	*sugar/candy [m: -kuài, -kē]*
wěiba	尾巴	noun	1.8.	*tail [m: -tiáo, -gè]*
Táiběi	台北/臺北	pn	2.9.	*Taipei (city in Taiwan)*
Táiwān	台湾/臺灣	pn	2.9.	*Taiwan*
Tàiyuán	太原	pn	2.9.	*Taiyuan (city in Shanxi)*
ná	拿	verb	2.8.	*take, hold*
luōsuo	罗嗦/囉嗦	adj	1.4.	*talkative*
gāo	高	adj	1.6.	*tall*
chá	茶	noun	2.8.	*tea [m: -bēi]*
jiāo=shū	教书/教書	vobj	2.2.	*teach (in a school setting)*
lǎoshī	老师/老師	adr	0.1.	*teacher*
lǎoshī	老师/老師	noun	0.1.	*teacher [m: -gè, -wèi]*
jiàoxué	教学/教學	noun	2.2.	*teaching*
diànhuà	电话/電話	noun	2.6.	*telephone [m: -bù]*
gàosu	告诉/告訴	verb	2.6.	*tell, relate, inform*
wàn	万	num	2.7.	*ten thousand, 10,000*
shí	十	num	2.6.	*ten, 10*
xièxie	谢谢/謝謝	phr	0.8.	*thanks (accept with gratitude)*

adj=adjective; *adr*=term of address; *adv*=adverb; *co-v*=co-verb; *comp*=complement; *conj*=conjunction; *dem*=demonstrative; *fam*=family name; *intr*=interjection; *mark*=grammatical marker; *mdl*=modal; *meas*=measure; *mnde*=modifying noun; *mptc*=modification particle; *nphr*=noun phrase; *num*=number; *phr*=phrase; *plce*=place; *plwd*=place word; *pn*=place name; *pre*=prefix; *prep*=preposition; *prn*=proper noun; *pron*=pronoun; *prvb*=pre-verb; *ques*=question word/phrase; *sptc*=sentence particle; *sufx*=suffix; *sv*=state verb; *timd*=time-(duration) word; *time*=time word; *timp*=time phrase; *tsfx*=time suffix; *vdir*=verb of direction; *vobj*=verb with set object; *vpot*=verb with potential

nà/nèi	那	dem	1.6.	*that*
Tāng tài tàng le!	汤太烫了！/ 湯太燙了！	phr	0.6.	*The soup is scalding hot!*
nàli	那里/那裏	plwd	2.6.	*there, that place*
nàr	那儿/那兒	plwd	2.6.	*there, that place*
tāmen	她们/她們	pron	1.4.	*they, them (female)*
tāmen	他们/他們	pron	1.4.	*they, them (gender free)*
dōngxi	东西/東西	noun	2.8.	*thing [m: -gè]*
sà	卅	num	1.5.	*thirty*
zhè/zhèi	这/這	dem	1.6.	*this*
qiān	千	num	2.7.	*thousand, 1,000*
sān	三	num	2.6.	*three, 3*
Tiānjīn	天津	pn	2.9.	*Tianjin (city in China)*
Xīzàng	西藏	pn	2.9.	*Tibet (region in China)*
piào	票	noun	2.8.	*ticket [m: -zhāng]*
jiǎnpiàokǒu	剪票口	plwd	2.3.	*ticket gate [m: -gè]*
chuāngkǒu	窗口	plwd	2.3.	*ticket window [m: -gè]*
lèi	累	adj	1.4.	*tired*
Dōngjīng	东京/東京	pn	2.1.	*Tokyo*
tài	太	adv	2.3.	*too, excessive*
<u>V</u> yíxià	<u>V</u>一下	timd	1.9.	*try to <u>V</u>, <u>V</u> for a while*
Qīngdǎo	青岛/青島	pn	2.2.	*Tsingtao (city in Shandong)*
Qīngdǎo píjiǔ	青岛啤酒/ 青島啤酒	noun	2.9.	*Tsingtao beer [m: -píng, -bēi, -tǒng, -guàn(r)]*
liǎng + <u>measure</u>	俩+<u>量词</u>/ 俩+<u>量詞</u>	num	2.7.	*two of, a couple of*
èr	二	num	2.6.	*two, 2*

adj=adjective; *adr*=term of address; *adv*=adverb; *co-v*=co-verb; *comp*=complement; *conj*=conjunction; *dem*=demonstrative; *fam*=family name; *intr*=interjection; *mark*=grammatical marker; *mdl*=modal; *meas*=measure; *mnde*=modifying noun; *mptc*=modification particle; *nphr*=noun phrase; *num*=number; *phr*=phrase; *plce*=place; *plwd*=place word; *pn*=place name; *pre*=prefix; *prep*=preposition; *prn*=proper noun; *pron*=pronoun; *prvb*=pre-verb; *ques*=question word/phrase; *sptc*=sentence particle; *sufx*=suffix; *sv*=state verb; *timd*=time-(duration) word; *time*=time word; *timp*=time phrase; *tsfx*=time suffix; *vdir*=verb of direction; *vobj*=verb with set object; *vpot*=verb with potential

nánkàn	难看/難看	adj	1.6.	*unattractive, ugly*
bù-qīngchu	不清楚	phr	1.7.	*unclear, unaware*
dǒng	懂	sv	0.7.	*understand*
Měiguó	美国/美國	pn	2.2.	*United States, America*
dàxué	大学/大學	plce	1.9.	*university [m: -suǒ, -gè]*
bù-shūfu	不舒服	adj	1.4.	*unwell, indisposed, uncomfortable*
yòng	用	verb	1.8.	*use*
yòng	用	verb	2.6.	*use*
<u>V</u> le méiyǒu?	<u>V</u>了没有?/ <u>V</u>了沒有?	ques	2.4.	*<u>V</u> done yet?*
shūcài	蔬菜	noun	2.9.	*vegetable [m: -zhǒng]*
hěn	很	adv	1.4.	*very (pre-adjective)*
tǐng	挺	adv	2.1.	*very, really*
děng	等	verb	2.3.	*wait*
yào	要	verb	2.8.	*want, require, demand, order (food), = xūyào*
Huáshèngdùn	华盛顿/華盛頓	pn	2.1.	*Washington D.C.*
wǒmen	我们/我們	pron	1.7.	*we, us*
zánmen	咱们/咱們	pron	1.7.	*we, us (includes the addressee)*
huānyíng	欢迎/歡迎	phr	1.9.	*welcome (to outsiders)*
shénme	什么/甚麼	ques	1.3.	*what*
<u>X</u> de shì zěnmeyàng le?	<u>X</u>的事怎么样了?	phr	2.7.	*What about the matter of <u>X</u>?*
Nǐ kàn zěnmeyàng?	你看怎么样?/ 你看怎麼樣?	phr	2.3.	*What do you think?*
<u>X</u> zhǎngde zěnmeyàng	<u>X</u>长得怎么样/ <u>X</u>長得怎麼樣	phr	1.6.	*What does <u>X</u> look like?*

adj=adjective; *adr*=term of address; *adv*=adverb; *co-v*=co-verb; *comp*=complement; *conj*=conjunction; *dem*=demonstrative; *fam*=family name; *intr*=interjection; *mark*=grammatical marker; *mdl*=modal; *meas*=measure; *mnde*=modifying noun; *mptc*=modification particle; *nphr*=noun phrase; *num*=number; *phr*=phrase; *plce*=place; *plwd*=place word; *pn*=place name; *pre*=prefix; *prep*=preposition; *prn*=proper noun; *pron*=pronoun; *prvb*=pre-verb; *ques*=question word/phrase; *sptc*=sentence particle; *sufx*=suffix; *sv*=state verb; *timd*=time-(duration) word; *time*=time word; *timp*=time phrase; *tsfx*=time suffix; *vdir*=verb of direction; *vobj*=verb with set object; *vpot*=verb with potential

gàn shénme?	干什么？/ 幹什麼？	phr	2.4.	*What is (somebody)* *doing?*
guìxìng	贵姓/貴姓	phr	1.2.	*What is your family* *name?*
lúnzi	轮子/輪子	noun	1.8.	*wheel [m: -gè]*
nǎli	哪里/哪裏	ques	2.1.	*where*
nǎr	哪儿/哪兒	ques	2.1.	*where*
shénme dìfang	什么地方/ 甚麼地方	phr	2.1.	*where, what place*
nǎ/něi	哪	dem	1.7.	*which*
nǎguó/něiguó	哪国/哪國	ques	2.2.	*which country*
nǎge/něige	哪个	ques	1.7.	*which one*
nǎwèi/něiwèi	哪位	ques	1.7.	*which person, who*
shéi/shuí	谁/誰	ques	1.3.	*who, whom*
fūren	夫人	noun	2.4.	*wife (formal)*
qīzi	妻子	noun	2.4.	*wife (formal)*
nǔde	女的	noun	1.6.	*woman [m: -gè]*
nǔrén	女人	noun	1.6.	*woman [m: -gè]*
gōngzuò	工作	verb	2.2.	*work*
zuò X gōngzuò	做 X 工作	phr	2.2.	*work at/as X*
gōngzuò	工作	noun	2.2.	*work, job*
gōngrén	工人	noun	2.7.	*worker [m: -gè, -wèi]*
xiě	写/寫	verb	2.6.	*write, compose*
bǐ	笔/筆	noun	2.6.	*writing instrument* *[m: -zhī]*
yuànzi	院子	noun	1.8.	*yard [m: -gè]*
nǐ	你	pron	0.1.	*you*
nǐmen	你们/你們	pron	0.1.	*you (pl.)*

adj=adjective; *adr*=term of address; *adv*=adverb; *co-v*=co-verb; *comp*=complement; *conj*=conjunction; *dem*=demonstrative; *fam*=family name; *intr*=interjection; *mark*=grammatical marker; *mdl*=modal; *meas*=measure; *mnde*=modifying noun; *mptc*=modification particle; *nphr*=noun phrase; *num*=number; *phr*=phrase; *plce*=place; *plwd*=place word; *pn*=place name; *pre*=prefix; *prep*=preposition; *prn*=proper noun; *pron*=pronoun; *prvb*=pre-verb; *ques*=question word/phrase; *sptc*=sentence particle; *sufx*=suffix; *sv*=state verb; *timd*=time-(duration) word; *time*=time word; *timp*=time phrase; *tsfx*=time suffix; *vdir*=verb of direction; *vobj*=verb with set object; *vpot*=verb with potential

nín	您	pron	1.2.	*you (polite)*
niánqīng	年轻/年輕	adj	1.6.	*young (human)*
zhìzi	稚子	noun	1.5.	*young child*
xiǎo + <u>surname</u>	小	adr	1.1.	*younger friend*
mèizi	妹子	noun	2.5.	*younger sister [m: -gè]*
Yúnnán	云南/雲南	pn	2.9.	*Yunnan (province in China)*
líng	零	num	2.6.	*zero, 0*
Zhèjiāng	浙江	pn	2.9.	*Zhejiang (province in China)*

adj=adjective; *adr*=term of address; *adv*=adverb; *co-v*=co-verb; *comp*=complement; *conj*=conjunction; *dem*=demonstrative; *fam*=family name; *intr*=interjection; *mark*=grammatical marker; *mdl*=modal; *meas*=measure; *mnde*=modifying noun; *mptc*=modification particle; *nphr*=noun phrase; *num*=number; *phr*=phrase; *plce*=place; *plwd*=place word; *pn*=place name; *pre*=prefix; *prep*=preposition; *prn*=proper noun; *pron*=pronoun; *prvb*=pre-verb; *ques*=question word/phrase; *sptc*=sentence particle; *sufx*=suffix; *sv*=state verb; *timd*=time-(duration) word; *time*=time word; *timp*=time phrase; *tsfx*=time suffix; *vdir*=verb of direction; *vobj*=verb with set object; *vpot*=verb with potential

AUDIO PROGRAM FOR
CHINESE: COMMUNICATING IN THE CULTURE (C3)

File#	File Name	File #	File Name	File #	File Name
01	u0s1 coaching.mp3	20	u1s1 coaching.mp3	37	u2s1 coaching.mp3
02	u0s1 Rehearsal.mp3	21	u1s1 Rehearsal.mp3	38	u2s1 Rehearsal.mp3
03	u0s2 coaching.mp3	22	u1s2 coaching.mp3	39	u2s2 coaching.mp3
04	u0s2 Rehearsal.mp3	23	u1s2 Rehearsal.mp3	40	u2s2 Rehearsal.mp3
05	u0s3 coaching.mp3	24	u1s3 coaching.mp3	41	u2s3 coaching.mp3
06	u0s3 Rehearsal.mp3	25	u1s3 Rehearsal.mp3	42	u2s3 Rehearsal.mp3
07	u0s4 coaching.mp3	26	u1s4 coaching.mp3	43	u2s4 coaching.mp3
08	u0s4 Rehearsal.mp3	27	u1s4 Rehearsal.mp3	44	u2s4 Rehearsal.mp3
09	u0s5 coaching.mp3	28	u1s5 coaching.mp3	45	u2s5 coaching.mp3
10	u0s5 Rehearsal.mp3	29	u1s6 coaching.mp3	46	u2s5 Rehearsal.mp3
11	u0s6 coaching.mp3	30	u1s6 Rehearsal.mp3	47	u2s6 coaching.mp3
12	u0s6 Rehearsal.mp3	31	u1s7 coaching.mp3	48	u2s6 Rehearsal.mp3
13	u0s7 coaching.mp3	32	u1s7 Rehearsal.mp3	49	u2s7 coaching.mp3
14	u0s7 Rehearsal.mp3	33	u1s8 coaching.mp3	50	u2s7 Rehearsal.mp3
15	u0s8 coaching.mp3	34	u1s9 coaching.mp3	51	u2s8 coaching.mp3
16	u0s8 Rehearsal.mp3	35	u1s9 Rehearsal.mp3	52	u2s8 Rehearsal.mp3
17	u0s9 coaching.mp3	36	u1s10 selftest.mp3	53	u2s9 coaching.mp3
18	u0s9 Rehearsal.mp3			54	u2s10 selftest.mp3
19	u0s10 selftest.mp3			55	u2s10 selftest answer.mp3

You can listen to the MP3 files of the C3 Audio Program on computer audio systems, or sync the CD contents to an iPod (MP3 player).

The audio program is the key component of a course of study of a spoken language. The "language" you need to learn is there. The other components of C3–print, graphics, video–exist to help you comprehend, reproduce, and expand on the Chinese you encounter here. The more you hear and speak, the faster you will learn to use the language. These materials are based on two assumptions: 1) that learning to speak a language requires you to develop the ability to learn efficiently and accurately with your ears, and 2) that you learn better when you understand what the language is being used to accomplish. Therefore, there are ample oral descriptions of the intentions and structure of the C3 language sample found in this program.

The C3 Audio Program has two basic presentational modes: coaching and rehearsal. Coaching will include English explanations and suggestions for performing the language. In Unit Zero, you will be coached to use the instructional expressions in your sessions with your instructors. Unit One and Unit Two include coaching through the conversations and drills and through the introduction to the pronunciation and romanization of Mandarin. Use the coaching as many times as necessary to become familiar with the language and the communicative intentions of the speakers.

Rehearsal presents the Mandarin Chinese in these materials without the English support. After you familiarize yourself with the content of the lessons, use rehearsal to repeat the essence of the lessons as many times as you can, developing your listening comprehension and speaking performances to the highest level you can reach. The rehearsal mode should be the basic tool for preparing for your instructional sessions.

Each unit concludes with a self-test where you can evaluate your command of the content presented in the unit.